A Gift for:

_____

From:

_____

HOPE
FOR EACH DAY

Words of Wisdom and Faith

BILLY GRAHAM

THOMAS NELSON
Since 1798

Therefore I live for today—
Certain of finding at sunrise
Guidance and strength for the way.
Power for each moment of weakness,
Hope for each moment of pain,
Comfort for every sorrow,
Sunshine and joy after rain!

—Anonymous

For many years I have sought to walk with God every day. What a joy it is to wake up in the morning and know He is with me, no matter what the day has in store. What a joy it is to look back in the evening and be able to thank Him for His faithfulness and to experience His peace. What a joy it is to know that someday soon the burdens of this life will be over and I will awaken in His presence!

When I think about God's love, I tend to dwell upon all the good things He has done for me. But then I must stop and realize that even when circumstances have been hard or the way unclear, God has still surrounded me with His love. God's love is just as real and just as powerful in the darkness as it is in the light. And that is why we can have hope!

Every day I turn to the Bible to give me strength and wisdom for the day and hope for the future. Its words have seen me through good times and bad—through times of happiness and grief, health and sickness, victory and disappointment. God's Word can do the same for you.

May God use these daily selections to encourage you and give you hope. May they also challenge you both to live more fully for Christ each day and to trust His great love—no matter what comes your way.

—BILLY GRAHAM

JANUARY

*I cried out to You, O L*ORD*:*
I said, "You are my refuge,
My portion in the land of the living."

PSALM 142:5

IN TUNE WITH THE MASTER

You shall surround me with songs of deliverance.
PSALM 32:7

Out West an old sheepherder had a violin, but it was out of tune. He had no way of tuning it, so in desperation he wrote to one of the radio stations and asked them at a certain hour on a certain day to strike the tone "A." The officials of the station decided they would accommodate the old fellow, and on that particular day the true tone of "A" was broadcast. His fiddle was thus tuned, and once more his cabin echoed with joyful music.

When we live apart from God, our lives get out of tune—out of harmony with others and with God. But if we live in tune with the Master, we, too, will find ourselves surrounded by His beautiful music.

As this new year begins, ask God to help you tune your life every day to His Word, so you can bring harmony and joy to those around you.

HOPE FOR TODAY

Are you feeling weary and worn? Are you desperate for something to change? Ask God to reveal where your life may be out of tune. He will be faithful to you.

THE SUN STILL SHINING

They looked . . . and behold, the glory of the LORD appeared in the cloud.

EXODUS 16:10

Without the clouds we wouldn't be shielded from the burning sun. Without the clouds there would be no lavish sunsets, no beneficial rain, no beautiful landscapes.

The same is true with life's clouds. When hard times come, we easily get discouraged. But behind the clouds God is still present, and can even use them to water our souls with unexpected blessings. Longfellow once wrote, "Be still, sad heart, and cease repining; behind the clouds is the sun still shining." As God's people wandered in the wilderness, He declared, "Behold, I come to you in the thick cloud" (Exodus 19:9).

Each of us experiences clouds in life—sometimes slight, but sometimes dark and frightening. Whatever clouds you face today, ask Jesus, the light of the world, to help you look behind the cloud to see His glory and His plans for you.

HOPE FOR TODAY

Help me, Lord, not to allow the clouds of the day prevent me from seeking Your face. May I, like Moses, be bold enough to approach the thick darkness (Exodus 20:21) if that is where Your presence is found.

3

A SPRING FOR THE SOUL

For with You is the fountain of life;
In Your light we see light.
PSALM 36:9

Sadly, many people get their happiness only from outward circumstances. As long as their lives are untroubled, they feel happy. But when illness strikes, or a relationship breaks down, or any of a thousand other unexpected troubles engulf them, then happiness flees.

Near my home is a spring that never varies its flow. Floods may rage, but its output doesn't increase. A long summer's drought may come, but it won't decrease. Its flow is steady, reliable, and unending.

Such is the peace we all yearn for—and such is the peace Jesus promises to all who trust in Him: "The water that I shall give him will become in him a fountain of water springing up into everlasting life. . . . My peace I give to you" (John 4:14; 14:27).

Have you come to that unending spring, which is Christ? Are you coming to Him each day?

HOPE FOR TODAY
The world attempts to woo people with its version of happiness. Today, spend some time alone with Christ and experience joy that is full and pleasures that are eternal.

THE PROMISE IS OURS

"I am with you always, even to the end of the age."

MATTHEW 28:20

When David Livingstone returned to his native Scotland after sixteen difficult years as a missionary and explorer in Africa, his body was emaciated by the ravages of some twenty-seven fevers that had coursed through his veins during the years of his service. His left arm hung useless at his side, the result of his being mangled by a lion.

Speaking to the students at Glasgow University, he said, "Shall I tell you what sustained me during the hardship and loneliness of my exile? It was Christ's promise, 'Lo, I am with you always, even to the end of the age.'"

That promise is ours as well. No matter what trials we face, Christ never leaves us. He is with us every step of the way! Keep that promise before you today—and always.

HOPE FOR TODAY

Have you had a loved one leave? A friend prove fickle? Unlike people, Christ's presence is a guarantee. One day, we'll look back on every trial and see that Jesus was always with us.

HE IS HERE TO HELP

Who shall separate us from the love of Christ?
ROMANS 8:35

After His resurrection Jesus came to His disciples, meeting them between the garden with its empty tomb and the city with its mob still passionate with hate. He said to them, "Do not be afraid. Go and tell My brethren" (Matthew 28:10).

In the midst of a world filled with danger, hatred, and war, the words of our Lord Jesus Christ are just as relevant as when He spoke them. He still says to all who love Him, "Do not be afraid."

He comes to you in the hospital room or in the midst of a family tragedy. He comes to you in the midst of an unexpected business reversal or physical crisis. And He says, "Don't be afraid. I'm alive, and I'm here to help you. The Cross shows the depth of My love, and the Resurrection shows the depth of My power. Nothing can ever separate you from Me!"

HOPE FOR TODAY

Thank You, Jesus, that Your love is as lavish and Your power is as unmatched as ever. Though the storms may rage and the enemy may taunt, You can still speak peace to me.

THE GLORY OF GOD

"In My Father's house are many mansions. . . . I go to prepare a place for you."
JOHN 14:2

There was once a little boy who was riding alone on a train, and the scenery was not too interesting. A woman sitting beside him asked, "Are you tired of the long ride?"

The boy smiled and said, "I'm a little tired, but I don't mind it much. You see, my father is going to meet me when I get there."

Sometimes we get tired of the burdens of life, but we know that Jesus Christ will meet us at the end of our life's journey—and that makes all the difference. Paul wrote, "Therefore we do not lose heart. . . . For the things which are seen are temporary, but the things which are not seen are eternal" (2 Corinthians 4:16, 18). Knowing we will be with Christ forever far outweighs our burdens today! Keep your eyes on eternity!

HOPE FOR TODAY

What are you focused on today? Perhaps you need to ask God to help you keep your eyes on Him and the eternal hope He has given His followers. Your Father is waiting for you.

A SPIRIT OF THANKFULNESS

I have learned the secret of being content
in any and every situation.

PHILIPPIANS 4:12 NIV

Some years ago I visited a man who was wealthy and successful, the envy of all his friends and business associates. But as we talked, he broke down in tears, confessing that he was miserable inside. Wealth had not been able to fill the empty place in his heart.

A few hours later I visited another man who lived only a few miles away. His cottage was humble, and he had almost nothing in the way of this world's possessions. Yet his face was radiant as he told me about the work he was doing for Christ and how Christ had filled his life with meaning and purpose.

I went away convinced that the second man was really the rich man. Although he had very little, he had learned to be thankful for everything God had given him. A spirit of thankfulness makes all the difference.

HOPE FOR TODAY

Worldly wealth can never compare with the treasures found in Christ. When we decide to walk with Jesus, our hearts can be filled to overflowing, even when our bank accounts are not.

THE TRIUMPHS OF GRACE

"I, even I, am He who blots out your transgressions."

ISAIAH 43:25

When Charles Wesley experienced the joy of divine forgiveness, he told a Moravian friend of his new sense of pardon and added, "I suppose I had better keep silent about it."

"Oh, no, my brother," came the reply. "If you had a thousand tongues, you should go and use them all for Jesus."

Charles Wesley went home and wrote the great hymn: "Oh for a thousand tongues to sing my great Redeemer's praise, the glories of my God and King, the triumphs of His grace!"

To a burdened, benighted world, crushed under the weight of its own wickedness, God says, "I, even I, am He who blots out your transgressions." This is glorious news, and it applies to all people—everywhere—including you. Have you received God's gift of forgiveness? If you have, thank Him for it—and if not, by faith invite Christ into your life today.

HOPE FOR TODAY

God offers forgiveness and freedom to those shackled by sin and shame. Today, through Christ, you have the option of letting go of guilt and embracing grace.

9

SET FREE FROM SIN

In Him we have redemption through His blood.
EPHESIANS 1:7

A loving mother who saved her little girl from a burning house suffered severe burns on her hands and arms. When the girl grew older, not knowing how her mother's arms had become so seared, the girl was ashamed of those scarred, gnarled hands and always insisted that her mother wear long gloves to cover up the ugliness.

But one day the daughter asked her mother how her hands had become so scarred. The mother, for the first time, told her the story of how she had saved the daughter's life with those hands. The daughter wept tears of gratitude and said, "Oh, Mother, those are beautiful hands, the most beautiful in the world. Don't ever hide them again!"

Just so, the blood of Christ may seem to be a grim, repulsive subject to those who do not realize its true significance; but to those who have been rescued from sin's chains, Christ's nail-pierced hands are beautiful beyond measure, for they tell us of His love and His willingness to save us regardless of the cost.

HOPE FOR TODAY

Thank You, Jesus, for the beauty of Your bloodstained Cross. I will not be ashamed, and I will not look away. May Your Cross be the centerpiece of my life.

THINK ETERNITY

"Seek first the kingdom of God."
MATTHEW 6:33

King George V wrote on the flyleaf of the Bible of a friend: "The secret of happiness is not to do what you like to do, but to learn to like what you have to do."

Too many people think happiness is an elusive, will-o'-the-wisp thing to be found only by constant pursuit and relentless searching. But happiness is not an end in itself; it is the by-product of something far greater. Jesus told His disciples: "Seek first the kingdom of God and His righteousness, and all these things shall be added to you" (Matthew 6:33). The "things" He spoke of were the basic needs of life: food, drink, clothes, shelter. He told us not to make these things the chief goal of our lives, but to "seek . . . the kingdom."

There, if we will take it, is the secret of happiness: "Seek first the kingdom of God . . ." How do we do this? By submitting ourselves without reserve to Jesus Christ as King of our lives every day. This is the path of true happiness.

HOPE FOR TODAY

In what ways have you been trying to create happiness in your life? Ask God to redirect your efforts and to give you a heart that seeks His kingdom more than worldly pleasures.

FAITH GROWS BY EXPRESSION

You are the light of the world.

MATTHEW 5:14

Tom Allan, Scotland's famous preacher, was brought to Christ while a soldier was singing, "Were you there when they crucified my Lord?" He said it was neither the song nor the voice, but the spirit in which that soldier sang—something about his manner, something about his sincerity of expression—that convicted Allan of his wicked life and turned him to the Savior.

Jesus said, "You are the light of the world. . . . Let your light so shine before [others], that they may see your good works, and glorify your Father in heaven" (Matthew 5:14, 16).

Our faith becomes stronger as we express it; a growing faith is a sharing faith. Pray now for those you know who need Christ, and ask God to help you be a witness to them—by the life you live and the words you speak.

HOPE FOR TODAY

The enemy wants you to think that, before telling anyone about Christ, you must have all of the answers and a pristine past to boot. The truth is that simplicity and godly sincerity go a long way (2 Corinthians 1:12).

ALL FOR JESUS

We are in Him who is true, in His Son Jesus Christ.

1 JOHN 5:20

In His Steps, by Charles M. Sheldon, tells of a pastor who challenged his congregation to pledge for one year not to do anything without first asking the question: "What would Jesus do?"

This challenge was kindled when a shabby man, mourning his wife who had died in poverty, stumbled into a wealthy church and addressed the congregation. He said, "I heard some people singing at a church prayer meeting the other night: 'All for Jesus! All for Jesus! All my being's ransomed powers; all my thoughts and words and doings, all my days and all my hours.' I kept wondering as I sat on the steps outside just what they meant by it. It seems to me there's an awful lot of trouble in the world that somehow wouldn't exist if all the people who sing such songs went and lived them out."

If someone posed the same question to us, what would be our response? Do we live our lives with the thought, *What would Jesus do*? Do we put it into practice every day?

HOPE FOR TODAY

In Philippians 2, Paul encourages believers to be like Christ. This goes against the way of the world and of our own flesh. In what areas do you need to go against the grain and be more like Jesus?

God's Hand of Blessing

Every good gift and every perfect gift is from above.
JAMES 1:17

In the midst of the Lord's Prayer are these familiar words: "Give us this day our daily bread" (Matthew 6:11). They remind us that we are dependent on God for everything, and that He is the giver of every blessing. "Every good gift and every perfect gift is from above, and comes down from the Father of lights" (James 1:17).

Some people say, "Why should I pray for my daily bread? I can take care of my own needs!" But listen: if it weren't for God's love and grace, you wouldn't have anything. We need to pray this prayer every day, because we need to be reminded to trust God in everything.

This prayer reminds us also of Jesus' words: "I am the bread of life. He who comes to Me shall never hunger" (John 6:35). Thank God for all His gifts—especially Christ, the greatest gift of all.

Hope for Today

There is freedom in acknowledging that we are completely dependent upon God for our daily bread and breath. Today, you can let go of the illusion of control and embrace the freedom of trusting His provision.

CHRIST PROVIDES THE CURE

If anyone is in Christ, he is a new creation.

2 CORINTHIANS 5:17

Wouldn't it be wonderful if we could find a medicine that would absolutely cure human nature's weaknesses and failures? Conflict, discontent, and unhappiness plague people everywhere. But suppose a cure could be found for humanity's ills. It would cause a worldwide stampede!

The most thrilling news in the world is that there is a cure! God has provided the medicine—and that "medicine" is Christ. Through Him our sins can be forgiven, and by His Holy Spirit within us our lives can be changed and renewed.

Sin, confusion, and disillusionment can be replaced by righteousness, joy, and hope. Our souls can know peace, a peace that is not dependent on outward circumstances. This cure was provided two thousand years ago by Jesus Christ's death and resurrection for us. Is He working daily in your life, changing you and making you more like Him?

HOPE FOR TODAY

Have you ever felt as if you weren't experiencing the promises of God in your life? Perhaps you've just been looking in the wrong places. Scripture tells us that all of God's promises find their yes in Christ.

LOOKING FOR LASTING JOY

May the God of hope fill you with all joy.
ROMANS 15:13

How often have you found what you were looking for in life, only to realize it didn't bring you the satisfaction you thought it would?

It is life's ultimate frustration—thinking we will find fulfillment in the things of this world. But they can never bring lasting happiness. As one bumper sticker I saw expressed it, "All I want is a little more than I have now."

We look for love, security, and happiness through our jobs, our possessions, our relationships—but if they really brought lasting joy, wouldn't we have testimonies to that effect from millions of people all over the world? Instead, we find emptiness, discontent, and hopelessness.

Try putting Christ first and watch how your life is turned around. You will discover that He alone is the source of the love, peace, and joy you have been searching for.

HOPE FOR TODAY

No person, possession, or earthly pleasure can bring us the joy our souls crave; they offer temporary happiness at best. Pure and permanent joy is only found in the presence of Christ.

ENJOYING GOD'S PRESENCE

In Your presence is fullness of joy.

PSALM 16:11

Have you ever watched a young couple communicate their love for each other without even saying a word? Maybe you have experienced it yourself. Every glance, every touch, every smile conveys love. People deeply in love find absolute bliss simply being in each other's presence.

In the same way, simply being in the presence of God brings us great joy. It happens as we listen to Him speak in His Word; it happens as we pray. But it also happens as we simply enjoy His presence—meditating on His goodness, delighting in the beauty of His creation, rejoicing in the life of a new baby or the surprise of an unexpected blessing. The Bible says, "Be still, and know that I am God" (Psalm 46:10).

Someday we will be in His presence forever; the Bible says, "God Himself will be with them" (Revelation 21:3). What joy that will be! But in the meantime, delight in His presence right now, for He is with you every hour of the day.

HOPE FOR TODAY

Are you ever guilty of taking God's presence for granted? Perhaps you've lost a little of the awe and wonder. Take a moment to rekindle the passion and ponder anew the glory of Immanuel—God with us.

SERVING ETERNALLY

You have a better and an enduring possession for yourselves in heaven.
HEBREWS 10:34

S ome people think Heaven will be dull and boring, but nothing could be further from the truth. The Father's house will be a happy home because there will be work to do there. John wrote in Revelation 22:3, "His servants shall serve Him." Each one will be given exactly the task that suits his powers, his tastes, and his abilities.

And the Father's house will be a happy home because friends will be there. Have you ever been to a strange place and had the joy of seeing a familiar face? Not one of us who enters the Father's house will feel lonely or strange, for we who have put our trust in Christ are part of His family, sharing Heaven's joys forever with all our brothers and sisters in Christ.

Alexander MacLaren described Heaven this way: "The joys of heaven are not the joys of passive contemplation, of dreamy remembrance . . . but they are described thus, 'They rest not night or day,' and 'His servants serve Him and see His face.'" In the midst of earth's turmoil, keep your eyes on Heaven!

HOPE FOR TODAY
There is joy in using our God-given gifts and talents to serve others; it is exhilarating and energizing. Imagine how much more joy and fulfillment there is when we are using those gifts to serve God Himself!

GOD'S PRESENCE

"I am with you always, to the very end of the age."
MATTHEW 28:20 NIV

These words are Christ's promise to all His disciples, and it is a promise that is marvelously inclusive. No situation is excluded; no challenge is omitted.

Dr. Handley Moule, the noted Greek scholar and Anglican bishop of Durham (England) in another generation, maintained that the words always could be paraphrased to mean, "I am with you all the days, all day long." That means we can count on Christ's presence not only every day but every moment of every day.

Of the fact of His presence there can be no doubt, for His Word cannot fail. What we need is to cultivate the sense of His presence, every day, every hour, every moment. This happens as we speak to Him in worship and prayer, and listen to Him speak to us through His Word, the Bible.

HOPE FOR TODAY

Christ's presence means that you will never face anything alone. He is with you in the valley and marches with you into battle. It's never you against the world; it's you with the One who has overcome the world.

THE TUG OF GOD'S LOVE

The Spirit Himself bears witness with our spirit that we are children of God.
ROMANS 8:16

Whenever anyone asks me how I can be so certain about who and what God really is, I am reminded of the story of the little boy who was out flying a kite. It was a fine day for kite flying. The wind was brisk, and large billowy clouds were blowing across the sky. The kite went up and up until it was entirely hidden by the clouds.

"What are you doing?" a man asked the little boy.

"I'm flying a kite," he replied.

"Flying a kite?" the man said. "How can you be sure? You can't see the kite."

"No," said the boy, "I can't see it, but every little while I feel a tug, so I know for sure that it's there!"

Don't take anyone else's word for God. Find Him for yourself by inviting Jesus Christ to come into your life. Then you, too, will know by the wonderful, warm tug on your heartstrings that He is there for sure.

HOPE FOR TODAY

It doesn't matter what you've done; you can have an intimate relationship with the Father. As the old hymn assures, "There is room at the cross for you."

REST FOR THE WEARY

"Come to Me, all you who labor and are heavy laden, and I will give you rest."
MATTHEW 11:28

Few people know how to rest these days. Even on vacation, many people rush to cram in as much as they can before returning to their jobs, where they spend twice as much energy catching up on the work and mail that have piled up in their absence. Many of us need vacations just to rest from our vacations! Perhaps we have been looking for rest in the wrong places.

Jesus said, "Come to Me . . . and I will give you rest." Like peace, rest and contentment can be found only in one place, from one source, and that is the Lord Jesus Christ.

Jesus gives us the ultimate rest, the confidence we need, to escape the frustration and chaos of the world around us. Rest in Him and don't worry about what lies ahead. Jesus Christ has already taken care of tomorrow.

HOPE FOR TODAY

How do you handle weariness: a cup of coffee, a power nap, or a weekend away? These things, at best, offer temporary rest for our bodies. What Christ offers is rest for our souls; we just need to come to Him.

KEEP ON BEING FILLED

Be filled with the Spirit.

EPHESIANS 5:18 NIV

The command to "be filled with the Spirit" actually has the idea of continuously being filled, in the original Greek language. We are not filled once for all, like a bucket. Instead, we are to be filled constantly. This verse might be translated, "Be filled and keep on being filled."

The Late Dr. Merrill C. Tenney once compared this to the situation of an old-time farmhouse kitchen. In one corner was a sink; above it was a pipe through which came a continuous stream of water from the spring outside. The water, by running constantly, kept the sink brimful of good water.

In the same way, we are not to let ourselves be filled and then emptied of the Spirit—like a leaky bucket—only to be refilled later on, again and again. Rather, the Holy Spirit should flow within us constantly—and He will, as we yield ourselves to Christ's presence and power every day.

HOPE FOR TODAY
Do you find yourself returning to something that refreshes momentarily but leaves you empty in the long run? Christ promises that those who come to Him will receive living water that springs up from within.

CHILDREN OF LIGHT

You, brethren, are not in darkness. . . . You are all sons of light.

1 THESSALONIANS 5:4–5

The born-again Christian sees life not as a blurred, confused, meaningless mass, but as something planned and purposeful. His eyes have been opened to spiritual truth.

In Christ's first sermon at Nazareth, He said that one of the reasons He had come to earth was to preach "recovery of sight to the blind" (Luke 4:18). By nature we are all spiritually blind because of sin. But the Spirit of God helps us see our sin and our helplessness and shows us God's redeeming grace in Christ. The Spirit reveals the truth of Jesus' declaration: "I am the light of the world. He who follows Me shall not walk in darkness, but have the light of life" (John 8:12).

In the Bible we are called "children of light and children of the day" (1 Thessalonians 5:5 NRSV), because it pleased God to share His mysteries and secrets with us. We are no longer in the dark—we know where we came from, we know why we are here, and we know where we are going. In the midst of a world living in spiritual darkness, walk as a child of the light!

HOPE FOR TODAY

The enemy wants to keep you in the dark where shame and confusion rule the day. Christ came so that you would know the truth; you were created to live in the light.

LIFE AFTER DEATH

For to me, to live is Christ, and to die is gain.
PHILIPPIANS 1:21

I have asked a number of scientists questions concerning life after death, and most of them say, "We just do not know." Science deals in formulas and test tubes. But there is a spiritual world science knows nothing about.

Because many do not believe in life after death, their writings are filled with tragedy and pessimism. The writings of William Faulkner, James Joyce, and many others are filled with pessimism, darkness, and tragedy. Sadly, the same was often true of their lives.

How different from Jesus Christ, who said, "I am the resurrection and the life. He who believes in Me, though he may die, he shall live. And whoever lives and believes in Me shall never die" (John 11:25–26). Our hope of immortality is based on Christ alone—not on our desires, longings, arguments, or instincts of immortality. And because we know Christ is alive, we have hope—hope for the present and hope for life beyond the grave.

HOPE FOR TODAY

Jesus came to break every chain. He conquered the grave so that you wouldn't live in fear of death any longer (Hebrews 2:15). To live is Christ and to die is gain (Philippians 1:21); it's a win-win for Christ followers.

BECAUSE OF PRAYER

The effective, fervent prayer of a righteous man avails much.

JAMES 5:16

John Knox prayed, and the results caused Queen Mary to say that she feared the prayers of John Knox more than she feared all the armies of Scotland. John Wesley prayed, and revival came to England, sparing that nation the horrors of the French Revolution. Jonathan Edwards prayed, and revival spread throughout the American colonies.

History has been changed time after time because of prayer. I tell you, history could be changed again if people went to their knees in believing prayer. Even when times are bleak and the world scorns God, He still works through the prayers of His people. Pray today for revival in your nation, and around the world.

HOPE FOR TODAY

Prayer is a powerful and, often, unused tool in the life of the saint. Is there something in your life that you've been trying to work out? Try praying about it instead.

SUFFERING AND SUCCESS

Whenever you face trials of any kind, consider it nothing but joy.
JAMES 1:2 NRSV

Before the power of the atom was discovered, science had to devise a way to smash the atom. The secret of the atom's immeasurable and limitless power was in its being crushed.

Some of the most godly people I've ever known were men and women who were called upon to endure great suffering. They could have grown bitter and resentful . . . yet, because they knew Christ and walked in the joy of His presence every day, God blessed them and turned them into people who reflected Christ.

Dr. Edward Judson, at the dedication of a church in New York City, said, "Suffering and success go together. If you are succeeding without suffering, it is because others before you have suffered; if you are suffering without succeeding, it is that others after you may succeed."

Admittedly it's hard to "count it all joy" when suffering comes. But when it does, ask God to sanctify it and use it to make you steadfast in your faith.

HOPE FOR TODAY

We are told, Lord, that it is a privilege to suffer on Your behalf (Philippians 1:29). May You receive glory in every season of my life whether I'm enjoying success or enduring sorrow.

WHEN CHRIST COMES

Abide in Him, that when He appears, we may . . . not
be ashamed before Him at His coming.
1 JOHN 2:28

Almost two thousand years ago Jesus Christ won the decisive battle against sin and Satan through His death and resurrection. Satan did his best to defeat God's plans, but he could not win against God's overwhelming power.

Yet the war continues, for although Satan is a defeated foe, he is still alive and does everything he can to block God's work. But when Christ comes again, the war will be over. His victory over evil will be complete, and He will usher in an age in which sin and death will no longer rule, and cruelty and suffering will no longer exist.

For you who believe in Jesus Christ, the future is assured. Tomorrow belongs to you! You await the distant trumpet announcing the coming of Jesus Christ. In the meantime, let nothing discourage you. Keep your eyes on Christ and live each day as if He were coming tomorrow. After all, He might!

HOPE FOR TODAY
Life may be uncertain, but for followers of Christ, eternity is not. We win because we get Him! We just need to keep our eyes on the prize; Jesus is on His way.

ABOVE THE DIN

Let this mind be in you which was also in Christ Jesus.

PHILIPPIANS 2:5

We Christians are not to be conformed to this world in the way we think. The world by its advertisements, its conversation, and its philosophy is engaged in a gigantic brainwashing. Not always consciously but sometimes unconsciously, the Christian is beset by secular and worldly propaganda, calling us to live for ourselves and to put things and selfish pleasures ahead of God. The world's sewage system threatens to contaminate the stream of Christian thought.

However, above the din we can hear the voice of Scripture: "Do not be conformed to this world, but be transformed by the renewing of your mind, that you may prove what is that good and acceptable and perfect will of God" (Romans 12:2).

Time yourself the next time you read the Bible and pray. Compare it to the amount of time you spend watching television or surfing the Internet. Is God getting His share of your time and attention?

Is the world shaping your mind—or is Christ?

HOPE FOR TODAY

The mind of the believer is a battleground. Every thought must either honor Christ or be taken captive until it does (2 Corinthians 10:5). Who's winning the war in *your* mind?

BORROWED TROUBLES

Let your requests be made known to God; and the peace
of God . . . will guard your hearts and minds.

PHILIPPIANS 4:6–7

No troubles distress the mind and wear upon the nerves like borrowed troubles. As someone has written, "Worry is an old man with a bent head, carrying a load of feathers he thinks is lead."

Worry about what might happen makes even the smallest trouble seem huge. Nervously anticipating troubles that may never happen can crush our spirit. Instead of "borrowing trouble" by constantly worrying about the future, listen instead to Jesus' promise: "Peace I leave with you, My peace I give to you; not as the world gives do I give to you. Let not your heart be troubled, neither let it be afraid" (John 14:27).

Whatever is worrying you right now, give it to Jesus and trust Him to take care of it. Let His peace replace your worry.

HOPE FOR TODAY
Think about the amount of time you spend worrying about the future. How would your life change if you spent those moments in worship? Beginning today, choose to be a worshiper instead of a worrier.

GLORIOUS RESPONSIBILITIES

"If anyone serves Me, him My father will honor."
JOHN 12:26

Young people seek adventure and excitement, but youth wants more—it wants something to believe in; it wants a cause to give itself to and a flag to follow. Without a purpose greater than themselves, young people know they will end up with empty hearts and meaningless lives.

The only cause that is big enough to satisfy the yearning of our hearts is the cause of Jesus Christ; and its flag is the blood-stained body that was lifted on the Cross of Calvary for the redemption of the world.

This invitation to discipleship is the most thrilling cause we could ever imagine. Think of it: the God of the universe invites us to become His partners in reclaiming the world for Him! We can each have a part, using the unique gifts and opportunities God has given us.

Christ's call is for us to be His disciples every day. How are you responding to His call?

HOPE FOR TODAY

Every moment lived for the Lord has the potential to be heavy with glory. When we pick up our crosses and follow Him, our days will never be mundane, and our lives will definitely matter.

LIVING STONES

You also, as living stones, are being built up a spiritual house.
1 PETER 2:5

I have a friend who lost his job, a fortune, his wife, and his home. But he tenaciously held to his faith in Christ—the only thing he had left. Like Job in the Old Testament, he would not abandon God, no matter what happened. And yet, like Job, he couldn't help but wonder why.

One day he stopped to watch some men doing stonework on a huge church. One of them was chiseling a triangular piece of stone.

"What are you going to do with that?" asked my friend.

The workman said, "See that little opening away up there near the spire? Well, I'm shaping this down here so it will fit in up there."

Tears filled my friend's eyes as he walked away, for it seemed that God had spoken through the workman to explain the ordeal through which he was passing: "I'm shaping you down here so you'll fit in up there."

HOPE FOR TODAY

I will focus on You, Lord, when I'm left confused and wondering, *Why?* I will trust that there is purpose in my pain and that my circumstances are causing me to look a little more like You.

GODLY THOUGHTS

Be transformed by the renewing of your mind.
ROMANS 12:2

The Bible teaches that our minds are to be brought under the control of Christ. The reason? How we act will be determined by how we think. If God is to change our lives, He must first change our minds.

The human mind cannot exist as a vacuum. It will be filled either with good or evil. It will be filled either with Christ or with carnality. What will make the difference? It depends on us, and on what we allow to enter our minds.

Negatively, our minds must be turned away from evil. We must be careful what kind of television programs we see, what kind of books we read, the things that occupy our thoughts.

But it isn't enough to put bad thoughts out of our minds. Positively, they must be replaced with good thoughts—thoughts that are shaped by God and His Word, by prayer and worship, by fellowship with other Christians.

Deliberately turn away from every evil thought today and ask God to fill your mind instead with Himself from this moment on.

HOPE FOR TODAY

It is a dangerous thing to go out into the world empty; everything the enemy presents will seem sweet (Proverbs 27:7). Choose to fill yourself with the things of God so that you won't be tempted by the world's offerings.

FEBRUARY

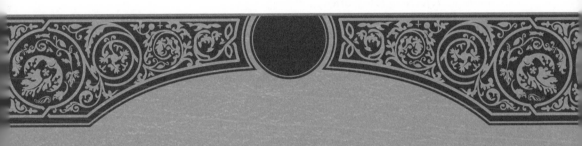

"No more shall every man teach his neighbor, and every man his brother, saying, 'Know the Lord,' for they all shall know Me, from the least of them to the greatest of them, says the LORD. For I will forgive their iniquity, and their sin I will remember no more."

JEREMIAH 31:34

A GLORIOUS OPPORTUNITY

May the glory of the LORD endure forever;
May the LORD rejoice in His works.
PSALM 104:31

C. T. Studd, the famous Cambridge cricketer and missionary pioneer, wrote the following couplet while still a student at Cambridge:

> Only one life, 'twill soon be past;
> Only what's done for Christ will last.

Life is a glorious opportunity if it is used to condition us for eternity. If we fail in this, though we succeed in everything else, our life will have been a failure. There is no escape for the man who squanders his opportunity to prepare to meet God.

You will never live this day again; once it is gone, it is gone forever. How will you spend it—for yourself, or for Christ? Remember: "Only what's done for Christ will last."

HOPE FOR TODAY

What can you do to love the Lord and to love your neighbor? Worldly accomplishments are soon forgotten, but today is a glorious opportunity to live for Christ and be a part of something that will last forever.

ALWAYS WITH US

No good thing will He withhold
From those who walk uprightly.
PSALM 84:11

Many times we make the mistake of thinking that Christ's help is needed only for sickrooms or in times of overwhelming sorrow and suffering. This is not true. Certainly, God is with us in times of distress, and that is a comforting truth. But listen: Jesus wants to be part of every experience and every moment of our lives.

He went to the wedding at Cana as well as to the home of Mary and Martha when Lazarus died. He wept with those who wept and rejoiced with those who rejoiced. Someone has said, "There are just as many stars in the sky at noon as at midnight, although we cannot see them in the sun's glare."

I seriously doubt if we will ever understand our trials and adversities until we are safely in Heaven. Then when we look back, we are going to be absolutely amazed at how God took care of us and blessed us even in the storms of life. But God is with us in the good times also, and we should thank Him for them and commit them to Him just as surely as we do the hard times.

HOPE FOR TODAY

Thank You, Lord, for being completely invested in the lives of Your people. You are intimately acquainted with the joys and sorrows of the flesh, and You have promised to be present with us through it all.

ABOVE THE CLOUDS

Your faithfulness reaches to the clouds.
PSALM 36:5

My home is on a mountain nearly four thousand feet high. Many times I can see below me the clouds in the valley. Some mornings I wake up to find that I am in lovely sunshine, but the valley below is covered with clouds. At other times thunderstorms come up, and I can see the lightning flash and hear the thunder roar down below while I am enjoying beautiful sunlight and clear skies above.

Many times I have sat on my rustic front porch and watched the clouds below. I have thought of the clouds of discouragement and suffering that temporarily veil the sunlight of God's love from us. Many people live with a cloud hanging over their lives.

The Bible has a great deal to say about clouds, for they sometimes symbolize the spiritual forces that obscure the face of God. But He has not abandoned us. He is still there, and in faith we know we can trust His promise: "I will never leave you nor forsake you" (Hebrews 13:5).

HOPE FOR TODAY
Have you ever felt as if others were enjoying sunshine while clouds obscured your view? Remember that the clouds that seem to hide God's presence can never hinder His power. He has not lost sight of you.

LOVE DEMONSTRATED

He loved us and sent His Son to be the propitiation for our sins.

1 JOHN 4:10

The word *love* is used to mean many different things. We say that we "love" the house that we have just bought or that we "love" a particular vacation spot or that we "love" a peanut butter and jelly sandwich. We also "love" a certain television program, and we "love" our husband or wife. Hopefully we don't love our spouse the same way we love a peanut butter and jelly sandwich!

The greatest love of all, however, is God's love for us—a love that showed itself in action. A friend once observed, "Love talked about is easily ignored, but love demonstrated is irresistible." The Bible says, "God demonstrates His own love toward us, in that while we were still sinners, Christ died for us" (Romans 5:8). Now, that is real love! How will you respond to His love today?

HOPE FOR TODAY

Teach me to love as You love, Lord. Give me the boldness to bring Your light into dark places and the compassion to carry Your beauty to broken people. May my life be evidence of Your irresistible love.

LONGING FOR GOD

My heart and my flesh cry out for the living God.
PSALM 84:2

Have you ever been under water for a period of time that is longer than you had expected? You know, as the time ticks away, how desperate you become to reach the surface and breathe the air. The greater the time you are under water, the more you long for a breath of air, until that desire overwhelms you, and you rush to get to the surface as rapidly as possible. You have no other thoughts but quenching your need for air.

That is what it means to "long for God," to feel unfulfilled without Him. It means we know we desperately need Him, even more than we need air, and we yearn to be filled with His presence. "My heart and my flesh cry out for the living God."

God wants us to be satisfied with nothing less than Himself. And we are never more fulfilled than when we know Him. Ask God to give you a new hunger for Him, so you may become filled with "the fullness of Christ" (Ephesians 4:13).

HOPE FOR TODAY
How many times have you felt something missing in your life but couldn't seem to fill the void? You've tried possessions, people, and prestige, but at the end of the day, the longing remains. Only Christ can fill the emptiness within.

TRIUMPH AND GLORY

The day of the Lord so comes as a thief in the night.

1 THESSALONIANS 5:2

Christians have no cause to go around wringing their hands, wondering what they will do in the face of the present world situation. The Scripture says that in the midst of persecution, confusion, wars, and rumors of wars, we are to comfort one another with the knowledge that Jesus Christ is coming back in triumph, glory, and majesty.

Many times when I go to bed at night, I think that before I awaken Christ may come. Sometimes when I get up and look at the dawn, I think that perhaps this is the day He will return.

But until that day, God is still working—and so should we. In a world filled with turmoil and hopelessness, we are to pray, and we are to do all we can to alleviate suffering and bring Christ's love to others. May Jesus' words become true in your life: "Let your light so shine before men, that they may see your good works and glorify your Father in heaven" (Matthew 5:16).

HOPE FOR TODAY

It's tempting to sit back, study the signs, and attempt to guess when Christ will return. But our command is to keep working until He comes (Luke 19:13). Let's be about our Father's business.

THE BREAD OF LIFE

He who wins souls is wise.

PROVERBS 11:30

We have bread to give to a hungry world—the Bread of Life, Jesus Christ. People may be so busy feeding on other things that they ignore Him or refuse Him, but we must keep offering Christ to a spiritually dying world.

We have water to give to a thirsting world—the Living Water, Jesus Christ. People may seek to quench the thirst of their souls in a hundred other ways, but we must keep crying out, "Ho, everyone who thirsts, come to the waters" (Isaiah 55:1). Sometimes they can't come, and we have to carry it to them.

We must persevere. We must never give up. Christ never gave up, but "became obedient to the point of death" (Philippians 2:8).

All around you are people who hunger and thirst for God, although they may not even realize it. Will you point them to Christ, who alone can satisfy their deepest longings?

HOPE FOR TODAY

Who do you know who is hungry for something more? Who around you is parched and longing for something to refresh their spirits? Don't let them leave your presence without a catching a glimpse of Christ.

THE STORM IS BEHIND US

You have cast all my sins behind Your back.
ISAIAH 38:17

We shall never understand the extent of God's love in Christ at the Cross until we understand that we shall never have to stand before the judgment of God for our sins. All our sins—without exception—were placed on Christ, and He took the judgment we deserve. He finished the work of redemption.

Once while crossing the North Atlantic in a ship, I looked out my porthole when I got up in the morning and saw one of the blackest clouds I had ever seen. I was certain that we were in for a terrible storm. I ordered my breakfast sent to my room and spoke to the steward about the storm. He said, "Oh, we've already come through that storm. It's behind us."

If we are believers in Jesus Christ, we have already come through the storm of judgment. It happened at the Cross. Don't be bound by your guilt or your fears any longer, but realize that sin's penalty has already been paid by Christ—completely and fully.

HOPE FOR TODAY

Guilt is the game of the enemy; he wants you to focus on every wrong you've done or had done to you. Choose, instead, to be consumed with the Cross of Christ and embrace the grace available to you.

POWER TO CHANGE THE WORLD

You are my hope, O Lord GOD;
You are my trust from my youth.
PSALM 71:5

We still wrestle with the same problems that preoccupied Plato and Aristotle centuries ago: Where did we come from? Why are we here? Where are we going? We search for answers, but the signs all seem to say "no exit."

But the Cross boldly stands against the confusion of our world, a beacon of hope in the midst of darkness and doubt. In the Cross, Christ not only bridged the gap between God and us, but there we find the answers to life's deepest questions. There we discover our true identity: forgiven sinners who now belong to God. There we discover our true destiny: a glorious eternity with God in Heaven. There we discover our true purpose: to love God and serve Him with all our might.

Never underestimate what Christ did for us through the Cross. By His death our salvation was won, and by it our lives—and our world—can be transformed. What difference does the Cross make in your life?

HOPE FOR TODAY
The Cross made clear Your love for me, God. No matter what comes my way, I will never question the sincerity of Your love or the lengths to which You would go to make me Your own.

THE MASTER KEY

The LORD our God we will serve, and His voice we will obey!
JOSHUA 24:24

I knew a wealthy father who refused to get his son a bicycle because the boy's report card showed disgracefully low marks, the yard was not raked, and other assignments had not been carried out. I'm sure the father would not have been wise to lavish gifts upon such a disobedient and ungrateful son. He wasn't being cruel or stingy; he simply knew his son needed to learn responsibility.

God, too, wants us to learn responsibility. Yes, we are saved by His grace—but we are also called to be responsible disciples, learning to follow Christ by obeying God's will. The Bible warns, "If you do not obey the voice of the LORD, but rebel against the commandment of the LORD, then the hand of the LORD will be against you" (1 Samuel 12:15).

If you want God to hear your prayers, surrender your selfishness and stubbornness to Him, and then humbly seek His will. Obedience is the master key to effective prayer.

HOPE FOR TODAY

Do you want to unleash the power of prayer in your life? Ask God to open your eyes to any area of disobedience that may be hindering your efforts. Then, watch what He can do with the prayers of a righteous person.

NOT FAITH BUT SIGHT

"The Son of Man will come in the glory of His Father with His angels."
MATTHEW 16:27

Today, Christ is hidden from our view (although through the Holy Spirit He lives in our hearts). Today is the day of faith; as Paul wrote, "We walk by faith, not by sight" (2 Corinthians 5:7). Only in the future will we "see Him as He is" (1 John 3:2).

Christ's first appearing was quiet, almost unnoticed—a humble manger, simple shepherds, an insignificant corner of the Roman Empire. His second appearing will be glorious and universal. He will be accompanied by His angels and will defeat every enemy until He subdues the whole earth.

How easily the events of the moment crowd out the promise of eternity! The present seems so real; the unseen future seems so illusory. But in reality the opposite is true. Don't let the present consume you. Instead, "seek those things which are above, where Christ is" (Colossians 3:1).

HOPE FOR TODAY

The things of this world, both the pleasures and the pains, are temporary. Learn to look beyond them and to seek your Father's face. His presence is a constant in an ever-changing world.

WE WAIT ON GOD

But those who wait on the LORD
Shall renew their strength;
They shall mount up with wings like eagles.
ISAIAH 40:31

Nowhere does the Bible teach that Christians are exempt from tribulation and natural disaster. We live in a world infected with the disease of sin, and we share in its misery and pain.

But the Bible does teach that we can face trials with a power others do not have—the power of God. As we trust Him, God helps us endure, and even discern His purposes in the midst of suffering. Christiana Tsai, the Christian daughter of a former governor in China, wrote, "Throughout my many years of illness [53], I have never dared to ask God why He allowed me to suffer so long. I only ask what He wants me to do."

The eagle has the unique ability to lock its joints and soar effortlessly on an updraft instead of flapping its wings. As we wait on God, He helps us use the winds of adversity to soar above our problems. As the Bible says, "Those who wait on the LORD . . . shall mount up with wings like eagles."

HOPE FOR TODAY

It is human nature, when trials come, to be consumed with trying to figure out the *why*. What if we, during those difficult seasons, chose to remind ourselves *Who* is in control and ask *what* He would have us to do?

45

A JOYFUL LIFE

Rejoice in the Lord always.

PHILIPPIANS 4:4

When our hearts are surrendered totally to the will of God, then we delight in seeing Him use us in any way He pleases. Our plans and desires begin to agree with His, and we accept His direction in our lives. Our sense of joy, satisfaction, and fulfillment in life increases, no matter what the circumstances, if we are in the center of God's will.

The Christian life is a joyful life. Christianity was never meant to be something to make people miserable. The ministry of Jesus Christ was one of joy. The Bible teaches that a life of inward peace and outward victory is a Christian's birthright.

"What a witness to the world Christians would be," wrote Amy Carmichael, "if only they were more evidently very happy people." Joy is one of the marks of a true believer. Will others see the joy of Christ in your life today?

HOPE FOR TODAY

Moses' shining face was evidence of his time with God. Peter's and John's courage let people know they had been with Jesus. Would people know you are a Christ follower by your fruit (Matthew 7:19)?

CHRISTIAN VIRTUES AT HOME

*"I am the vine, you are the branches. He who abides
in Me, and I in him, bears much fruit."*

JOHN 15:5

How we live at home is the acid test for any Christian man or woman. It is far easier to live an excellent life among our friends, when we are putting our best foot forward and are conscious of public opinion, than it is to live for Christ in our home.

Our own family circle sees us in our unguarded moments. They see us when exhaustion and stress fray our nerves. Our own family circle knows whether Christ lives in and through us.

If I am a true Christian, I will not give way at home to bad temper, impatience, faultfinding, sarcasm, unkindness, suspicion, selfishness, or laziness. Instead, each day my life will display the fruit of the Spirit, which is "love, joy, peace, patience, kindness, goodness, faithfulness, gentleness, and self-control" (Galatians 5:22–23 NIV). How different would your home be if you consistently practiced these Christlike virtues?

HOPE FOR TODAY

Lord, I don't want to portray something in public that I don't live up to in private. Help me to live out the fruit of Your Spirit wherever I am each and every day.

THIRSTING AFTER RIGHTEOUSNESS

They were all filled with the Holy Spirit.
ACTS 2:4

The early Christians had no buildings, no airplanes, no automobiles, no printing presses or television or radio or social media. Yet they turned their world "upside down" for Christ. They started a spiritual revolution that shook the very foundations of the Roman Empire.

In the face of opposition and overwhelming odds, they stayed courageous, bold, dauntless, and full of faith. They lived their lives daily for Christ, no matter what others thought. They gladly suffered scorn, persecution, and even death for their faith in Christ.

What was their secret? The Bible gives us the key: "They were all filled with the Holy Spirit." The Holy Spirit changed their lives, and those they met couldn't help but be impressed by their love and the quality and purity of their lives. What keeps us from turning our world upside down for Christ?

HOPE FOR TODAY
Paul told the believers in Thessalonica not to quench the Holy Spirit. What would happen if all believers gave the Holy Spirit free reign in their lives?

SERVING GOD FOREVER

Because of His great love . . . [He] . . . made us alive together with Christ.

EPHESIANS 2:4–5

Your life may seem monotonous and filled with drudgery. Yet remember, if you are a Christian, you are not working for an hour or for a day but for eternity. When this body of corruption shall take on immortality, another part of our work will begin, for the Scripture teaches that God's servants shall serve Him forever. The difference is that in Heaven we will never grow bored or weary!

Some time ago a man said to me, "You might be mistaken, for no one has ever come back from the grave to tell us."

I replied, "Sir, that's exactly where you are wrong. Someone has returned— His name is Jesus Christ, our Lord."

That makes all the difference! Because Christ is alive, we have "an inheritance incorruptible and undefiled . . . reserved in heaven" (1 Peter 1:4). And this helps us persevere, even when life seems dull.

HOPE FOR TODAY

The birth of Christ was announced to shepherds in a field doing what they did every other evening. God isn't looking for flashy people doing extraordinary things; He reveals Himself to those who are faithful in the ordinary.

POWER FOR LIFE

"The Spirit of truth . . . dwells with you and will be in you."
JOHN 14:17

Walter Knight tells the story about a little boy who had recently received Christ. "Daddy, how can I believe in the Holy Spirit when I have never seen Him?" asked Jim.

"I'll show you how," said his father, who was an electrician. The father took Jim to a power plant and showed him the generators. "This is where the power comes from to heat our stove and to give us light. We can't see the power, but it's in that machine and in the power lines," said the father.

"Now, son, let me ask you a question: Do you believe in electricity?" he asked.

"Yes, I believe in electricity," said Jim.

"Of course you do," said his father, "but you don't believe in it because you see it. You believe in it because you see what it can do. Likewise, you can believe in the Holy Spirit not because you see Him, but you see what He does in people's lives when they are surrendered to Christ and possess His power."

HOPE FOR TODAY
Lord, there is evidence of You everywhere. You enable me to praise when in pain and to have peace in times of chaos. One day I will see You as clearly with my eyes as I have felt You in my heart.

GOD TAKES THE BURDEN

As a father pities his children,
so the LORD pities those who fear Him.
PSALM 103:13

As God's children, we are His dependents. Dependent children spend little time worrying about meals, clothing, and shelter. They assume—and they have a right to—that their parents will provide everything they need.

Jesus said, "Do not worry, saying, 'What shall we eat?' or 'What shall we drink?' or 'What shall we wear?' . . . But seek first the kingdom of God . . . and all these things shall be added to you" (Matthew 6:31, 33).

Unfortunately, worry is an ingrained habit for most of us. But because we are God's children, He is responsible for our welfare. That is why you should be "casting all your care upon Him, for He cares for you" (1 Peter 5:7). In other words, let God do the worrying! He says, "I'll take the burden—don't give it a thought—leave it to Me."

Never forget: God is bigger than your problems. Whatever worries press upon you today, put them in God's hands—and leave them there.

HOPE FOR TODAY

What would we be free to do if we were free from worry? The next time anxiety creeps in, let's choose to worship or be in God's Word instead. It's a far better use of our time.

A Formula for Peace

Great peace have those who love Your law,
And nothing causes them to stumble.
PSALM 119:165

God has a plan for peace, and it is found in His Son, whom the Bible calls the "Prince of Peace" (Isaiah 9:6). But we have rejected God's plan. Wars still ravage our world—and our lives.

Why? Jesus said the problem is within us: "Out of the heart . . . proceed evil thoughts, adulteries, fornications, murders, thefts, covetousness, wickedness, deceit, lewdness, an evil eye, blasphemy, pride, foolishness" (Mark 7:21–22). What a list! Our real war is a rebellion against God—and it brings unending misery.

But God longs to see this rebellion cease. That is why Christ came. By His death He provided the way for us to be reconciled to God. And when we have peace with God, we have peace in our hearts—and peace with each other.

This happens as we repent and receive Christ. The war is over, for God extends a peace treaty to all who come to Christ.

Hope for Today
God promises perfect peace to those whose minds are fixed on Him. Who doesn't desire perfect peace? If we are focused on God and His Word, no financial woe, health crisis, or family drama will cause us to stumble.

A WARNING LIGHT

If your heart is wise, My heart will rejoice.
PROVERBS 23:15

One of the ways God has revealed Himself to us is in the conscience. Conscience has been described as the light of the soul. Even when it is dulled or darkened by sin, it can still bear witness to the reality of good and evil, and to the holiness of God.

What causes this warning light to go on inside me when I do wrong? It is my conscience, given by God to steer me away from evil and toward good. Conscience can be our gentlest teacher and friend—and sometimes our worst enemy (or so we think) when we sin.

The Scripture says, "Man's conscience is the lamp of the eternal" (Proverbs 20:27 MOFFATT). In other words, conscience is God's lamp within the human breast. In his *Critique of Pure Reason*, Immanuel Kant said there were just two things that filled him with awe—the starry heavens above and the human conscience within.

Persistent sin can dull or even silence our conscience. On the other hand, persistent attention to God's Word will sharpen our conscience and make us more sensitive to moral and spiritual danger. Is this happening in your life?

HOPE FOR TODAY

Thank You, God, for loving me enough to prick my conscience when I'm being led astray. May I remain sensitive to the Spirit's guidance so that I remain close to Your side.

PRAY ANYWHERE, ANYTIME

Rejoice always, pray without ceasing.
1 THESSALONIANS 5:16–17

Prayer is an essential part of a healthy Christian life. Just as omitting an essential vitamin from our diet will make us physically weak, so a lack of prayer will make us spiritually anemic.

The Bible says, "Pray without ceasing." It isn't enough to get out of bed in the morning, quickly bow our heads, and repeat a few sentences. Instead, we need to set aside specific times to be alone with God, speaking to Him in prayer and listening to Him speak through His Word. If you set aside special times for prayer, your unconscious mind will be saturated with prayer all day long.

For the overworked mother or other busy person, this may seem impossible (although even a few minutes alone with God can reap rich rewards). But even when we are busy, we can "pray without ceasing" in our hearts and minds. We can pray anywhere, anytime—and God will hear us. Today let prayer saturate your life "without ceasing."

HOPE FOR TODAY
Prayer is not an isolated activity; it is ongoing throughout the day. When we seek to hear from God, we will find that He is always available and ever eager to speak to His children. We pray with our words and find answers in His Word.

TRUST CROWDS OUT WORRY

Commit your way to the LORD . . .
And He shall bring it to pass.
PSALM 37:5

You cannot stop a baby's cry by giving him a rattle when he is hungry. He will keep on crying until his hunger is satisfied by the food his little body demands. Neither can the soul of a mature person be satisfied apart from God. David described the hunger of every human being when he said, "As the deer pants for the water brooks, so pants my soul for You, O God" (Psalm 42:1).

Two conflicting forces cannot exist in one human heart. When doubt reigns, faith cannot abide. Where hatred rules, love is crowded out. Where selfishness rules, there love cannot dwell. When worry is present, trust cannot crowd its way in.

In the same way, God will not share His rightful place in our lives with anything or anyone less than Himself. Is anything crowding God out of your heart today? Don't give first place to anything less than Christ, but "commit your way to the LORD."

HOPE FOR TODAY

Are you prone to worry? Quick to become angry? Generally impatient? Perhaps it's time to put Christ back in control and allow the fruit of His Spirit to fill every nook and cranny of your heart.

LET IT SHINE!

The light of the righteous rejoices.

PROVERBS 13:9

We are holding a light. We are to let it shine! Though it may seem but a twinkling candle in a world of blackness, it is our business to let it shine. Light dispels darkness, and it attracts people in darkness to it.

We are blowing a trumpet. In the din and noise of battle, the sound of our little trumpet may seem to be lost, but we must keep sounding the alarm to those who are in spiritual danger.

We are kindling a fire. In this cold world full of hatred and selfishness, our little blaze may seem to be unavailing, but we must keep our fire burning.

A light, a trumpet, a fire . . . they seem so little amidst the darkness and violence of the world. But "with God all things are possible" (Matthew 19:26), and He will bless our efforts to bring the good news of Jesus to a weary and strife-torn world.

HOPE FOR TODAY

A single flame may not be much, but a multitude of flames would be unstoppable. There are no solo acts in the body of Christ. Who do you need to link arms with today?

No Bargain, No Barter

"Come, buy . . .
Without money and without price."
Isaiah 55:1

God does not bargain with us, nor can we barter with Him. He holds our eternal salvation in His omnipotent hand, and He bids us take it as a free gift, "without money and without price."

Yet this is hard for us to accept. Surely something as precious as salvation must cost us greatly! Surely God must demand we work for it!

But that is wrong—and the reason is because the price has already been paid! Salvation is free—but it wasn't cheap. It cost the dear Son of God His very life.

Only cheap, tawdry things have a price tag on them.

The best things in life are free—the air we breathe, the stars at night, the wonder of human love. But the greatest gift of all is our salvation, purchased for us by Jesus Christ. "Thanks be to God for His indescribable gift!" (2 Corinthians 9:15).

Hope for Today

The Philippian jailer asked Paul what he must do to be saved (Acts 16:30). Do you wonder that as well? The answer is the same for people today as it was for the prison guard: we just have to believe and receive.

THE DIVINE FLAME

"You shall receive power when the Holy Spirit has come upon you; and you shall be my witnesses."
ACTS 1:8

Simon Peter was so spiritually weak before Pentecost that, in spite of his bragging to the contrary, he swore and denied Christ. He was cowed by the crowd, shamed by a little servant girl, and took his place with the enemies of Christ.

But see him after he has been baptized with fire—the fire of the Holy Spirit! He stands boldly before the same rabble that had crucified Jesus, looks into their faces, and fearlessly proclaims the good news of salvation (see Acts 2:36). Peter, the weak, was transformed into Peter, the rock.

So it was with the early disciples. The Holy Spirit changed them from ordinary individuals into firebrands for God. Their faith and zeal started a conflagration that spread throughout the Roman Empire.

Their secret? Total submission to Jesus Christ and His will. What keeps you from being used of God to touch your world for Christ?

HOPE FOR TODAY

Would you be so bold as to ask God to use you? To put no caveats or limitations on *how* He may choose to do so? Revival begins when believers stand and say, "Here I am, Lord. Send me."

THE HAND OF GOD

No good thing will He withhold
From those who walk uprightly.
PSALM 84:11

In the midst of sorrow and trouble, this life has many blessings and enjoyments that have come from the hand of God.

Think of the blessings we so easily take for granted: life itself; preservation from danger; every bit of health we enjoy; every hour of liberty; the ability to see, to hear, to speak, to think, and to imagine—all this comes from the hand of God. Even our capacity to love is a gift from God. Most of all, God has given us the gift of Christ.

What should our response be? We can put it in one word: *gratitude.* But how do we show our gratitude? By giving back to God a part of what He has given us.

What have you done lately to show your gratitude to God for all that He has done, and is doing, for you?

HOPE FOR TODAY

In Scripture, God commands His people to tell future generations about all that He has done for them. We can express gratitude to God by telling others and, in the process, reminding ourselves of His faithfulness to us.

A PREPARED PLACE

"In My Father's house are many mansions."
JOHN 14:2

As much as our homes mean to us, they are not permanent. Sometimes I look at my own adult children and can hardly believe they are all grown and on their own. The house that once rang with the laughter of children now seems empty.

Those disciples who for Christ's sake gave up houses and lands and loved ones knew little of home life or home joys. It was as if Jesus were saying to them, "We have no lasting home here on earth, but my Father's house is a home where we will be together for all eternity."

The venerable Bishop Ryle is reputed to have said, "Heaven is a prepared place for a prepared people, and those who enter shall find that they are neither unknown nor unexpected."

Even life's happiest experiences last but a moment, yet Heaven's joy is eternal. Someday we will go to our eternal Home—and Christ will be there to welcome us!

HOPE FOR TODAY

Many songs, books, and movies have been written around the theme of going home and the emotions that accompany it. None of them can hold a candle to the heavenly homecoming that awaits us in glory!

A Passion to Please God

I have learned in whatever state I am, to be content.

PHILIPPIANS 4:11

Popularity and praise can be far more dangerous for the Christian than persecution. They can turn us away from God without our even being aware of it, making us like those in Jesus' day who "loved the praise of men more than the praise of God" (John 12:43).

Unfortunately, it is easy when all goes well to lose our perspective. Instead, we must learn like Paul to be content in whatever state we find ourselves. The important thing is to have one consuming passion: to please Christ. Then, whatever happens, we know He has permitted it to take place to teach us and to perfect us for His service. He will enrich our circumstances, be they pleasant or disagreeable, by His presence with us.

Ask God to keep you from worrying about what others think, and to make you content with whatever He sends your way. All the tomorrows of our lives have to pass Him before they get to us!

Hope for Today

Peace comes when we abandon our people-pleasing efforts and focus on Christ instead. Love the Lord. Love your neighbor. Obey the Lord. Show mercy. The things that please Christ never change.

MARCH

Only fear the LORD, and serve Him in truth with all your heart; for consider what great things He has done for you.

1 SAMUEL 12:24

IN THE WORLD, NOT OF THE WORLD

They are of the world. . . . We are of God.
1 JOHN 4:5–6

The Gulf Stream flows in the ocean, and yet it is not absorbed by it. It maintains its warm temperatures even in the icy waters of the North Atlantic.

Believers are in the world, and yet they must not be absorbed by it. If Christians are to fulfill their purposes in the world, they must not be chilled by the indifferent, godless society in which they live. The Bible says, "Do not be conformed to this world" (Romans 12:2). It is true that Jesus dined with publicans and sinners, but He did not allow the social group to overwhelm Him and conform Him to its ways. Instead, He seized every opportunity to present spiritual truth and to lead a soul from death to life.

Our social contacts should not only be pleasant, they should be opportunities to share our faith with those who do not yet know Christ. As you have contact with others this day, will they sense the warmth of Christ's presence through you?

HOPE FOR TODAY

It's possible for us to interact with an unbelieving world, to love our neighbors, to share Christ, and, yet, still to be set apart. We can go into all the world (Mark 16:15) while not looking anything like it.

PEOPLE OF PRAYER

Lord, teach us to pray.
LUKE 11:1

Thousands pray only in times of great stress, danger, or uncertainty. I have flown through bad storms and found myself surrounded by people praying for the first time in their lives. It is instinctive for us to pray in times of trouble. Only then do we realize our helplessness.

But Christ instructed His followers to pray at all times, both by His teaching and His example. So fervent and so direct were His prayers that once, after He finished praying, His followers pleaded, "Lord, teach us to pray." They yearned to be in touch with God, as they knew Christ was.

Have you ever said, "Lord, teach me to pray"? Prayer shouldn't be casual or sporadic, dictated only by the needs of the moment. Prayer should be as much a part of our lives as breathing. Never has our world stood in greater need of people who will pray. Will you be one of them?

HOPE FOR TODAY

Do your prayers feel forced or ineffective? Do you long for more intimacy with God? All you have to do is ask (Matthew 7:7), and your Father will show you how to speak to and hear from Him.

WE CAN COUNT ON HIM

Blessed is the man whose strength is in You.
PSALM 84:5

Someone has written a little verse that goes like this:

> Said the robin to the sparrow,
> I should really like to know,
> Why these anxious human beings
> Rush about and worry so.
> Said the sparrow to the robin,
> Friend, I think that it must be,
> That they have no heavenly Father
> Such as cares for you and me.

Jesus used the carefree attitude of the birds to underscore the fact that worrying is unnatural. "Look at the birds of the air, for they neither sow nor reap; . . . yet your heavenly Father feeds them" (Matthew 6:26). If He cares for tiny birds and frail flowers, why can't we count on Him for every aspect of our lives? After all, He loves us so much that He sent His Son into the world to save us. We are that valuable to Him!

HOPE FOR TODAY

We can rest easy knowing that our loving Father is in control of His creation and of our circumstances.

LIFE PLUS LOVE

All the law is fulfilled in one word; . . . "love your neighbor as yourself."
GALATIANS 5:14

Suppose I gave everything I had to charity. You probably would say I was a very good person—a fine Christian. But Paul said that unless I acted out of love, "I am nothing" (1 Corinthians 13:2). George Sweeting has said, "Life minus love equals nothing!"

Do you have this kind of love—a love that puts others ahead of yourself? Without Jesus Christ in your heart, without the Holy Spirit in your life, you can't produce this love. This is the kind of love Jesus had for us, when He willingly left the glory of Heaven and went to the Cross for our salvation.

Only God can give us a selfless love for others, as the Holy Spirit changes us from within. This is one reason we must receive Christ, for apart from His Spirit we can never be freed from the chains of selfishness, jealousy, and indifference. Will others see Christ's love in your life today?

HOPE FOR TODAY

Forgive me, Lord, for the times I have done good things with a bad attitude. I know that You judge my motives and not just my movements. Teach me to love as You love.

THE SPIRIT OF GOD

*"I will pray the Father, and He will give you another
Helper, that He may abide with you forever."*
JOHN 14:16

During His lifetime on earth, Christ's presence could be experienced only by a small group of people at any given time. Now Christ dwells through the Spirit in the hearts of all who have received Him as Savior and Lord. The apostle Paul wrote, "Do you not know . . . that the Spirit of God dwells in you?" (1 Corinthians 3:16).

The Holy Spirit is given to every believer—not for a limited time, but forever. If He left us for one moment, we would be in deep trouble. But He doesn't! He is there to give you both the gifts and the power to work for Christ. He is there to give you strength in the moment of temptation. He is there to produce the fruit of "love, joy, peace, longsuffering, kindness, goodness, faithfulness, gentleness, self-control" (Galatians 5:22–23).

You will never have more of the Holy Spirit than you do right now. But will He have more of you?

HOPE FOR TODAY

Do you know people who seem to have more of the Holy Spirit than you? More peace, patience, kindness? They don't have more Spirit; they are just more surrendered to Him. Ask God to take complete control of your life.

GLORIOUS GIVING

"Give, and it will be given to you."
LUKE 6:38

"Give," Christ commanded. Yet it was more than a command. It was an invitation to glorious and abundant living. If we get our attitude toward money right, it will help straighten out almost every other area of our lives.

Have you ever realized just how cruel and deceptive a master money can be? Some people spend their entire lives slavishly serving it—often without even realizing it. No wonder Jesus warned, "You cannot serve both God and Money" (Matthew 6:24 NIV).

The chief motive of the selfish, unregenerate person is to "get." The chief motive of the dedicated Christian should be to "give." Jesus said, "Give, and it will be given to you." It's a promise, and we know Jesus never breaks His promises. Getting . . . or giving? Which is true of you?

HOPE FOR TODAY

We strive to get things, and we struggle to keep them. It is so much easier to give things away. An open palm takes far less energy than a clenched fist. Our God designed us to be givers!

LIFE IN CHRIST WORKS

I know whom I have believed.
2 TIMOTHY 1:12

Does Christianity work? Does anything really happen when a person repents of sin and receives Christ by faith?

I can only tell you that it worked in my own life. I was reared during the Depression on a farm in North Carolina. My parents weren't able to give me the advantages most young people enjoy today. I grew up in a Christian home, but by the time I was fifteen, I was in full revolt against all religion—against God, the Bible, the church.

But one night I committed my life to Jesus Christ, and He gave me a whole new direction. My grades picked up. My attitude toward others changed. I began to seek God's will instead of my own way. No, I didn't become perfect, but my life was changed.

I have been all over the world, and I have never met anyone who regretted giving his or her life to Christ. And neither will you.

HOPE FOR TODAY
Of all the things you may regret, choosing Christ will never be one of them. You will never be abandoned, unloved, or misunderstood by Him. You will have purpose and passion. You will always have a place to call home.

THE BRIGHTNESS OF GOD'S LOVE

My flesh and my heart fail;
But God is the strength of my heart.
PSALM 73:26

Trouble will not hurt us unless it does what many of us too often allow it to do—harden us, making us sour, bitter, and skeptical. But it need not be this way. Troubles we bear trustfully can bring us a fresh vision of God and a new outlook on life—an outlook of peace and hope.

If we make our troubles an opportunity to learn more of God's love and His power to aid and bless, then they will teach us to have a firmer confidence in His providence. As a result, the brightness of His love will fill our lives.

Learn to trust God with a childlike dependence on Him as your loving heavenly Father, and no trouble can destroy you. In those darkest hours before the Cross, Jesus could still say, "I am not alone, because the Father is with Me" (John 16:32).

The same is true for you. Even in that last dark hour of death, when your flesh and your heart fail, you will be able to depend in peace upon Him who "is the strength of my heart and my portion forever" (Psalm 73:26).

HOPE FOR TODAY

I can endure anything, Lord, as long as I know You are near. Give me the wisdom to seek You in every trial and the courage to follow wherever You lead. Give me the grace to finish well.

THE MIND OF CHRIST

Let this mind be in you which was also in Christ Jesus.
PHILIPPIANS 2:5

Jesus had the most all-encompassing mind this world has ever seen. His convictions were so strong, so unswerving that He was not afraid to mingle with any group, secure in the knowledge that He would not be contaminated or swayed.

Fear makes us unwilling to give voice to our convictions or to listen to those of others—fear of rejection, fear our beliefs will be attacked, fear our faith might be shaken. But if that is the case, perhaps we need to examine just how deep our convictions really are.

Jesus had no such fear, no need to fence Himself off from others for His own protection. He knew the difference between graciousness and compromise, and we would do well to follow His example.

Jesus alone is "the way, the truth, and the life" (John 14:6). Never lose your confidence in the truth of the gospel! But—like Jesus—may you always be "speaking the truth in love" (Ephesians 4:15).

HOPE FOR TODAY
Believers must spend time in prayer and in God's Word in order to know truth. Then, we can remain confident in what we've been taught and interact with the world without being led astray (2 Corinthians 11:3).

A MIGHTY FORTRESS

He is my refuge and my fortress;
My God, in Him I will trust.
PSALM 91:2

A refuge is a place safely out of harm's way. A fortress is a fortified building that is virtually impenetrable by conventional means.

Martin Luther wrote a wonderful hymn that says, "A mighty fortress is our God; a bulwark never failing. Our helper He amidst the flood; of mortal ills prevailing." What a statement about the magnificent power and protection of God!

Does God care for you and me? Can we turn to Him in trust and faith when troubles and temptations threaten to overwhelm us? Yes—a thousand times yes! What greater proof do we need than that He sent His Son, Jesus Christ, to die in our place?

HOPE FOR TODAY

Where do you go when life gets hard? To whom do you turn when things fall apart? Your heavenly Father waits with open arms to comfort and protect you. Run to Him; there is no safer place.

COME BOLDLY

"Ask, and it will be given you; seek, and you will find."
MATTHEW 7:7

Children are not bashful about asking for things. They would not be normal if they did not boldly make their needs known.

God has said to His children, "Let us . . . come boldly to the throne of grace, that we may obtain mercy and find grace to help in time of need" (Hebrews 4:16). God is keenly aware that we are dependent upon Him for life's necessities. It was for that reason that Jesus said, "Ask, and it will be given to you; seek, and you will find; knock, and it will be opened to you" (Matthew 7:7).

What is troubling you today? Is your heart burdened because of some problem that threatens to overcome you? Are you filled with anxiety and worry, wondering what will happen next? Listen—as a child of God through faith in Christ, you can turn these over to Christ, knowing that He loves you and is able to help you. Don't carry your burden any longer, but bring it "boldly to the throne of grace"—and leave it there.

HOPE FOR TODAY

It pleases God when we bring our burdens to Him, and we don't need to be bashful about it. He says, "Come boldly! Make your requests known." He can handle the hopes and hurts of His children.

GOD'S KINGDOM, GOD'S WAY

Your throne, O God, is forever and ever.

PSALM 45:6

Many intellectuals are asking where history is going. Will society get better and better-—or will we end up destroying ourselves?

Christ prayed, "Thy kingdom come. Thy will be done in earth, as it is in heaven" (Matthew 6:10 KJV). Someday that prayer—a prayer that you and I often pray—is going to be answered. The last chapter of history will not be written by any human leader, however good or bad. Only God will write it. And write it He will.

Someday, when the human race stands at the edge of the abyss of self-destruction, God will intervene. It may be tomorrow; it may be a thousand years from now. But the outcome is certain—the future belongs to the kingdom of God.

Never forget: if you belong to the King, you are on the winning side!

HOPE FOR TODAY

Satan is a vanquished foe, but he wants people to believe otherwise. Too many lead defeated lives because they have believed the lies of the enemy. All who belong to Christ are victorious!

DYNAMIC AND DEDICATED

Stand fast in the Lord.
PHILIPPIANS 4:1

A bar of raw steel may be purchased for a few dollars. But when that bar of steel has been thrust into the fires and processed, when it has been tempered and forged and made into tiny watch springs for expensive watches, it is worth thousands of dollars. Fire and the skilled hands of master artisans made the difference, enhancing the value.

Just as the sun by its heat and light performs a thousand miracles a day in the plant kingdom, God through the refining fire of His Spirit performs a thousand miracles a day in the spiritual realm. His regenerating power can take the dull and ordinary things of our lives—even the burned-out ashes of our past—and forge them into something useful, even beautiful, for His purposes.

HOPE FOR TODAY
God is still in the business of raising up dry bones and making beauty from ashes. The same God who called forth Lazarus can take what is dead in your life and make it live again.

RESCUING ANGELS

The angel of the LORD encamps all around those who fear Him,
And delivers them.

PSALM 34:7

During World War II, Captain Eddie Rickenbacker and his crew ran out of fuel and ditched their B-17 in the Pacific Ocean. For weeks nothing was heard of him, and across the country thousands of people prayed.

Then he returned, and in an article told what had happened. "And this part I would hesitate to tell," he wrote, "except that there were six witnesses who saw it with me. A gull came out of nowhere, and lighted on my head—I reached up my hand very gently—I killed him and then we divided him equally among us. We ate every bit, even the little bones. Nothing ever tasted so good." This gull saved them from starvation.

Years later I asked him to tell me the story personally, because it was through this experience that he came to know Christ. He said, "I have no explanation except that God sent one of His angels to rescue us." We may never see them, but God still sends His angels to surround and protect His children—including you.

HOPE FOR TODAY

Can you think of a time when you were spared from potential harm or a situation turned out better than expected? One day, we will look back and see evidence of God's protective hand throughout our lives.

JOYOUS OPTIMISM

My soul shall be joyful in the LORD.
PSALM 35:9

When Jesus Christ is the source of our joy, no words can describe it. It is a joy "inexpressible and glorious" (1 Peter 1:8 NIV). Christ is the answer to the sadness and discouragement, the discord and division in our world. He can take discouragement and despondence out of our lives and replace them with optimism and hope.

If our hearts have been attuned to God through an abiding faith in Christ, the result will be joyous optimism and good cheer. The reason? Because we know He loves us, and nothing "shall be able to separate us from the love of God which is in Christ Jesus our Lord" (Romans 8:39).

When our confidence is in Him, discouragement gets crowded out. May that be true in your life today!

HOPE FOR TODAY

Lord, give me a joy that isn't dependent on circumstances. Give me a joy that can't be shaken or quenched. Give me a joy, God, that doesn't make sense to the world—a joy that is only found in Your presence.

RIGHT ON THE BEAM

"Narrow is the gate and difficult is the way which leads to life."
MATTHEW 7:14

O nce when we were on a flight from Korea to Japan, we ran through a rough snowstorm. When we arrived over the airport in Tokyo, visibility was almost zero, so the pilot had to make an instrument landing. I sat up in the cockpit with him and watched him sweat it out as the watchful men in the airport tower guided him in.

I did not want these men to be broad-minded. I did not want them to say to the pilot, "Oh, well, just land any way you want to. We don't think it'll matter what altitude you keep or how fast you land." I knew that our lives depended on their precise instructions.

Just so, when we come in for the landing in the great airport of Heaven, I don't want any broad-minded advice. I don't want anyone to tell me that it doesn't really matter what I believe, as long as I'm sincere—for Jesus said otherwise. I want to come in on the beam, and even though I may be considered narrow-minded here, I want to be sure of a safe landing there. And I am sure, because Christ has gone before me and has provided the way.

HOPE FOR TODAY

Children thrive in environments with clear boundaries. A world without rules is a scary place. It's the same for God's people; we must follow His instructions so that we don't wander onto the broad path that leads to destruction.

UNLOAD YOUR DISTRESS

[Cast] all your care upon Him, for He cares for you.
1 PETER 5:7

I've been told that the French translation of the phrase "Cast all your care upon Him" is "Unload your distresses upon God."

Have you ever seen a dump truck get rid of its load? The driver simply pushes a button or pulls on a lever and the heavy load is discharged at the prescribed spot. The truck would be of no use if it carried its burden forever.

We were never meant to be crushed under the weight of care. We can push the button of faith or pull the lever of trust, and our burden is discharged upon the shoulder of Him who said He would gladly bear it. Unload the anxieties of the present moment upon Him, for He cares for you. If He loved you enough to take away the burden of your sins, can't you trust Him to take away every lesser burden as well?

HOPE FOR TODAY

Imagine carrying a heavy suitcase filled with useless things everywhere you went. Why would someone do that? That is what we do when we carry the burdens of worry and anxiety. It's unnecessary and does us no good.

MATERIAL GODS

"What will it profit a man if he gains the whole world, and loses his own soul?"
MARK 8:36

The Bible does not condemn money or material possessions. Money and possessions can do great good when they are used wisely and kept in proper perspective. Some of the great people of the Bible were very rich. Abraham, Isaac, and Solomon were perhaps the richest men of their day.

God's quarrel is not with material goods but with material gods. Materialism has become the god of too many of us. Our material possessions are elevated to the central place in our lives, and we give them the attention only God deserves.

The Bible teaches that preoccupation with material possessions is a form of idolatry. And God hates idolatry. It poisons every other phase of our lives, including our family life.

The problem, the Bible says, is not with money itself, but with our love of money: "The love of money is a root of all kinds of evil" (1 Timothy 6:10). Don't let money, or anything else, take God's rightful place in your life.

HOPE FOR TODAY

We were created to worship. If we fail to do it correctly, our worship will be corrupted. We can keep a proper perspective on material possessions when we give our praise to God alone.

SOARING IN VICTORY

"Unless one is born again, he cannot see the kingdom of God."
JOHN 3:3

In the third chapter of John, Jesus teaches that the new birth is something God does for us as we yield ourselves to Him and put our faith and trust in Christ. We do not have within ourselves the seed of the new life; this must come from God.

One day an ugly caterpillar climbs into a tree and spins a silky robe about itself. It goes to sleep, and in a few weeks emerges a beautiful butterfly.

So we—discouraged, unhappy, hounded by guilt, confused, depressed, vainly looking for an escape—can come by faith to Christ and emerge a new person. We can be born again! It sounds incredible, even impossible—and yet it is precisely what happens. We become members of God's family, looking forward to our eternal home in Heaven.

Do you feel you are in a cocoon? Turn to Christ and ask Him to give you your beautiful wings so that you might soar above your problems and be victorious over them.

HOPE FOR TODAY

One of the most glorious truths about coming to Christ is that we don't have to be who we've been in the past. We are not repurposed versions of our old selves. We are brand-new creations (2 Corinthians 5:17).

LIFE WITH A CAPITAL "L"

"The Son gives life to whom He will."
JOHN 5:21

The moment you come to Christ, the Spirit of God brings the life of God into you and you begin to live. For the first time you begin to live with a capital "L." There's a spring in your step, a joy in your soul, and a peace in your heart. Life has taken on a new outlook.

There's a whole new direction to your life, because now the Spirit of God has implanted within you the very life of God Himself, who is eternal. And that means you will live as long as God lives!

Too many Christians let themselves get bogged down by the cares and routines of daily living. Don't let that happen to you. Ask God to help you live each day with eternity in view.

HOPE FOR TODAY

Lord, help me to see beyond today. Let me view whatever comes my way in light of the glories that await me in eternity. Remind me that I am only passing through this place.

GOD'S GREAT HEART

"Love the Lord your God with all your heart . . . and your neighbor as yourself."
LUKE 10:27

Divine love, like a reflected sunbeam, shines down before it radiates out. Unless our hearts are conditioned by the Holy Spirit to receive and reflect the warmth of God's compassion, we cannot love others as we ought.

Jesus wept tears of compassion at the graveside of a friend. He mourned over Jerusalem because its people had lost their sensitivity to God and His Word. His great heart was always sensitive to the needs of others. When challenged to state the most important commandment, He replied, "You shall love the Lord your God with all your heart . . . [and] your neighbor as yourself" (Matthew 22:37, 39).

Jesus' love was more than human compassion, however; it was in the fullest sense divine love, for He was God in human flesh. This is the kind of love He calls us to have—and the kind He will give us as we seek it from Him.

HOPE FOR TODAY

Only through the Holy Spirit can we truly weep with those who weep and rejoice with those who rejoice. Ask God to help you take your flesh out of the equation and to love as God loves.

EARNEST PRAYER

Continue earnestly in prayer, being vigilant in it with thanksgiving.
COLOSSIANS 4:2

Today we have learned to harness the power of the atom, but very few of us have learned how to develop fully the power of prayer. We have not yet learned that a person can be more powerful on his or her knees than behind the most powerful weapons ever developed.

We have not learned that a nation is more powerful when it unites in earnest prayer to God than when its resources are channeled into weapons. We have not discovered that the answer to our problems can come through contact with the living God.

Weapons by themselves will not keep us safe or solve the world's problems. Our basic problems are spiritual in nature, and only spiritual solutions will solve them. That is why prayer is so vital, for only God can change the human heart.

Who knows what might happen if millions of believers around the world availed themselves of the greatest privilege this side of Heaven—the privilege of intercessory prayer? Will you be one of them?

HOPE FOR TODAY

How often do we view a situation as helpless, throw up our hands, and walk away? Or we say, "All we can do now is pray." Prayer should be our first line of defense, not a last resort!

CLAIM A LARGER BLESSING

Through God we will do valiantly.
PSALM 108:13

There are two ways of getting out of a trial. One is to simply try to get rid of the trial, and be thankful when it is over. The other is to recognize the trial as a challenge from God to claim a larger blessing than we have ever had.

Sometimes God removes our trials, and it isn't necessarily wrong to ask Him to do that. But often the trials remain, and when they do, we should accept them and ask God to teach us from them.

As Peter Marshall once put it, "God will not permit any troubles to come upon us, unless He has a specific plan by which great blessing can come out of the difficulty."

It is through the suffering, the tests, and the trials of life that we can draw near to God. A. B. Simpson once heard a man say something he never forgot: "When God tests you, it is a good time for you to test Him by putting His promises to the proof, and claiming from Him just as much as your trials have rendered necessary."

HOPE FOR TODAY

What do you need to endure your current trial? Strength, comfort, patience, the ability to forgive? Whatever the need, boldly approach the throne and make your requests known.

THE VICTORIOUS CHIME

"I, even I, am the LORD,
And besides Me there is no savior."
ISAIAH 43:11

It is said that during Napoleon's Austrian campaign his army advanced to within six miles of the town of Feldkirch. It looked as though his men would take it without resistance. But as Napoleon's army advanced toward their objective in the night, the Christians of Feldkirch gathered in their little church to pray. It was Easter eve.

The next morning at sunrise, the bells of the village pealed out across the countryside. Napoleon's army, not realizing it was Easter Sunday, thought that in the night the Austrian army had moved into Feldkirch and the bells were ringing in jubilation. Napoleon ordered a retreat, and the battle at Feldkirch never took place. The Easter bells caused the enemy to flee, and peace reigned in the Austrian countryside.

As Easter is celebrated each year, churches and cathedrals around the world will ring their bells—not to sound Christ's death knell but to declare Christ's victory over death. He is the risen Lord, and because of Him our final enemy—death—has been defeated, and peace reigns in our hearts!

HOPE FOR TODAY

Every person faces different trials and circumstances in life. But, when Christ conquered the grave, He defeated the one enemy that every person was going to have to face. Oh, death, where is your sting?

THE ANSWER TO FEAR

"Do not be afraid."
MATTHEW 28:10

Months after the September 11, 2001, terrorist attacks on New York and Washington, psychiatrists reported that people who lived thousands of miles away from those tragic events were still coming to them, unable to sleep and paralyzed by fear. We live in a world shaken by fear, apprehension, and anxiety.

What is the answer to this stifling fear? After Jesus had been put to death, His disciples huddled in fear behind closed doors, filled with uncertainty and despair. But suddenly they found themselves in the presence of their living Lord, and at His first words their fears disappeared: "Peace to you" (Luke 24:36). The answer to our individual fears is found in a personal faith in the living, glorified Lord.

And the answer to collective fear is a corporate faith in the living, glorified Lord. The answer to national and international tensions and fears is for the world to know Him who is alive forevermore. We do not worship a dead Christ. We worship a risen Christ, who has broken the power of sin and death and hell and is alive forevermore. Why then should we fear?

HOPE FOR TODAY
Uncertainty breeds fear, and the world is an uncertain place. Focus, instead, on the steadfast Savior, who ever lives and ever reigns. There is nothing to fear when our faith is in the One who controls it all.

COWARDLY OR COURAGEOUS?

If God is for us, who can be against us?

ROMANS 8:31

The chairman of the history department of one of our great universities once stated his opinion to me: "We have become a nation of cowards." I challenged his statement, but he argued that many people have become reluctant to follow a course if it isn't popular. I had to admit he was right.

Even if deep inside we know it to be right, we draw back because we are afraid of the consequences. If the odds are in our favor, we will take a stand; but if there is any risk involved in standing up for what we know to be right, we will play it safe.

How different from the early Christians! From one end of the Roman Empire to the other, they boldly proclaimed the gospel in the face of hostility, persecution, scorn, and even death. The apostle Paul knew the key: "For God has not given us a spirit of fear, but of power and of love and of a sound mind" (2 Timothy 1:7).

You may never face the same dangers those early Christians did, but don't take the road of cowardice; don't give in to fear. Remember: "If God is for us, who can be against us?"

HOPE FOR TODAY

Are you currently avoiding a conversation or situation out of fear? Ask God to give you the same attitude as Paul had among the Thessalonians (1 Thessalonians 2:2–7)—bold, but gentle—and, remember: God is for you.

CHRIST IS RISEN

He is not here, but is risen!
LUKE 24:6

Easter Sunday is the most triumphant and joyous day in the calendar of the Christian church—and it should be!

For many people the resurrection of Jesus Christ is symbolized by new Easter clothes, the bright color of daffodils, and beautiful white Easter lilies. But most of all, the wonder of His resurrection is symbolized in the hope that beats in the hearts of believers everywhere as they sing triumphantly: "Christ the Lord is risen today."

It is the message "Jesus is alive!" that lifts Christianity out of the category of dead superstitions and archaic religions and makes it the abiding faith of millions. The angel's message is true: "He is not here, but is risen!" And now God's promise is for you: "If you confess with your mouth the Lord Jesus and believe in your heart that God has raised Him from the dead, you will be saved" (Romans 10:9).

HOPE FOR TODAY

How are we to endure suffering? By remembering Jesus Christ, risen from the dead (2 Timothy 2:8). How can we maintain faith during dark times? By remembering Jesus Christ, risen from the dead. He is risen; He is risen indeed.

PEACE WITH GOD

Let the peace of God rule in your hearts.

COLOSSIANS 3:15

Science has confirmed what the Bible taught centuries ago: there is a close relationship between our minds and bodies. Proverbs puts it this way: "A cheerful heart is good medicine, but a crushed spirit dries up the bones" (Proverbs 17:22 NIV).

But there is also a close relationship between our mental and physical health and the health of our spiritual lives. Guilt, fear, jealousy, bitterness, futility, escapism—these and a host of other problems are spiritual ills, brought about by the disease of sin. Like poison, they can sicken us in mind and body.

But when Christ comes into our lives, He removes our guilt and takes away our fears. He gives us love for others and a new purpose in life. His joy and peace neutralize sin's poison—and that promotes emotional and physical health.

Does that mean our emotional and physical problems will vanish? Not necessarily. But like a spring of pure water, God's peace in our hearts brings cleansing and refreshment to our minds and bodies.

HOPE FOR TODAY

The weight of worldly concerns can crush our spirits. We get bogged down in life and forget what has been given to us. Ask the Lord to restore to you the joy of your salvation and refresh your spirit.

A Purpose and a Power

Go quickly and tell . . . that He is risen from the dead.
MATTHEW 28:7

When Samuel Morse, inventor of the telegraph, sent his first message, he telegraphed these words: "What hath God wrought!"

The greatest news ever sent tells of a far greater event God has wrought: Christ is risen. On that first resurrection day, the angel at the tomb delivered the most important message anyone can ever hear: "He is not here; for He is risen" (Matthew 28:6).

When Adam and Eve first sinned, God's warning became a reality: "You shall surely die" (Genesis 2:17). From that moment on, death reigned over the human race—and with it fear, dread, and superstition.

But Christ's resurrection changed all that, bringing hope and salvation to all who put their trust in Him. Listen: Death is a defeated foe! Christ has won the victory. That is why Paul could say, "Thanks be to God, who gives us the victory through our Lord Jesus Christ" (1 Corinthians 15:57). Is your confidence in Jesus Christ, the risen Lord?

HOPE FOR TODAY
Who, in your life, needs to know that Jesus Christ is risen from the dead and that they are free from the fear of death through Him? Listen to the words of the angel at the tomb: "Go quickly and tell."

HE SUFFERED FOR YOU

His visage was marred more than any man.

ISAIAH 52:14

When Jesus Christ was on the Cross, His blood draining the life from His body, He knew what it was like to be alone and racked with pain. But Jesus' pain was far more than just physical pain, for He was suffering God's judgment on all the sins of the ages—the greatest darkness of the soul ever known. As the divine Son of God, He was perfect and without sin. But all our sins were placed on Him, and He took the judgment and hell we alone deserve. He died in our place.

Why did Jesus suffer? For you. For me. That we might have eternal life and have His peace in the midst of life's storms. That we might know that He understands our pain and suffering and stands ready to help.

Why did Jesus suffer? Because God loves us. Because God loves you, Christ willingly went to the Cross for you. There was no other way for sin's penalty to be paid, and for us to be redeemed. The Cross is the measure of God's love.

How will you respond to His love, poured out on the Cross for you?

HOPE FOR TODAY

Nothing could have kept Christ from the Cross; His love for us is that great. No physical pain, no mocking crowd, no fickle followers could change His mind. We are loved with an everlasting love.

"IT IS FINISHED"

He was wounded for our transgressions.
ISAIAH 53:5

On a hill overlooking the harbor of Macao, Portuguese settlers built a massive cathedral. But over time it fell in ruins, except for one wall. On the top of that high, jutting wall, challenging the elements down through the years, was a huge bronze cross.

It is said that when Sir John Bowring saw it, he was moved to write these words: "In the cross of Christ I glory, tow'ring o'er the wrecks of time."

When Jesus lifted up His voice and cried, "It is finished," He did not mean His life was ebbing away or God's plan had been foiled. Though death was near, Jesus realized the last obstacle had been hurdled and the last enemy destroyed. He had successfully and triumphantly completed the task of redemption. With the words "It is finished," He announced that Heaven's door was open.

Kingdoms and empires come and go, but the Cross and all it stands for will always remain, "tow'ring o'er the wrecks of time."

HOPE FOR TODAY

Thank You, Lord, that nothing the enemy attempts can undo what You have accomplished. Through the Cross, You forever conquered death and hades. The veil was torn, and the gates of Heaven swung wide.

APRIL

And let us not grow weary while doing good, for in due season we shall reap if we do not lose heart.

GALATIANS 6:9

THE LIVING CHRIST

It is no longer I who live, but Christ lives in me.
GALATIANS 2:20

Jesus Christ was crucified between two thieves on a rugged Cross on Calvary, just outside Jerusalem. Think of it: the very Son of God came down from Heaven and "humbled Himself and became obedient to the point of death, even the death of the cross" (Philippians 2:8).

Jesus gave His head to the crown of thorns for us. He gave His face to human spittle for us. He gave His cheeks and His beard to be plucked out for us. He gave His back to the lash for us. He gave His side to the spear for us. He gave His hands and feet to the spikes for us. He gave His blood for us. Jesus Christ, dying in our place, taking our sins on that Cross, is God's love in action.

But that's not the end of the story. He rose again, and He is the living Christ. If Christ is not alive, there is no hope for any of us. But He is alive! And because He is, "he is able to save completely those who come to God through him, because he always lives to intercede for them" (Hebrews 7:25 NIV). Hallelujah!

HOPE FOR TODAY

Had Jesus come to earth but not died, His life here would have been pointless. Had He died but not resurrected, His death would have been powerless. Praise the Lord, Jesus accomplished everything He set out to do, and we are free.

A LIVING SACRIFICE

Present yourselves to God as being alive . . . and your members as instruments of righteousness to God.

ROMANS 6:13

The apostle Paul, who was a splendid example of a disciplined Christian, said, "I beseech you therefore, brethren, by the mercies of God, that ye present your bodies a living sacrifice, holy, acceptable unto God, which is your reasonable service" (Romans 12:1 KJV).

If we have given ourselves to Christ, then He has come to live within us, and our bodies are now the temples—the dwelling places—of the Holy Spirit. Now we must act worthy of Him who lives within us, disciplining both our bodies and minds so we do not bring dishonor to Him. We must pray as Jeremy Taylor once prayed, "Let my body be a servant of my spirit, and both body and spirit servants of Jesus."

Paul knew Christ had sacrificed His body for his salvation, and the only reasonable thing to do in response was to give his body as a living sacrifice to Christ.

Let me challenge you to commit your body and your mind to Christ, "which is your reasonable service."

HOPE FOR TODAY

There is nothing God could ask of us that would be "unreasonable" considering the sacrifice He made for us. How are we using our body, our gifts, and our resources to honor Him? Are we holding anything back?

THE RESURRECTION AND THE LIFE

"He who believes in me will live . . . and . . . will never die."
JOHN 11:25–26 NIV

We have three great enemies: sin, Satan, and death. Because Christ rose from the dead, we know that sin and Satan and death have been decisively defeated. And because Christ rose from the dead, we know there is life after death, and that if we belong to Him, we need not fear death or Hell.

Jesus said, "I am the resurrection and the life. He who believes in me will live, even though he dies; and whoever lives and believes in me will never die" (John 11:25–26 NIV). He also promised, "If I go and prepare a place for you, I will come back and take you to be with me that you also may be where I am" (John 14:3 NIV).

How hopeless our lives would be if these words were not true. Every cemetery and every grave site would be a mute witness to the futility and despair of human life. But Jesus' words are true! By God's power, Jesus rose from the dead and hundreds became witnesses to His resurrection (see 1 Corinthians 15:1–8).

What a glorious hope we have because Jesus is alive!

HOPE FOR TODAY

The message of the Cross never changes: Christ died for us. The promise of the empty tomb is the same: death has been conquered. Though we've heard it many times, our hearts never tire of hearing of His love for us.

REFINED AND PURIFIED

When He has tested me, I shall come forth as gold.

JOB 23:10

Affliction can be a means of refining and of purification. Just as ore must pass through the refiner's furnace before it can yield up its gold, so our lives must sometimes pass through God's furnace of affliction before they can bring forth something beautiful and useful to Him.

We might never have had the songs of Fanny Crosby had she not been afflicted with blindness. George Matheson would never have given the world his immortal song, "O Love That Will Not Let Me Go," had it not been for the pain of personal tragedy and heartache. The "Hallelujah Chorus" was written by Handel when he was poverty-stricken and suffering from a paralyzed right side and right arm.

Affliction can also make us stronger in our faith and develop our confidence in God's watch care over us. It may also drive us back to the right path when we have wandered. David said, "Before I was afflicted I went astray, but now I keep your word" (Psalm 119:67).

Whatever the reason, if God sends affliction your way, take it in faith as a blessing, not a curse.

HOPE FOR TODAY

Anything that comes our way has been filtered through the loving hands of our Father. Knowing that, we can trust that our pain has purpose and our struggles are never in vain.

THE LIGHT OF GOD'S LOVE

O LORD my God, You are very great. . . .
You who laid the foundations of the earth.
PSALM 104:1, 5

God's love did not begin at Calvary. Before the morning stars sang together, before the world was baptized with the first light, before the first blades of tender grass peeped out, God was love.

Turn back to the unwritten pages of countless eons before God spoke this present earth into existence, when the earth was "without form, and void" (Genesis 1:2) and the deep, silent darkness of space stood in stark contrast to the brilliance of God's glory and His cherubim and seraphim.

Even then, God was love. Before the worlds were created, He knew all about us and the need we would have someday for Christ to die for us. So in His love "he chose us in him before the creation of the world" (Ephesians 1:4 NIV).

God does not change—and neither does His love. He loved you before you were born . . . He loves you now . . . and He will love you forever. Will you love Him in return?

HOPE FOR TODAY

Lord, we are only able to love because You first loved us. Help us to love You in return with all of the passion and faithfulness that You deserve.

THE FUTURE LIFE

As for man, his days are like grass;
As a flower of the field, so he flourishes.
PSALM 103:15

The Bible reminds us that our days are as grass. For a brief time we flourish, but soon we wither and die. Yet the minutes of our lives can be flecked with the gold of eternity. Instead of wasting our lives—as we so easily do—God exhorts us to redeem the time.

But our lives are also immortal. God made us different from the other creatures. He made us in His own image, a living soul. Don't let anyone tell you that we are simply a higher species of animal. If you believe that, you will begin to act like one. No! You are far greater.

One thousand years from this day you will be more alive than you are at this moment. The Bible teaches that life does not end at the cemetery. There is a future life with God for those who put their trust in His Son, Jesus Christ. There is also a future Hell of separation from God where all are going who have refused, rejected, or neglected to receive His Son, Jesus Christ.

Make sure of your relationship to Christ, and then ask God to help you live each day for His glory.

HOPE FOR TODAY

Our choices have consequences and blessings that ripple far into the future. The things we see are only temporary; the things that truly matter are eternal.

WE CAN'T OUT-GIVE GOD

The generous soul will be made rich.

PROVERBS 11:25

The Bible teaches that blessings follow those who give liberally. Proverbs 11:25 says, "The generous soul will be made rich, and he who waters will also be watered himself."

I've heard countless testimonies from men and women who were afraid to put to the test God's promise to bless those who are generous. They feared they would not have enough. Then, when at last they decided to tithe (to give a tenth of their income) in accordance with the Bible's standard, they began to prosper. They discovered what countless others have known across the ages: you can't out-give God.

What keeps you from being more generous in supporting God's work? Selfishness? Fear? Insecurity? Even a sinful habit you would rather support? Whatever the reason, repent of it and discover the blessedness of generosity. Remember: "God loves a cheerful giver" (2 Corinthians 9:7).

HOPE FOR TODAY

The cure for greed is giving. Every time we're tempted to cling to money or material possessions, we should instead look for opportunities to be generous. Watch God open His storehouses of blessings (Malachi 3:10).

GOD CARES FOR YOU

God is not the author of confusion but of peace.

1 CORINTHIANS 14:33

Who of us has not asked in times of affliction and difficulty, "Does God care for me?" The Psalmist said, "Refuge failed me; no man cared for my soul" (Psalm 142:4 KJV). Martha, overly concerned with her workaday duties, said to Jesus, "Lord, do You not care?" (Luke 10:40). How many faithful, loving mothers, overwhelmed by the burdens of motherhood, have cried anxiously, "Lord, do You not care?"

That question is forever answered in those reassuring words of Peter: "He cares for you" (1 Peter 5:7). This is the Word of God. Even if the world passes away, it will not change.

You can be confident God cares for you. If He didn't, would He have sent Christ into the world to die for you? Of course not! That is why you can always turn to Him for the strength and encouragement you need.

Yes, life can be overwhelming at times. But when it is, remember this: God knows what you are facing, and "He cares for you."

HOPE FOR TODAY

There is immense comfort in knowing that God always cares for us. He is never caught off guard or left wondering what to do. He is, not only aware of our needs, but willing and able to meet them.

THE GOOD SHEPHERD

The good shepherd lays down his life for the sheep.
JOHN 10:11 NIV

One of the figures of speech Jesus applied to Himself was that of a shepherd. He said, "I am the good shepherd. The good shepherd lays down his life for the sheep. The hired hand is not the shepherd who owns the sheep. . . . I know my sheep and my sheep know me" (John 10:11–14 NIV).

Note four things about Jesus, the Good Shepherd. He owns the sheep; they belong to Him. Next, He guards the sheep; He never abandons them when danger approaches. Also, He knows the sheep; He calls them by name and they follow Him. Finally, He lays down His life for the sheep; their salvation is His primary concern.

The Bible says, "We are His people and the sheep of His pasture" (Psalm 100:3). Because we belong to Christ, we can be secure and at rest.

HOPE FOR TODAY
We're not simply a mass of faces to God. He knows each of His children intimately and individually. He loves each of us so much that He would leave the ninety-nine to run to your side if necessary (Luke 15:4).

THE MESSAGE OF EASTER

He has risen! He is not here.

MARK 16:6 NIV

The message of Easter is the central focus of Christianity.

The apostle Paul said, "If Christ has not been raised, your faith is futile; you are still in your sins" (1 Corinthians 15:17 NIV). It is as simple as that. If Christ is still dead, then He cannot be our Savior, for He was not the Son of God, and He died like all men. More than that, Heaven's doors are still locked.

But if Christ is risen, as the Scriptures teach and as hundreds of witnesses testified (none of whom ever recanted that testimony despite threats and death for many of them), then we have the ultimate hope of humanity-—eternal life with the God who made us and the certainty of life beyond the grave.

What does Easter mean to you? It should mean everything, because Christ has conquered death! And that makes all the difference—now and forever!

HOPE FOR TODAY

The Cross shows there isn't anything Christ would not do for us. The tomb tells us there isn't any place He won't go for us. The resurrection promises that there isn't anything that can separate us from Him.

RISEN AND RETURNING

This same Jesus . . . will so come in like manner as you saw Him go.
ACTS 1:11

The resurrection of Jesus Christ is the key to God's plan for the future. Unless Christ was raised from the dead, there can be no future kingdom and no returning King. Unless Christ was raised from the dead, sin and death still reign, and God's plan of redemption remains unfulfilled. But Christ has been raised!

As the disciples stood watching after Jesus ascended into the heavens, the angels assured them that the risen Christ would someday be the returning Christ. "Men of Galilee, why do you stand gazing up into heaven? This same Jesus, who was taken up from you into heaven, will so come in like manner as you saw Him go into heaven" (Acts 1:11).

Just as surely as Christ rose from the dead, so He will return and take us to Himself. Every promise—without exception—will be fulfilled.

HOPE FOR TODAY

Have you ever felt the pain of someone leaving? Perhaps you didn't know when or if you would see that loved one again. Jesus wants us to be very clear on one thing: He is coming back soon (Revelation 22:7).

A CERTAIN HOPE

Blessed is the man who trusts in the LORD,
And whose hope is the LORD.
JEREMIAH 17:7

One of the great hymns of the church, "The Solid Rock," by Edward Mote and William Bradbury, begins, "My hope is built on nothing less, than Jesus' blood and righteousness; I dare not trust the sweetest frame, but wholly lean on Jesus' name. On Christ, the solid Rock, I stand; all other ground is sinking sand."

On what is your hope built? You may hope for a raise in pay at work. You may hope that you pass an exam at school. You may even hope that you win a contest you have entered. Such hopes are based on externals over which we have little control: a favorable view of our work by the boss, the "right" questions being asked by the professor, our name being drawn among thousands of entries.

But all these "hopes" fade into insignificance when compared with the greatest hope of all—our hope of salvation in Christ. And that hope is an absolute certainty, because it is based not on ourselves or our good works, but squarely on "Jesus' blood and righteousness."

HOPE FOR TODAY

Circumstances change, people leave, and possessions get destroyed. If any of these are the source of our hope, we are in for a lot of heartache. Thank You, Lord, that a hope in You never disappoints.

WHY DID HE DIE?

The message of the cross . . . is the power of God.
1 CORINTHIANS 1:18

We can never grasp the horror of human sin until we realize it caused the Son of God to be crucified. Not Pilate, not Judas, not the mob—but sin.

The ravages of war and poverty, the wrenching pain of loneliness and rejection. The haunting cry of the orphan and widow, the dying gasps of the world's starving—these and a thousand other tragedies all bear witness to the fact that we live in a world poisoned by sin.

And that is why Jesus died. The terrible, bitter cup of humanity's sin sent Him to the Cross. Jesus prayed in those last hours, "O My Father, if it is possible, let this cup pass from Me; nevertheless, not as I will, but as You will" (Matthew 26:39). There was no other way. Why did He drink that awful cup? So you and I would not have to.

Sin is the second most powerful force in the universe, for it sent Jesus to the Cross. Only one force is greater—the love of God.

HOPE FOR TODAY

Jesus rebuked the devil when he tried to tempt Him with riches and earthly power and said, "It is written, Man shall live. . . by every word that proceeds from the mouth of God" (Matthew 4:4). We should strive to live by the authority of God's own Word.

FORGIVENESS AND FELLOWSHIP

"I will forgive their iniquity, and their sin I will remember no more."

JEREMIAH 31:34

There is no possibility of true happiness until we have established friendship and fellowship with God. And there is no possibility of establishing this fellowship apart from the Cross of His Son, Jesus Christ.

God says, "I will forgive you, but I will forgive only at the foot of the Cross." He says, "I will fellowship with you, but I will fellowship with you only at the Cross."

Why is this? Because only through Christ's death on the Cross can we be forgiven and reconciled to God.

This is why we must come to the Cross, repenting of our sins and trusting Christ alone to save us. Human pride gets in the way; we don't want to admit we are sinners, or that we are too weak to save ourselves. Only when we leave our pride at the Cross can our hearts be open to God's redeeming grace.

When we come to Christ, God imparts His righteousness to us. It is as if an accounting entry had been made in the books of Heaven, declaring us righteous for Christ's sake. The Divine Bookkeeper cancels our debt!

HOPE FOR TODAY

Other religions have people spending lifetimes attempting to reach God and hoping they've done *enough*. Through Christ, God made Himself accessible to all who would come to the Cross. Those who do will find that the Cross is always enough.

HEAVENLY NEWS

God both raised up the Lord and will also raise us up by His power.
1 CORINTHIANS 6:14

The angel who came to the garden where Jesus' body lay rolled away the stone and permitted fresh air and morning light to fill His tomb.

The sepulcher was no longer an empty vault or dreary mausoleum; rather, it was a life-affirming place that radiated the glory and power of the living God. No longer was the tomb a dark, fearsome prison but a transformed reminder of the celestial light that sweeps aside the shadows of death. Jesus' resurrection changed all that—forever!

An unknown poet has said of the tomb, "'Tis now a cell where angels used to come and go with heavenly news." No words of men or angels can adequately describe the height and depth, the length and breadth of the glory to which the world awakened when Jesus came forth to life from the pall of death.

Jesus' promise has been fulfilled: "Because I live, you will live also" (John 14:19).

HOPE FOR TODAY

Is there something in your life that seems dead? Do you fear something or someone is too far gone? God is still in the resurrection business. He can breathe fresh life into places that once held the stench of death.

THE GREATEST MESSAGE

I know that you seek Jesus who was crucified.
MATTHEW 28:5

On the third day after Christ's death, the Bible says, "And behold there was a great earthquake; for an angel of the Lord descended from heaven, and came and rolled back the stone from the door, and sat on it. His countenance was like lightning, and his clothing as white as snow. And the guards shook for fear of him, and became like dead men" (Matthew 28:2–4).

As Mary looked into the tomb, she saw "two angels in white sitting, one at the head and the other at the feet, where the body of Jesus had lain" (John 20:12). Then one of the angels who was sitting outside the tomb proclaimed the greatest message the world has ever heard: "He is not here; for He is risen" (Matthew 28:6). Those few words changed the history of the universe. Darkness and despair died; hope and anticipation were born in the hearts of men.

With those few words, joy and new life now dawn in the hearts of all who believe. Don't leave Jesus in the manger . . . or on the Cross . . . or in the tomb. He is alive, and even now He wants to walk beside you every day.

HOPE FOR TODAY

Lord, may I always be found seeking You. When trials come and there are none who understand, I will remember that You were raised from the dead (2 Timothy 2:8) and know that I am never alone.

PATIENCE AND PRAYER

We . . . do not cease to pray for you.

COLOSSIANS 1:9

Some years ago a woman wrote me that she had pleaded for ten years for the conversion of her husband, but that he was more hardened than ever. I advised her to continue to plead. Sometime later I heard from her again. She said her husband was gloriously and miraculously converted in the eleventh year of her prayer vigil. How thankful she was that she had kept on praying!

Scripture says, "Pray without ceasing" (1 Thessalonians 5:17). This should be the motto of every true follower of Jesus Christ. Never stop praying, no matter how dark and hopeless your case may seem. Your responsibility isn't to tell God when He must act or even how He must act. Your responsibility is simply to "pray without ceasing," trusting Him to act according to His perfect will.

HOPE FOR TODAY

Frustration comes when we take more of the burden than we were meant to bear! We don't have to understand why something happens or how it is to be fixed. We are to pray and watch and trust God to do what only He can do.

A SURE SUPPLY

My God shall supply all your need.

PHILIPPIANS 4:19

One lesson that Jesus would teach us is to have confidence that God answers every true petition. Skeptics may question it, humanists may deny it, and intellectuals may ridicule it. Yet here is Christ's own promise: "If you abide in Me, and My words abide in you, you will ask what you desire, and it shall be done for you" (John 15:7).

Does this verse mean God gives us a blank check (so to speak) when we pray? Does He promise to give us anything we want, if we just keep asking? No. God loves us too much to answer prayers that are foolish or might harm us. But the closer we get to Him—the more we abide in Him and the more His Word abides in us—the more we will desire what He desires, and the more our prayers will reflect His will.

The Bible promises, "No good thing does he withhold from those whose walk is blameless" (Psalm 84:11 NIV). Trust that promise with all your soul.

HOPE FOR TODAY

God longs to bless His children and bestow on them every good and perfect gift (James 1:17.) In order to receive and enjoy His gifts, draw near to Him, spend time in His Word, and walk in obedience with Him daily.

SHINING LIGHTS

"Let your light so shine before men, that they may . . . glorify your Father in heaven."
MATTHEW 5:16

Our Lord regarded His followers as a select company who belonged to a different world from the rest of humanity. Many of the religious people of His day were worldly and unspiritual, publicly parading their religion to impress others while privately dominated by pride, ambition, greed, and falsehood.

Jesus told His disciples they could not make their light shine by sinking to the world's low level. It was only by abiding in Christ and living under the ruling power of His Holy Spirit that they could rise above the world. Only in that way could they be salt and light to a decaying and darkened world.

Our influence on society depends on our likeness to Jesus Christ. We cannot elevate others higher than we ourselves have gone. The first-century Christians out-thought, out-lived, and out-loved their neighbors, and by their example of purity and compassion attracted countless thousands to the Christian faith.

What do others see in your life that would attract them to Christ?

HOPE FOR TODAY

Many will shy away from a light that exposes their guilt. Teach me, Lord, to shine Your light in a way that highlights the grace of God that takes away a person's shame.

The Call to Discipleship

"Take My yoke upon you and learn from Me."

MATTHEW 11:29

A generation ago, Jim Elliot went from Wheaton College to become a missionary to the Aucas in Ecuador. Before he was killed, he wrote, "He is no fool who gives what he cannot keep to gain what he cannot lose."

The Christian faith brings its own "blood, sweat, and tears" to those who would follow Jesus Christ. Christ calls us to discipleship. When we come to Him, He takes away one set of burdens—the burden of sin, the burden of guilt, the burden of separation from God, the burden of hopelessness.

But He also calls us to follow Him, to renounce our selfish desires, and to seek His will above all else. He calls to us: "Take My yoke upon you and learn from Me."

So are we simply exchanging one burden for another—the burden of sin for the burden of obedience? No! It is no burden to follow Christ. Instead, we become the bearers of joy—because now we are yoked to the very Son of God. Nor is it too heavy to bear, for Christ bears it with us: "My yoke is easy and My burden is light" (Matthew 11:30).

With whom are you yoked—the world or Christ?

Hope for Today

Are you feeling as if your load is too heavy? Does it seem more than you can bear? Perhaps you're still attempting to carry a burden that Christ has already taken off your shoulders.

GOD NEVER CHANGES

God is Spirit, and those who worship Him must worship in spirit and truth.
JOHN 4:24

I was reared in a small Presbyterian church in Charlotte, North Carolina. Before I was ten years of age my mother made me memorize the "Shorter Catechism," a summary of basic Christian beliefs in the form of questions and answers. In the catechism we were asked to define God. The answer we learned was, "God is a Spirit—infinite, eternal, and unchangeable."

Those three words beautifully describe God. He is infinite—not body-bound. He is eternal—He has no beginning and no ending. He is unchangeable—never changing, never capricious, never unreliable. As the Bible says, with God "there is no variation or shadow of turning" (James 1:17). He is forever self-existent.

People change, fashions change, conditions and circumstances change, but God never changes. His love never changes. His holiness never changes. His purpose never changes. His glory never changes. He is the same yesterday, today, and forever.

Can you think of any reason not to trust Him? Neither can I!

HOPE FOR TODAY
Thank You, God, that I don't have to wonder if You still love me, if You're still good, or if You're still in control. Because of this, I can trust You no matter what comes my way.

THE HOPE OF THE CENTURIES

It is good that one should hope and wait quietly
For the salvation of the LORD.

LAMENTATIONS 3:26

The promised coming of Christ has been the great hope of believers down through the centuries. The ancient Nicene Creed affirms, "He shall come again with glory."

Charles Wesley wrote seven thousand hymns; five thousand mention the coming of Christ. As the archbishop of Canterbury crowned Queen Elizabeth II, he stated, "I give thee, O Sovereign Lady, this crown to wear until He who reserves the right to wear it shall return."

But until that time, our world remains in the grip of violence and despair. One noted columnist summed it up this way: "For us all, the world is disorderly and dangerous; ungoverned, and apparently ungovernable." Someday, however, the King will return. Someday the heavens will shout, "The kingdoms of this world have become the kingdoms of our Lord and of His Christ, and He shall reign forever and ever!" (Revelation 11:15).

Christ alone is the answer to the burdens of our hearts and the hopelessness of our world.

HOPE FOR TODAY

Let's live in anticipation of the Messiah coming again, knowing that, at any moment, the King could make an appearance.

COMFORTING OTHERS

Comfort each other and edify one another.

1 THESSALONIANS 5:11

It is an undeniable fact that usually those who have suffered most are best able to comfort others who are suffering. They know what it is to suffer, and they understand more than others what a suffering person is experiencing—physically, emotionally, and spiritually. They are able to empathize as well as sympathize with the afflictions of others because of what they have experienced in their own lives.

Our sufferings may be rough and hard to bear, but they teach us lessons that in turn equip and enable us to help others. Our attitude toward suffering should not be, "Grit your teeth and bear it," hoping it will pass as quickly as possible. Rather, our goal should be to learn all we can from what we are called upon to endure, so that we in turn can "comfort each other and edify one another."

HOPE FOR TODAY

As bad as our suffering may seem, it would be far worse for it to be in vain. Ask God to reveal ways your trials can serve to comfort others and to glorify Him.

WALK WITH GOD

My eyes shall be on the faithful of the land,
That they may dwell with me.
PSALM 101:6

Walk with God as Noah did; when the flood came, Noah was saved amidst the scorn and rejection of his neighbors. Walk with God as Moses did in the solitude of the desert; when the hour of judgment fell upon Egypt, Moses was prepared to lead his people to victory.

Walk with God as David did as a shepherd boy; when he was called to rule his people, he was prepared for the task of kingship. Walk with God as Daniel and his three young friends did in the palace of Babylon's king; when the fiery furnace and the lions' den came, God was beside them and delivered them. No, God didn't always deliver His saints from adversity or even death, nor does He today. But because they had learned to trust Him in the light, they were prepared to follow Him in the darkness.

God has not promised to deliver us from trouble, but He has promised to go with us through the trouble. "Yea, though I walk through the valley of the shadow of death, I will fear no evil; for You are with me" (Psalm 23:4).

HOPE FOR TODAY

It's tempting to look at men and women in Scripture and think they were superhuman or ultra holy. The same God who walked with them walks with us; we just need to remain faithful, knowing His eyes are on us.

CORONATION DAY

Blessed is the man who endures trial for . . . he will receive the crown of life.
JAMES 1:12 RSV

To the Christian, death is said in the Bible to be a coronation. The picture here is that of a regal prince who, after his struggles and conquests in an alien land, returns to his native country and court to be crowned and honored for his deeds.

The Bible says we are pilgrims and strangers in a foreign land. This world is not our home; our citizenship is in Heaven. And someday all our battles on this earth will be over, and we will enter that heavenly home.

To the one who has been faithful Christ will give a crown of life. Paul said, "There is laid up for me the crown of righteousness, which the Lord, the righteous Judge, will give to me on that Day, and not to me only but also to all who have loved His appearing" (2 Timothy 4:8).

When D. L. Moody was dying, he looked up to Heaven and said, "Earth is receding, heaven is opening, this is my coronation day." Never forget: if you are a Christian, you are a child of the King!

HOPE FOR TODAY

We feel discouraged when we don't seem to fit in here; we become despondent at the thought of leaving. Both of these reactions come when we forget that we were only passing through. Our heavenly home awaits!

NOW IS THE TIME

You do not know what will happen tomorrow.

JAMES 4:14

Billy Bray, a godly clergyman of another generation, sat by the bedside of a dying Christian who had been very shy about his testimony for Christ during his life. The dying man said, "If I had the power I'd shout glory to God." Billy Bray answered, "It's a pity you didn't shout glory when you had the power."

I wonder how many of us will look back over a lifetime of wasted opportunities and ineffective witness, and weep because we did not allow God to use us as He wanted. "Night is coming, when no man can work" (John 9:4 NASB).

If ever we are to study the Scriptures, if ever we are to spend time in prayer, if ever we are to win souls for Christ, if ever we are to invest our finances for His kingdom—it must be now.

HOPE FOR TODAY

We don't have to wait until we get married, until the kids are grown or until we're financially stable. We must be about our Father's business, doing the work He sent us to do while it's still day.

CHRIST IS KING

Your kingdom is an everlasting kingdom.
PSALM 145:13

The government in God's kingdom is unique. It is not a democracy where the people govern, but a "Christocracy" where Christ is the supreme authority. In a society of unredeemed people, democracy is the only fair and equitable system. But no democracy can ever be better than the people who make it up. When citizens are selfishly motivated, the government will be inequitable. When people are dishonest, the government will be the same. When everyone wants his own way, someone is going to get hurt.

But in God's kingdom, Christ is King. He is compassionate, fair, merciful, and just. When He is sovereign in men's hearts, anguish turns to peace, hatred is transformed into love, and misunderstanding into harmony.

Is Christ the King of your motives and your attitudes?

HOPE FOR TODAY

When people are worried about being mistreated, self-preservation becomes the goal. As Christ followers, we can trust that God has our backs and knows what is best. We are then free to serve Him and love others better.

A Sealed Bargain

He . . . put his Spirit in our hearts as a deposit, guaranteeing what is to come.
2 Corinthians 1:21–22 niv

As we trust in Christ, God gives us the Spirit as a pledge, or, as some translations read, earnest or guarantee. "He . . . put his Spirit in our hearts as a deposit, guaranteeing what is to come."

In the apostle Paul's day, a deposit or pledge did three things: it was a down payment that sealed a bargain, it represented an obligation to buy, and it was a sample of what was to come.

As an illustration, suppose you decided to make a down payment on a new car. What does your deposit represent? First, it seals the transaction; from now on, both you and the seller are committed. Also, it shows that you have committed yourself to pay the rest of the purchase price. Finally, it enables you to take possession of the car right now (even though it still belongs to the bank!).

In the same way, the Holy Spirit in our hearts is God's pledge or deposit to us—sealing His commitment to save us, guaranteeing that someday our salvation will be complete, and enabling us to experience its joys right now.

Hope for Today

There is no fine print when we come to faith; there is no cancellation or return policy. When we come to Christ, the Holy Spirit is sealed within us, and nothing can ever take Him away.

123

LIVE FOR THE LORD

My days are swifter than a weaver's shuttle.
JOB 7:6

In North Carolina I have visited the textile mills and have watched the giant looms that turn out cloth for the nation. The shuttles move with the speed of lightning, scarcely visible to the naked eye.

Job said that his days were "swifter than a weaver's shuttle." Life passes so quickly it is almost over before we realize it. The Bible says this is the chronology of eternity. Though you live to be seventy, eighty, or ninety years old, that is but a snap of the finger compared to eternity.

Put your hand on your heart and feel it beat. It is saying, "Quick! Quick! Quick!" We have only a few brief years at the most. Let's live them for the Lord.

HOPE FOR TODAY

Christ knew that His days on earth were few; He had a mission to accomplish, and He wouldn't be distracted. We should live with that same determination and focus. Whether we have thirty or one hundred years, let's not waste a single moment.

THE SECRET OF PURITY

Who shall ascend the hill of the LORD? . . .
He who has clean hands and a pure heart.
PSALM 24:3–4 RSV

We live in the most permissive society since pagan times. Movie marquees, the covers of magazines, the Internet, billboards, television—all scream sensual messages at us. "If it feels good, do it" has become a national motto.

Yet, if you talk with people who have come to Christ out of deep sin, they will tell you they wish they had never fallen into such sin, and that they had come to Christ sooner.

Many Christian books tell of men and women who committed terrible crimes or were entangled in immorality or sensuality. We rejoice with them that Christ has redeemed and forgiven them. But how much better to have avoided such sin in the first place! God's standard has not changed: "You shall be holy, for I the LORD your God am holy" (Leviticus 19:2).

The secret of purity is God. When we are committed to Christ, we will shrink back from all that is impure. Instead, we will seek a pure heart—a heart cleansed by the Holy Spirit and the Word of God.

HOPE FOR TODAY

Have you seen something inappropriate on television and thought, *That's not too bad?* Be on the lookout for the enemy's attempts to desensitize you to blatant sin.

MAY

Remember His marvelous works which He has done,
His wonders, and the judgments of His mouth.

1 CHRONICLES 16:12

GOD'S KIND OF STRENGTH

They shall walk and not faint.

ISAIAH 40:31

Never in history have the nations of the world possessed so many lethal armaments, so many ways to bring death and destruction to the human race. Some of our most brilliant minds spend their entire lives developing new and more sophisticated ways to destroy life.

But have all our weapons brought us lasting security? On the contrary; if anything, they have made the world less secure. At any one time at least thirty wars rage in various parts of the world, in addition to countless instances of civil unrest. I am reminded of the false prophets of Jeremiah's day: "'Peace, peace,' they say, when there is no peace" (Jeremiah 8:11 NIV).

In the midst of an uncertain and threatening world, however, we can have peace. It comes from putting our trust in the living God. Isaiah's words—written in a time of great upheaval—still speak to us today: "Those who wait on the LORD shall renew their strength; . . . they shall walk and not faint" (Isaiah 40:31).

HOPE FOR TODAY

Defeating an earthly enemy will never bring peace; creating the most devastating weapon doesn't prove strength. People who learn to wait on the Lord will be the ones who experience perfect peace and a strength that doesn't fade regardless of world events.

OUR INFINITE GOD

Great is the LORD, and greatly to be praised.
PSALM 48:1

As a boy I grew up in the rural American South. My idea of the ocean was so small that the first time I saw the Atlantic I couldn't comprehend how any lake could be so big! The vastness of the ocean cannot be understood until it is seen.

This is the same with God's love. It passes knowledge. Until you actually experience it, no one can describe its wonders to you. The opening lines of one of our great old hymns declare, "O the deep, deep love of Jesus, vast, unmeasured, boundless, free! Rolling as a mighty ocean in its fullness over me."

Behind the love of God lies His omniscience—His ability to know and understand all. Omniscience is a quality of God that is His alone. God possesses infinite knowledge and an awareness that is uniquely His. At all times, even in the midst of any type of suffering, I can realize that He knows, loves, watches, understands, and, more than that, has a purpose.

No matter what comes your way . . . no matter how tempted you are to give in to despair . . . never forget: God's love for you can never be exhausted, for His love is beyond measure.

HOPE FOR TODAY

Marriage vows are possibly the strongest declaration of love: in sickness and in health, for rich or for poor. Yet, even this love is only until "death do us part." God promises that not even death can separate us from His love.

WALK IN THE SPIRIT

Walk in the Spirit, and you shall not fulfill the lust of the flesh.
GALATIANS 5:16

To walk means to place one foot in front of the other and to go forward one step at a time. If you stop doing this, you are no longer walking. You are standing still—or worse, going backward. Walking always implies movement, progress, and direction.

This is what it means to walk with God. It means moving forward in step with Him, confident that the way He is leading is best. The problem is that we are weak. We stumble or get diverted, or we get weary and stop moving forward. But that is one reason why the Holy Spirit has been given to us. Galatians 5:16 could be paraphrased this way: "Walk by means of the Spirit."

One of the highest commendations in the Bible is found in these words about Noah: "Noah was a just man, perfect in his generations. Noah walked with God" (Genesis 6:9). Could this be said of you?

HOPE FOR TODAY

Do you feel the enemy trying to lead you off God's path? Whatever you do, don't stop! Keep walking with God: be in His Word, pray continually, move forward in faith. Slow and steady still wins the race.

GOD'S PERFECT PLAN

Be transformed . . . that you may prove what is that . . . perfect will of God.

ROMANS 12:2

The Bible reveals that God has a plan for every life, and that if we live in constant fellowship with Him, He will direct and lead us in the fulfillment of this plan.

God does not reveal His plan through fortune-tellers, astrologers, soothsayers, and workers of hocus-pocus. His perfect will is reserved for those who have trusted Christ for salvation. He shares His secrets only with those who are redeemed and transformed, those who humbly seek His will for their lives.

You cannot know the will of God for your life unless you first come to the Cross and confess that you are a sinner and receive Christ as Lord and Savior. Once you do come to Him, you begin a whole new life—a life lived not for yourself but for Christ. From that moment on God, wants to show you His will. Whatever decisions you face today, commit them to God and ask Him to guide you—and He will.

HOPE FOR TODAY

God created us with a purpose; it's to His glory that we discover and live out that purpose. Do you want to know God's will for you? Come to Christ, and God will make known the mystery of His will (Ephesians 1:9).

CONFESSION AND CLEANSING

If we confess our sins, He is faithful and just to forgive us our sins.
1 JOHN 1:9

Corrie ten Boom used to tell a story of a little girl who broke one of her mother's demitasse cups. The little girl came to her mother, sobbing, "Oh, Mama, I'm so sorry I broke your beautiful cup."

The mother replied, "I know you're sorry and I forgive you. Now don't cry anymore." The mother then swept up the pieces of the broken cup and placed them in the trash can. But the little girl enjoyed the guilty feeling. She went to the trash can, picked out pieces of the cup, brought them to her mother, and sobbed, "Mother, I'm so sorry that I broke your pretty cup."

This time her mother spoke firmly to her. "Take those pieces and put them back in the trash can. Don't be silly enough to take them out again. I told you I forgave you, so don't cry anymore."

Don't keep holding on to your guilt. If you have confessed your sins to Christ, He has forgiven them and taken them away—forever.

HOPE FOR TODAY

When a person comes to Christ, he is a new creation. He is not a cleaned up, repurposed version of his old self. As believers, our stories are no longer ones of guilt but of grace.

PERFECT IN WEAKNESS

When I am weak, then I am strong.

2 CORINTHIANS 12:10

God's idea of strength and man's idea of strength are opposite. The Lord told Paul, "My strength is made perfect in weakness" (2 Corinthians 12:9). Having learned this lesson, Paul could then say, "When I am weak, then I am strong" (2 Corinthians 12:10). A paradox? Not really. Only when Paul admitted his own weakness and was willing to get out of the way could God take over and work.

If we try to do God's will in our own strength, then we can take the credit for whatever gets accomplished. But that isn't God's way! When we let His strength work through us, then He alone will get the glory—and that is as it should be.

In the Old Testament, God repeatedly told the leaders of Israel to reduce the size of their armies, or He announced in advance how their victory would be won. Why? So they would place their trust in Him and not in their own strength. As someone has said, "God's work, done in God's way, will never lack for God's provision."

HOPE FOR TODAY

God's will for our lives will always require God's presence to accomplish it. The next time you feel too weak for what God is calling you to do, just be obedient and watch what happens when God shows up.

LONGING FOR GOD

My soul thirsts for God, for the living God.
PSALM 42:2

These words of the psalmist sound strange to most people today: "My soul thirsts for God, for the living God." In an age preoccupied with the things of this world, God seems almost irrelevant.

But the psalmist had discovered what most people realize sooner or later (even if they refuse to admit it): the things of this world can never satisfy the longings of our souls.

Only God can meet our deepest yearnings. As Saint Augustine said centuries ago, "You have made us for Yourself, O God, and our hearts are restless until they find their rest in You."

What crowds out a yearning for God in your life? Don't let anything—or anyone—come between you and God. Isaiah wrote, "Why do you spend money for what is not bread, and your wages for what does not satisfy?" (Isaiah 55:2).

God wants you to know Him in a personal way, and He has made this possible through Jesus Christ. He loves you, and He will give you His peace.

HOPE FOR TODAY

Lord, we could gorge ourselves on the world's offerings, and our souls would still be starving for You. This world can never satisfy the longings of Your people. More of You, God. That's what we need—more of You.

LOUD AND CLEAR

The mystery . . . now has been revealed to His saints.

COLOSSIANS 1:26

Radio was just coming of age when I was a boy. We would gather around a crude homemade set and twist the tuning dials. Often the only sound was the squeak and squawk of static. It wasn't very exciting, but we kept at it. We knew that somewhere out there was the unseen transmitter, and if we established contact, we could hear a voice loud and clear.

Does God speak to us? Is He trying to reach us? Yes! The problem is not with Him, but with us. Like that crude radio, we aren't attuned to Him.

We could only know God in one way: if He revealed Himself to us. And that is what He has done. He revealed Himself in the world He created, and in a fuller way He revealed Himself in His written Word, the Bible. Centuries ago He spoke to the prophets and the apostles, and by the inspiration of the Holy Spirit, they wrote down His Word for us.

God is trying to break through to us—but we must "tune in" to His Word. Are you listening?

HOPE FOR TODAY

Long ago, God spoke to His people through the prophets (Hebrews 1:1). Today, we have direct access to Him through Christ and through His Word. Do you want to hear from God? Open the Bible; He is waiting to speak to you.

GOD'S SECRET AGENTS

He will give his angels charge of you
to guard you in all your ways.
PSALM 91:11 RSV

A secret agent is one who seeks to protect his country, his king, or his president against evil forces that are opposed to the one he serves. The American Secret Service is charged with protecting the president of the United States. They do an excellent job, but even they will tell you that someone who is fiercely determined to assassinate the president could be successful.

God has His own secret agents—the angels. Unseen and unrecognized by the world, they never fail in their appointed tasks. Much has been written recently about angels—often not based on the Bible but on popular legends. But angels are real, and God has commanded them to watch over us. Only in eternity will we know how many accidents they prevented, or how often they kept Satan's malicious spirits at bay. In the meantime, we can take comfort in their presence, and thank God for the love He expresses for us through their service.

HOPE FOR TODAY

If you've ever had to fill in for a coworker or hold down the fort while a spouse was away, you've likely been surprised by how much that person handles. Likewise, we will be amazed at how busy God's angels have been over our lifetimes.

IN THE PRESENCE OF CHRIST

The upright shall dwell in Your presence.
PSALM 140:13

What would you do if you were about to meet the Queen of England? I'm sure you would go out of your way to dress correctly and to be properly briefed so you didn't say the wrong thing or act in an improper way.

Someday you and I will meet a far greater Sovereign: the King of the universe. His dazzling glory far exceeds that of any earthly monarch, and in His presence we can only bow in humble worship and praise. Our cry will be that of Revelation: "You are worthy, O Lord, to receive glory and honor and power" (Revelation 4:11).

Are you prepared for that day when you will meet the King of kings face-to-face? No one knows the day or the hour when life will end. The time for you to prepare is now, by committing your life to Christ and beginning to live as a child of the King.

HOPE FOR TODAY

Christ is preparing us a place in Heaven; He's expecting us. What do we need to be doing to prepare ourselves and our hearts for Him? Are we living in a way that will say, upon His arrival, "I was expecting You"?

A STEP IN THE PROCESS

Blessed is the man whom You instruct, O LORD.
PSALM 94:12

A child develops muscles through exercise. Only when our muscles encounter resistance do they become stronger.

In the same way, the Bible tells us that we only become stronger spiritually through exercise—through using our spiritual muscles to meet the challenges of life. This is especially true when we face suffering and affliction, for they are one way God makes us strong. One reason God allows suffering to come to His people, the Bible says, is to discipline, chasten, and mold us.

In the last essay he wrote before he died, the great Christian writer C. S. Lewis said, "We have no right to happiness; only an obligation to do our duty." Sometimes our God-given duty will include suffering. When it does, ask God to teach you through it. Remember the psalmist's words I quoted above: "Blessed is the man whom You instruct, O LORD."

HOPE FOR TODAY
People post pictures of their breakfast, their new home, or a good parking spot on social media and call it blessed. If we were "instructed by God," how many of us would consider ourselves blessed?

A NEW CREATION

If anyone is in Christ, there is a new creation: everything old has passed away.

2 CORINTHIANS 5:17 NRSV

I once heard a carpenter say that it is always better, and usually more economical, to construct a new house than to patch up an old one. This is even more true in the spiritual realm.

The old nature, with its deceitfulness, its depravity, and its wickedness, must give way to a new nature. And this is exactly what God stands ready to do. God says, "I will give you a new heart and put a new spirit within you" (Ezekiel 36:26).

What a challenge! It is much more difficult to change our dispositions than it is our apparel. As a matter of fact, it is utterly impossible for us to change our dispositions in our own strength.

But God can! "If anyone is in Christ, there is a new creation." God doesn't just want to patch us up. He wants to remake us completely into the likeness of Christ! He wants to come into our lives and begin to change us from within. Have you asked Him to do that? He will!

HOPE FOR TODAY

The God who took a murderer named Saul and changed him into a missionary named Paul can do the same for anyone who comes to Him. In Christ, we don't have to be who we were yesterday; we can be brand-new.

AMBASSADORS UNDER AUTHORITY

We are ambassadors for Christ, as though God were pleading through us.
2 CORINTHIANS 5:20

What is an ambassador? He is a representative and servant of his government in a foreign land. He is not free to set his own policies or develop his own message, but must carry out the will of the government he represents. In other words, he is a person under authority.

In the same way we are called to live under the authority of Jesus Christ and the authority of the Scriptures. We are servants. We must live under the authority of the Word of God. We are called not to do our will, but Christ's.

The world today is looking for holy men and women who live under the authority of the Word of God. Unbelievers will not listen to what we say unless we back it up with the way we live. Are you a faithful ambassador for Christ to those around you?

HOPE FOR TODAY

Have you ever neglected to witness to someone for fear you wouldn't know what to say? We can be confident in the message of Christ because it's God's message. It's nothing we have to conjure up; we just speak the gospel.

LIVING A PEACEABLE LIFE

Lead a quiet and peaceable life in all godliness and reverence.

1 TIMOTHY 2:2

As Christians, we aren't to isolate ourselves from the world in which we live. We are part of society, and we share in its difficulties, problems, and hopes.

The Bible has much to say about our social responsibility. The Old Testament prophets condemned those who ignored the poor and exploited the weak. Not that it is easy. As Christians, we know human society is affected by sin, and any effort to improve society will always be incomplete and imperfect. We will never build a Utopia on earth.

But we must do all we can to alleviate suffering, and to strike at the root causes of injustice, racial prejudice, hunger, and violence. We are to work for a peaceable life and human dignity for others. Why? Because God loves this suffering world. Jesus saw the crowds and "was moved with compassion" (Matthew 9:36).

Christ is concerned about the whole person—including the society in which that person lives. Do we share His concern?

HOPE FOR TODAY

As believers, are we huddling in our churches, or are we helping our communities? The command was never to wait; it was to go and tell (Matthew 28:19).

A GREAT GIFT

The kingdom of God is . . . righteousness and peace and joy in the Holy Spirit.
ROMANS 14:17

To the great gift of forgiveness God adds the great gift of the Holy Spirit. He is the source of power who meets our need to escape from the miserable weakness that grips us. He gives us the power to be truly good as we yield ourselves to Him.

If we are to live a life of sanity in our modern world, if we wish to be men and women who can live victoriously, we need the two-sided gift God has offered us. First, the work of the Son of God for us; second, the work of the Spirit of God in us. In this way God has answered humanity's two great cries: the cry for forgiveness and the cry for goodness.

As a friend of mine has said, "I need Jesus Christ for my eternal life, and the Holy Spirit of God for my internal life." He might have added, ". . . so I can live my external life to the fullest."

HOPE FOR TODAY

God's love truly is the gift that keeps on giving. Through Christ, we have access to God and eternal life. Through the Holy Spirit, we have the guidance, comfort, and strength we need to navigate the journey to Heaven.

GOD'S WORK

As many as are led by the Spirit of God, these are sons of God.

ROMANS 8:14

The first key for usefulness in God's kingdom is humility. Pride cuts us off from God (and from other people), and deceives us into thinking we can do God's work without God's power. When we rely on the Holy Spirit, however, He sanctifies us and empowers us so we can be effective tools in God's hands.

But there is a second key, and that is faith—faith that God is sovereign, and that He is at work, even if we can't see it. Habakkuk complained to God that evil people were winning the day. But God replied, "I will work a work in your days which you would not believe, though it were told you" (Habakkuk 1:5).

God is at work, even in the midst of the problems, pessimism, and frustrations of our day. He alone is sovereign—and that is why we can trust Him, even when the way seems dark.

HOPE FOR TODAY

Lord, I long to be used by You; give me a teachable heart. Let me see You do a work in my day that many would not believe and that would not be possible apart from Your divine intervention.

CONFIDENCE AND PEACE

You will keep him in perfect peace,
Whose mind is stayed on You.
ISAIAH 26:3

Peace carries with it the idea of unity, completeness, rest, ease, and security. Many times when I meet Jewish friends, I greet them with *"Shalom,"* the Hebrew word for "peace." And often when I greet my Arab friends I use a similar term that they use for "peace," *"Salam."*

Notice the key phrase in that verse: "whose mind is stayed on You." When troubles hit, our minds naturally focus on them. When suffering comes, all we can think about is the pain. It takes a deliberate act of the will to turn away from the problem and focus our minds on God.

When our minds are stayed on God, we won't be worried about the future, because we know it is in His hands. We won't tremble over what might happen, because our lives are built upon the solid rock of Christ.

When you and I yield to worry, we deny our Guide the right to lead us forward in confidence and peace. Don't cause Him to grieve over you by indulging in worry, but trust everything into His all-loving care.

HOPE FOR TODAY

Choose the peace of Christ over today's problems. Focus on your faith instead of your feelings. Let worship be your first response instead of worry. Remind yourself that you know whom you have believed.

WITNESS TO THE WORLD

Rejoice with those who rejoice, and weep with those who weep.

ROMANS 12:15

Jesus ate with publicans and sinners. Nearly everyone He associated with was an outcast. But His relationship with them was not purely social; it was redemptive.

We must not get our worlds mixed up at this point. God meant that we are not to mingle with the world and be polluted by the world, but we are to witness to the world. We are to "weep with those who weep," suffer with those who suffer, and identify ourselves with the poor, the sick, and the needy in body, mind, and spirit. How else can we reach them for Christ?

We are to love those who are involved in the world without being contaminated, influenced, or swayed by them. We can do this only through a close walk with Christ. Like Him, we are to be in the world, but not of the world.

It is good for a ship to be in the sea, but bad when the sea gets into the ship.

HOPE FOR TODAY

We are not to avoid the world; we are to engage it with a godly purpose. How else are we to proclaim freedom to the captive except to meet them in their captivity?

DISCOVER GOD'S GRACE

We conducted ourselves in the world . . . by the grace of God.
2 CORINTHIANS 1:12

I s God's grace really sufficient in times of trouble? Can it sustain us in the midst of life's storms?

Yes—but to be honest, sometimes it's hard for us to rely on God's grace instead of ourselves. We think we have to grab control of our lives, and we believe the responsibility for shaping our future must be in our hands.

When troubles come, therefore, we resist them instead of depending on God to see us through. Alexander Maclaren, the distinguished British preacher of another generation, once wrote, "What disturbs us in this world is not trouble, but our opposition to trouble."

Put God to the test when troubles come. He won't let you down. In the midst of a painful illness Paul begged God to intervene and take it away. But God replied, "My grace is sufficient for you" (2 Corinthians 12:9). It was sufficient for Paul, and it will be for you.

HOPE FOR TODAY

When God says His grace is enough, it's true. It doesn't have to make sense in the moment; it may not take the pain instantly away. But we can trust in His love for us and know that we have everything we need to endure.

A Home in Heaven

"If I go and prepare a place for you, I will come again and receive you to Myself."

JOHN 14:3

During Christ's ministry on earth He had no permanent home. He once said, "Foxes have holes and birds of the air have nests, but the Son of Man has no place to lay his head" (Matthew 8:20 NIV).

What a contrast to the home He left in order to come to earth—His heavenly home. From all eternity His dwelling place had been filled with unimaginable glory and splendor. And yet, the Bible says He "emptied Himself . . . being born in human likeness" (Philippians 2:7 NRSV). Out of love for you and me, He left Heaven's glory for earth's misery.

But the story doesn't end there. Now He has returned to Heaven—and someday we will join Him. Think of it: He wants to share Heaven's glory with us!

One evening a little girl was taking a walk with her father. Looking up at the stars she exclaimed, "Daddy, if the wrong side of Heaven is so beautiful, what must the right side be like!"

HOPE FOR TODAY

Scripture says that God has set eternity in our hearts; it's that longing for Heaven that we don't fully understand. The truth is we're all just a little homesick and ready for our Father to welcome us home.

THE GREATEST SECURITY

He who dwells in the secret place of the Most High
Shall abide under the shadow of the Almighty.
PSALM 91:1

Someone has said that the only certainty in life is uncertainty—and it is true. Governments collapse, stock markets plummet, wars destroy, disasters strike, relationships end. As the writer of Hebrews put it, "Here we have no continuing city" (Hebrews 13:14).

Yet deep in the human heart is a yearning for security—a yearning that will not go away. We know we need a solid foundation to life, a foundation that cannot be shaken. Where will it be found?

Only God never changes. His love does not change, and neither do His promises. That is why we can look to Him for the security and stability we all seek. King David knew the secret: "He who dwells in the secret place of the Most High shall abide under the shadow of the Almighty."

Salvation is not an occasional, vague feeling of God's presence. It is actually dwelling with God, secure in His presence forever. Is your security in Christ?

HOPE FOR TODAY

Security is a big deal; it's why we seek committed relationships or high-paying jobs. That's also why it's devastating when spouses leave and jobs are eliminated. Christ is the only true source of security; He will never leave you or forsake you.

IN GIVING, WE RECEIVE

"Love one another as I have loved you."
JOHN 15:12

Saint Francis of Assisi had discovered the secret of happiness when he prayed:

> O Divine Master, grant that I may not so much seek
> To be consoled as to console,
> To be understood as to understand,
> To be loved as to love;
> For it is in giving that we receive;
> It is in pardoning that we are pardoned;
> It is in dying that we are born to eternal life!

Tears shed for self are tears of weakness, but tears of love shed for others are a sign of strength. I am not as sensitive as I ought to be until I am able to "weep o'er the erring one and lift up the fallen." And until I have learned the value of compassionately sharing others' sorrow, distress, and misfortune, I cannot know real happiness.

The opposite of love isn't hate. It's selfishness. Will you ask the Holy Spirit to free your life from selfishness and fill you instead with His love?

HOPE FOR TODAY

Lord, forgive me for the times I have chosen self over service or a grudge over grace. Give me a love that sees others as more important than myself.

A Positive Influence

Do not be conformed to this world, but be transformed.
ROMANS 12:2

I have found that the casual Christian has little or no influence for good upon others. Only the Christian who refuses to compromise in matters of honesty, integrity, and morality is bearing an effective witness for Christ.

The casual, worldly Christian is prepared to do as the world does and will condone practices that are dishonest and unethical because he is afraid of the world's displeasure. He ignores the Bible's clear command: "Do not be conformed to this world."

Only by a life of obedience to the voice of the Spirit, by a daily dying to self, by a full dedication to Christ and constant fellowship with Him are we enabled to live a godly life and have a positive influence on this present ungodly world. Is the world changing you . . . or are you changing the world?

HOPE FOR TODAY

The early church turned the world upside down for Christ. They endured beatings, imprisonments, and death. How can we hope to change our world for Christ when we're afraid to take a stand or to stand out?

CHOOSE LIFE

I have set before you life and death . . . therefore choose life.

DEUTERONOMY 30:19

I f God were to remove all evil from our world (but somehow leave human beings on the planet), it would mean that the essence of "humanness" would be destroyed. We would become robots.

Let me explain what I mean by this. If God eliminated evil by programming us to perform only good acts, we would lose this distinguishing mark—the ability to make choices. We would no longer be free moral agents. We would be reduced to the status of robots.

Let's take this a step further. Robots do not love. God created us with the capacity to love. Love is based upon one's right to choose to love. We cannot force others to love us. We can make them serve us or obey us. But true love is founded upon one's freedom to choose to respond.

Given the choice, I would rather be responsible for my actions than be a robot without responsibility! Are you using your ability to make decisions wisely—and using it for God?

HOPE FOR TODAY

Think about the number of choices you've made in the last twenty-four hours. What did you do with all of that freedom? How many of your choices were made with God and His will in mind?

VICTORY OVER SIN

In all these things we are more than conquerors through Him who loved us.
ROMANS 8:37

We sing "Onward Christian soldiers, marching as to war," but so often when Satan mounts an attack against us, we behave as if we were prisoners of war, or worse, conscientious objectors! But as Christians, we don't have to live defeated lives. God wants us to live victorious lives—lives that are constantly conquering sin.

There is only one way to have victory over sin. That is to walk so closely with Christ that sin no longer dominates your life. It becomes the exception rather than the rule.

Why does a close walk with Christ make the difference? Simply this: the closer we are to Christ, the farther we are from Satan. The Bible says, "Resist the devil and he will flee from you. Draw near to God and He will draw near to you" (James 4:7–8). Is the devil farther away from you today than he was a week ago? If not, why?

HOPE FOR TODAY

Because of Christ, we are conquerors, and the victory is ours. The blood of Jesus enables us to draw near to God and enjoy His protection, and we no longer have to fear the enemy.

RELINQUISH CONTROL

This is God, our God forever and ever;
He will be our guide, even to death.
PSALM 48:14

The story is told of a little girl whose father was an airline pilot. As they crossed the Atlantic, a storm came up. The flight attendant awakened the little girl and told her to fasten her seat belt because they were in some turbulent weather. The little girl opened her eyes, saw the lightning flashing around the plane, and asked, "Is Daddy at the controls?" The flight attendant replied, "Yes, your father is in the cockpit." The little girl smiled, closed her eyes, and went back to sleep.

God is at the controls of our lives. Or, rather, He wants to be at the controls. But He gives us the freedom to pilot ourselves as we wish. The problem is that we often crash, much as we would if we took the controls of an airplane we had not been taught to fly.

God knows us. He knows our strengths and weaknesses, and He knows what is best for us. If we will only relinquish the control of our lives to Him, He will see us safely home.

HOPE FOR TODAY

God is infinitely wise and good. He can't be caught off guard or unprepared. He never panics or quits, and best of all, He adores His children. Who better to chart our courses and guide our steps?

DEFLECT DESPAIR

[God] gives us the victory through our Lord Jesus Christ
1 CORINTHIANS 15:57 NIV

There is a story about Martin Luther going through a period of discouragement and depression. For days his long face darkened the family table and dampened the family's home life. One day his wife came to the breakfast table all dressed in black, as if she were going to a funeral service. When Martin asked her who had died, she replied, "Martin, the way you've been behaving lately, I thought God had died, so I came prepared to attend His funeral."

Her gentle but effective rebuke drove straight to Luther's heart, and as a result the great Reformer resolved never again to allow worldly care, resentment, depression, discouragement, or frustration to defeat him. By God's grace, he vowed, he would submit his life to the Savior and reflect His grace in a spirit of rejoicing, whatever came.

When was the last time you praised God in the midst of despair? Don't wait until you "feel like it," or you'll never do it. Do it, and then you'll feel like it!

HOPE FOR TODAY

There is one certainty regarding every trial you will ever face: God is still in control. You haven't encountered the one problem He can't fix. Seas still part and mountains still crumble at His command.

ONE WAY

"I am the way, the truth, and the life. No one comes to the Father except through Me."

JOHN 14:6

An old saying declares, "All roads lead to Rome." Perhaps it was true in the ancient world—but today, you can get lost anywhere! The road you are on may lead in exactly the opposite direction from your goal. The only sure way to reach your destination is to consult a GPS or ask someone who knows the way.

Not all roads lead to God, as some suggest. The reason? There is a roadblock that keeps man from reaching God—the roadblock of sin. But God has provided a map—the Bible—and He has provided us with One who knows the way and can give us directions—Jesus Christ.

Jesus did not say, "I am one of many roads to God." What He said was, "I am the way." That wasn't arrogance, or narrow-mindedness, or lack of compassion. It is truth—because only Christ came from Heaven to pay the price for our sins. Follow Christ and never be lost!

HOPE FOR TODAY

The lead car in a caravan must know the way, not get too far ahead, and keep an eye on the other cars. Christ knows how to lead His people, always watches over us, and *is* the way. We just have to follow faithfully.

FROM TRIAL TO TRIUMPH

Walk in wisdom . . . redeeming the time.

COLOSSIANS 4:5

The master musician knows that suffering precedes glory and acclaim. He or she knows the hours, days, and months of grueling practice and self-sacrifice that precede the one hour of perfect rendition when his efforts are applauded.

The master craftsman knows that years of work, sacrifice, and suffering as an apprentice precede his being promoted to the master of his trade.

The student knows that years of study, self-denial, and commitment precede the triumphant day of graduation with honors.

Astronauts spend years training for a flight that can be as short as a few days.

The Bible teaches that sacrifice and discipline are necessary if we are to be faithful servants of Christ. Paul wrote, "I discipline my body and bring it into subjection, lest, when I have preached to others, I myself should become disqualified" (1 Corinthians 9:27).

Discipline your time . . . discipline your eyes . . . discipline your mind . . . discipline your body . . . all for the sake of Christ.

HOPE FOR TODAY

How we spend our time, what we see (Psalm 119:37), and what we think about (2 Corinthians 10:5), matter. Our entire existence is to be a living sacrifice to the God who created us and awaits us in glory.

HOPE FOR THE HOME

He sets the poor on high . . .
And makes their families like a flock.
PSALM 107:41

One of the primary reasons for the breakdown of the home is that we have forgotten God's commands about marriage.

God gave marriage to us, and His standards have not changed. Jesus said, "A man shall leave his father and mother and be joined to his wife. . . . Therefore what God has joined together, let not man separate" (Matthew 19:5–6).

Divorce was not part of God's original design—nor is it now. The Bible declares, "The LORD God of Israel says that He hates divorce" (Malachi 2:16). Marriage is a symbol of the unity between Christ and His church—a unity that should never be torn.

No marriage is beyond repair with God's help. But we must humble ourselves and put aside our pride and self-will. We must put others ahead of ourselves.

If divorce has happened to you, God can forgive the past, heal the present, and give you hope for the future. But if you are married, treasure your spouse as a gift from God, and yield your marriage to Christ.

HOPE FOR TODAY
A great marriage is one filled with grace in which two imperfect people follow Christ together and forgive one another along the way.

JESUS WILL ANSWER

He will give His angels charge of you
to guard you in all your ways.
PSALM 91:11 RSV

Once a poor Chinese woman went up to the foothills to cut grass. Her baby was tied to her back, and a little child walked beside her.

Just as she reached the top of a hill, she heard a roar. Frightened, she turned and saw a mother tigress springing at her, followed by her two cubs.

The illiterate woman had never attended school or church, but a missionary once told her about Jesus, "who is able to help you when you are in trouble." As the tiger's claws tore into her arm, the woman cried out, "O Jesus, help me!" The tiger, instead of attacking again, suddenly turned and ran away.

What "beasts" are attacking you? Chances are you will never be attacked by a wild tiger, but you will be attacked by doubts, fears, worry, loneliness, or despair.

Cry out to Jesus and He will answer you just as surely as He heard and answered the Chinese woman's desperate cry.

HOPE FOR TODAY
What enemies have we faced and what pains have we endured because we failed to cry out to Jesus in our times of need? The next time you're tempted to tough it out, choose to cry out instead.

JUNE

Let your speech always be with grace, seasoned with salt, that you may know how you ought to answer each one.

COLOSSIANS 4:6

HIS MOST PRECIOUS BLOOD

Jesus Christ . . . loved us and washed us from our sins in His own blood.
REVELATION 1:5

When J. P. Morgan, the multimillionaire, died, it was found that his will consisted of about ten thousand words and thirty-seven articles. He made many transactions, some involving large sums of money.

But we are left in no doubt as to what he considered his most important transaction: "I commit my soul into the hands of my Savior, in full confidence that, having redeemed and washed it in His most precious blood, He will present it faultless before my heavenly Father; and I entreat my children to maintain and defend, at all hazard and at any cost of personal sacrifice, the blessed doctrine of the complete atonement for sin through the blood of Jesus Christ, once offered, and through that alone."

In the matter of his soul's eternal blessing, J. P. Morgan's vast wealth was powerless. He was just as dependent on God's mercy as was the dying thief at Calvary. No matter who you are or what you have done, only Christ can save you, for only "the blood of Jesus Christ . . . cleanses . . . from all sin" (1 John 1:7).

HOPE FOR TODAY

It's been said that the ground is level at the foot of the Cross. We all arrive equally guilty and sin-stained; we all leave equally forgiven and free. The same blood cleanses us all.

ASK AND RECEIVE

*"Whatever things you ask when you pray, believe that
you receive them, and you will have them."*

MARK 11:24

Someone has said that before our prayers can mean anything to God, they must first mean something to us. Mindlessly repeating a prayer we memorized in childhood, or vaguely asking God to bless everyone, everywhere—that isn't authentic prayer. Prayer is speaking to God about the deepest concerns of our hearts.

What is the source of true prayer? It is a heart attuned to God. It is a life lived in loving obedience to the Father. The Bible says, "And whatever we ask we receive from Him, because we keep His commandments and do those things that are pleasing in His sight" (1 John 3:22).

God delights in the prayers of His children—prayers that express our love for Him, prayers that share our deepest burdens with Him. Don't pray casually or thoughtlessly, but "come boldly to the throne of grace, that [you] may obtain mercy and find grace to help in time of need" (Hebrews 4:16).

HOPE FOR TODAY

God longs to hear from repentant sinners, and He delights in knowing that His children will trust Him with their heartfelt prayers guided by the Holy Spirit of God.

LIVING A HOLY LIFE

"Lay up for yourselves treasures in heaven."
MATTHEW 6:20

An old man, a great man of God, lay on his deathbed. He summoned his grandson to come to his side. Calling the boy's name, he said, "I don't know what type of work I will be doing in Heaven, but if it's allowed, I'm going to ask the Lord Jesus to let me help build your mansion. You be sure you send up plenty of the right materials."

Living a life of purity and love, leading others to Christ as we share our faith, doing good works in Christ's name—all of these things are materials that may be sent on ahead. These can never be touched by the fluctuations in the earthly economy, by natural disaster, or by thievery.

What kind of materials are you sending up to Heaven?

HOPE FOR TODAY

We plan for our earthly futures: college funds, retirement plans, and so forth. Are you putting the same planning into storing up treasures in Heaven? What have you done today that will be credited to your eternal account?

REST FOR THE WEARY

"Come to Me . . . and I will give you rest."
MATTHEW 11:28

We forget that Jesus was human as well as divine. He had calluses on His hands. If the chisel slipped and cut His finger, His blood was red and warm like ours. He knew what it meant to work long hours, to come in at night tired and weary.

That is one of the reasons Jesus could say with such appeal, "Come to Me, all you who labor and are heavy laden, and I will give you rest" (Matthew 11:28). When we are exhausted and hurting, we can take comfort from the fact that Jesus knows what it is to be exhausted and hurting also.

But the greatest work Jesus did was not in the carpenter's shop, nor at the marriage feast in Cana where He turned the water into wine. The greatest work Jesus did was not when He made the blind to see, the deaf to hear, the dumb to speak, nor even the dead to rise.

What was His greatest work?

His greatest work was what He accomplished through the Cross and resurrection. There the burden of our sins was placed on Him, and there He won our salvation. And that is why we can come by faith to Him, and He will give us rest.

HOPE FOR TODAY
God came to life and lived life as a man. Whatever we encounter, God says, "Come and rest. I know exactly how you feel."

More Attached to God

God is our refuge and strength,
an ever-present help in trouble.
PSALM 46:1 NIV

A young Irishman, Joseph Scriven (1820–1886), was deeply in love with a young woman, and their marriage plans had been made. The night before their wedding, however, she drowned in a tragic accident. For months Scriven was bitter, and in utter despair.

At last he turned to Christ, and through His grace, found peace and comfort. Out of this experience Scriven wrote the familiar hymn that has brought consolation to millions of aching hearts: "What a friend we have in Jesus, all our sins and griefs to bear!"

Sometimes our way lies in the sunlight. It was so for Joseph Scriven as he approached his wedding day. But like him, we may find that our path also leads through the dark shadows of loss, disappointment, and sorrow.

Yet even sorrows turn to blessings when they make us less attached to the earth and more attached to God. Then more than ever we discover that Jesus truly is our friend—"All our sins and griefs to bear!"

Hope for Today

Lord, may every earthly loss serve to lead me to the Cross. Whatever good things come and go in this life, let the cry of my heart always be, "God is all I need."

TAKE THE LEAP

By my God I can leap over a wall.
PSALM 18:29

The Bible confronts us with our moral independence within ourselves and our spiritual dependence upon God.

In the picturesque words of Psalm 18, David says, "By my God I can leap over a wall." We can jump over some barriers in life by our own will and our own efforts; God has not left us completely powerless. But some walls are so high we need more than this.

The psalmist knew such walls. They could be leaped only with the help of God. When we try to jump over them by ourselves, we repeatedly fall short. But with God's help, we can conquer them.

What walls do you need to jump over? A habit you cannot break? An emotion that defeats you? An attitude that separates you from others? A heart beset with doubt or discouragement or fear? Whatever it is, with God's help you can leap over that wall.

HOPE FOR TODAY

The enemy is great at distorting things. Like a funhouse mirror, he can make obstacles seem far larger than reality. We must remember, when our eyes play tricks on us, that nothing is impossible with God (Luke 1:37).

THE SEAL OF THE SPIRIT

Having believed, you were marked in him with a seal, the promised Holy Spirit.
EPHESIANS 1:13 NIV

God places a seal on us when we receive Christ. And that seal is a person—the Holy Spirit. By the Spirit's presence God gives us security and establishes His ownership over us.

The Spirit is also God's pledge. He not only seals the arrangement, but He represents God's commitment to see us through. And fellowship with the Spirit is a sample of what we can expect when we come into our inheritance in Heaven.

Finally, the Spirit witnesses to us, by the Scriptures and within our hearts, that Christ died for us and that by faith in Him we have become God's children.

What a wonderful thing to know the Holy Spirit has been given to us as a seal, a pledge, and a witness! May each of these give us new assurance of God's unchanging love for us, and give us confidence as we seek to live for Him.

HOPE FOR TODAY
Have you ever felt unexplainable peace in a difficult time? Inner conviction when tempted to go astray? Boldness to stand up for what is right? These are reminders from God that you belong to Him and He will not let you go.

A CLEAR CONSCIENCE

I myself always strive to have a conscience without offense toward God and men.

ACTS 24:16

Benjamin Franklin composed this little rhyme: "Keep conscience clear, then never fear." George Bernard Shaw, the great Irish writer, said, "Better keep yourself clean and bright; you are the window through which you must see the world."

If conscience was such a vital concept to these secular writers, how much more concerned should we as Christians be that our consciences are "without offense toward God and men"? Without a conscience, we would be like rudderless ships at sea, or missiles without a guidance system.

God has given our conscience to us. Its very presence is a reflection of God in the human soul. Sin, however, can dull or even distort our conscience, silencing its voice and leading us astray. But God's Word can purify and sharpen our conscience—and when that happens, "He leads [us] in paths of righteousness for His name's sake" (Psalm 23:3). Is this happening in your life?

HOPE FOR TODAY

We can know the will of God when we know the Word of God. Through reading and meditating on His precepts, we learn to recognize His voice and can follow the way of faithfulness (Psalm 119:30).

167

IN THE TIME OF TROUBLE

Cast your burden on the LORD,
And He shall sustain you.
PSALM 55:22

Years ago I came across this oft-quoted prayer: "God, grant me the serenity to accept things I cannot change, the courage to change the things I can, and wisdom to know the difference." This prayer expresses an important thought; one we should all pray—and live.

Some things in life cannot be changed—and some can. Some things God has given to us as fixed realities that we must accept. And some things He would have us not accept, but (with His help) work to change. If we fail to do both of these—to accept some things and work to change others—we will end up burdened with worry, undeserved guilt, and frustration.

Someone once said, "Worry is the interest paid on trouble before it comes due." Instead, God would have us learn to trust Him. "Cast your burden on the LORD, and He shall sustain you."

HOPE FOR TODAY
Is there a situation you've been fighting to change that God may be calling you to accept? Perhaps there is something you've "learned to accept" that He wants you to rise up against. Ask for wisdom to know the difference.

GOD'S GOOD PROMISE

Blessed be the LORD. . . . There has not failed one word of all His good promise.

1 KINGS 8:56

When we purchase something of great value—a house, for example—we are usually required to put down a deposit to indicate our sincerity and to promise that our intentions are serious. That deposit is a form of insurance, a guarantee that adds substance to our word.

God has made some incredible promises to us—-promises that stagger our imaginations. He has promised that we might have a relationship with Him through His Son. He has promised never to leave us or forsake us and to be with us always. He has promised to take us to Heaven when we die. The Bible is full of God's promises.

Someone might ask, "What insurance do we have that God is serious? How do we know His promises can be trusted?" God's deposit is the most precious investment anyone could make: His Son, who by His death and resurrection purchased our salvation—completely and fully. Not only is Jesus Christ a sufficient "down payment" on God's promises, He is, in fact, payment in full!

HOPE FOR TODAY

Every promise God has ever made to His people finds its fulfillment in the person of Jesus Christ (2 Corinthians 1:20). By studying Scripture, we see time and time again that our God is the great promise keeper.

THE PRIVILEGE OF PRAYER

"Ask, and you will receive, that your joy may be full."
JOHN 16:24

What a privilege is ours: the privilege of prayer! Just think of it: you and I have the incredible privilege of approaching the God of the universe, "the High and Lofty One who inhabits eternity, whose name is Holy" (Isaiah 57:15)! We can only do this because Jesus Christ has opened the way.

We are to pray in times of adversity, lest we become faithless and unbelieving.

We are to pray in times of prosperity, lest we become boastful and proud.

We are to pray in times of danger, lest we become fearful and doubting.

We are to pray in times of security, lest we become self-sufficient.

Pray, believing, in the promise of God's Word that "if we ask anything according to His will, He hears us" (1 John 5:14).

HOPE FOR TODAY

Can you imagine Moses turning down the chance to speak to God on the mountain? That is the choice we make when we neglect the privilege of prayer. Whatever is on your heart, joy or sorrow, your God wants to hear from you.

OVERFLOWING JOY

But the fruit of the Spirit is . . . joy.

GALATIANS 5:22

The word *joy* has all but disappeared from our current Christian vocabulary. One reason is because we have confused joy with happiness, and have come to believe it is found in pleasure, security, and prosperity. In doing this, however, we have believed a lie that Satan is constantly telling the world to believe.

But James did not say, "Count it all joy when you fall into an easy chair." He said, "Count it all joy when you fall into various trials" (James 1:2).

Joy is not the same as happiness—although they may overlap. Happiness depends on circumstances; joy depends on God. Happiness vanishes when life turns painful; joy keeps going and may even grow.

Joy comes from a living, vital relationship with God. It comes from knowing this world is only temporary and that someday we will be with God forever. It comes from the fact that although we do not yet see God, we "believe in him and are filled with an inexpressible and glorious joy" (1 Peter 1:8 NIV). It comes from a life of submission to the Holy Spirit—regardless of circumstances.

HOPE FOR TODAY

We've all heard it; some of us have surely said, "I just want to be happy." How sad that we would content ourselves with happiness when the joy of the Lord is ours for the taking. Choose joy.

A BEACON OF HOPE

"If I go and prepare a place for you, I will come again."
JOHN 14:3

In his remarkable book *Christian Behavior,* C. S. Lewis said, "Hope is one of the theological virtues." He meant that a continual looking forward to the eternal world is not, as some people think, a form of escapism or wishful thinking, but one of the things a Christian is meant to do.

This does not mean we are to leave the present world as it is. If you read history, you will find that the Christians who did the most for the present world were those who thought the most of the next. It is only since Christians have largely ceased to think of the next world that they have become so ineffective in this one. "Aim at heaven," said Lewis, "and you will get earth thrown in. Aim at earth, and you will get neither."

In the midst of the pessimism, gloom, and frustration of the present hour there is one bright beacon of hope—and that is the promise of Jesus Christ: "If I go and prepare a place for you, I will come again and receive you to Myself" (John 14:3).

HOPE FOR TODAY
Paul said that if Christ's death only brings us hope for this life, we are to be pitied (1 Corinthians 15:19)! Christ didn't die so that we could endure earth but so that we could expect heaven.

POWER FOR PROBLEMS

I can do all things through Christ who strengthens me.

PHILIPPIANS 4:13

A friend told me of a nonbeliever who came to him in the midst of a troubled day. Knowing my friend was a Christian, the man asked, "If I get born again, will all of my problems go away?"

"No," said my friend, "but you will have the power to deal with them."

God will give us wisdom and courage. He will surround us with brothers and sisters in Christ to help carry our burdens, and He will even provide us with insight and practical assistance.

Satan will always try to discourage those who belong to Christ. When problems persist, he may even whisper, "See, God doesn't care about you!" But with the Holy Spirit's help, we can combat the evil one and contradict his lies.

If God dismissed all our problems with a single stroke, we would be left defenseless, unequipped to meet the inevitable attacks of the enemy of our souls. But in the midst of life's problems God supplies everything we need to see us through.

HOPE FOR TODAY
Job had heard of God and lived a righteous life, but following his trials, he declared, "Now my eye sees you." Every time we face an obstacle and prevail, we see God at work, and our faith is strengthened.

ACCEPT GOD'S FREEDOM

Draw near to God and He will draw near to you.

JAMES 4:8

One day a little child was playing with a valuable vase. He put his hand into it and could not take it out. His father, too, tried his best to get the little boy's hand out, but all in vain. They were thinking of breaking the vase when the father said, "Now, my son, make one more try. Open your hand and hold your fingers out straight as you see me doing and then pull."

To the father's astonishment, the little fellow said, "Oh, no, Daddy! I couldn't put my fingers out like that because if I did I would drop my penny."

Smile if you will, but thousands of us are like that little boy. We are so busy holding on to the world's worthless trifles that we cannot accept God's freedom.

What "trifle" is keeping you from God? A sin you won't let go of? An unworthy goal you are determined to reach? A dishonorable relationship you won't give up? I beg you to drop that trifle in your heart. Surrender! Let go and let God have His way in your life.

HOPE FOR TODAY

Have you found yourself clinging to something that you know isn't good? For many, bondage is more familiar than freedom. Let go of anything that is holding you back and embrace the freedom of Christ.

NEARER THAN YOU THINK

His angels . . . keep you in all your ways.

PSALM 91:11

Occasionally I see reports of happenings that cannot be humanly explained—of visitors unexpectedly appearing to assist in times of crisis or warn of impending danger. These can only be explained as the intervention of God's angels.

In the Bible, angels occasionally assumed visible form—at the birth of Jesus, for example. But usually angels go about their business unseen and unrecognized. They never draw attention to themselves, but point us instead to Christ.

C. S. Lewis once said that we tend to make one of two errors about Satan: we either make too little of him, or we make too much.

The same could be said of angels. Don't make too little of them. God has given "His angels charge over you, to keep you in all your ways" (Psalm 91:11). On the other hand, don't worship them or become preoccupied with them. Instead, thank God for His angels and rejoice in their unseen watchfulness over you.

HOPE FOR TODAY

There is no such thing as a coincidence in the life of a Christian; God is actively involved in every aspect of our lives. Ask God to give you eyes that see, and you'll begin to see Him at work all around you.

GOD'S TRUE PURPOSES

"Whatever you ask in My name, that I will do."
JOHN 14:13

Prayer links us with God's true purposes, for us and for the world. It not only brings the blessings of God's will to our own personal lives, it brings us the added blessing of being in step with God's plan.

Prayer also—in ways we will never fully understand this side of eternity—makes us partners with God in what He is doing in the world. God works through our prayers!

The model prayer Jesus gave us concludes with, "Thine is the kingdom, and the power, and the glory for ever" (Matthew 6:13 KJV). Remember, that we must seek God's glory in our prayers and not just our own selfish desires. If we are to have our prayers answered, we must be willing to give God the glory when He acts—no matter what the result. Our Lord said to His disciples, "Whatever you ask in My name, that I will do, that the Father may be glorified in the Son" (John 14:13).

HOPE FOR TODAY

Our prayers cause things to happen in unseen places. Don't become discouraged; our greatest blessings may come through those times we don't see with our eyes the results of our prayers (John 20:29).

WHITE AS SNOW

Wash me, and I shall be whiter than snow.

PSALM 51:7

S now is so white that one can see almost anything that is dropped on it, even at great distances. We can take the whitest object we can find, like newly washed clothing, but when we place it next to snow it still looks dirty by comparison.

Our lives are like that. At times, we may think of ourselves as morally good and decent; we are content that we are "not like other men." But compared to God's purity, we are defiled and filthy.

In spite of our sins and uncleanness, God still loves us. And because He loves us, He decided to provide for us a purity we could never attain on our own. That is why He gave His Son, Jesus Christ, to die for us on the Cross. Only when our sins have been washed in the blood of Jesus Christ will we appear as white as snow in the eyes of God. Thank God today that you are now "whiter than snow," because "you were washed . . . in the name of the Lord Jesus and by the Spirit of our God" (1 Corinthians 6:11)!

HOPE FOR TODAY

God set the bar high on purpose. Being good will never be good enough; better than someone else simply won't cut it. Perfectly pure is the goal, and none of us can achieve it apart from Christ.

SINCERE DEVOTION

The fruit of the Spirit is love, joy, peace . . . gentleness, self-control.
GALATIANS 5:22–23

We should seek to produce the fruit of the Spirit in our lives. Or to put it more accurately, we should allow the Holy Spirit to produce His fruit in our lives.

You say, "I am powerless to produce such fruit. You don't know how weak and self-centered I am. It would be utterly impossible for me to do so!"

With that I agree! That is, we can't produce this fruit in our own strength. When the Spirit of God dwells in us and has control of our lives, He will produce that fruit. Our responsibility is to cultivate the soil of our hearts through sincere devotion and surrender, so He might find favorable ground to produce His fruit.

I might have a fruit tree in my yard, but if the soil isn't enriched and the bugs carefully destroyed, it will not yield a full crop. What keeps the Holy Spirit from producing His fruit in your life?

HOPE FOR TODAY

It's tempting to say, "I'm just not a patient or gentle person." On our own, none of us would consistently exhibit the fruit of the Spirit. It's God's fruit, and He will produce it if our hearts are yielded to Him.

THE BREVITY OF LIFE

What is your life? You are a mist that appears for a little while and then vanishes.

JAMES 4:14 NIV

Several years ago a university student asked me what had been my biggest surprise in life. Immediately, I replied, "The brevity of life." Almost before we know it, the years have passed and life is almost over.

On one hand, life's brevity should challenge us. If ever we are to live for Christ and share Him with others, it must be now. Jesus said, "The night is coming when no one can work" (John 9:4).

But life's brevity should also comfort us. Life is short—and before us is eternity! When sufferings overwhelm us or difficulties assail us, we know they will soon be over. Paul wrote, "Our light affliction, which is but for a moment, is working for us a far more exceeding and eternal weight of glory. . . . For the things which are seen are temporary" (2 Corinthians 4:17–18).

Don't live as if this life will continue forever. It won't. Live instead with eternity in view!

HOPE FOR TODAY

You promise a harvest, Lord, to those who don't give up (Galatians 6:9). Give me the endurance to finish strong; I want to look back and know that I didn't waste a single moment that You gave me.

FREE BUT NOT CHEAP

"If anyone desires to come after Me, let him . . . take up his cross, and follow Me."
MATTHEW 16:24

During the early years of the twentieth century, Bill Borden turned his back on one of America's great family fortunes to become a missionary to China. He only got as far as Egypt, where, still in his twenties, he died of typhoid fever. Before his death he wrote, "No reserves, no retreats, no regrets!"

Discipleship is always costly. No, it may not cost us our lives. But it will cost us. It will cost us our plans, our wills, our selfish desires. Jesus' standard has not changed: "If anyone desires to come after Me, let him deny himself and take up his cross, and follow Me" (Matthew 16:24). Instead of controlling our lives, we turn them over to Christ as Lord.

Someone has said, "Salvation is free but not cheap." It cost Jesus His life, and it will cost us as well. But could anything be greater? Could anything be more fulfilling?

Follow Christ, and at life's end you will be able to say, "No regrets!"

HOPE FOR TODAY
Everyone who follows Christ first picks up his cross, and no one's cross is light. What have you had to sacrifice in order to follow Him? Whatever it is, you can know that it was worth it.

Our Omnipotent Helper

"The Spirit of truth who proceeds from the Father, He will testify of Me."
John 15:26

God the Holy Spirit is equal with the Son and with the Father in every respect. Although the doctrine of the Trinity is difficult for us to understand, the Bible teaches that He is co-equal with God the Father and co-equal with God the Son.

The Bible also teaches that the Holy Spirit is a Person. He is never to be referred to as "it." He is not an impersonal power or force, nor is He just a divine influence or agent. He is a mighty Person, the Holy Spirit of God.

The Bible tells us as well that the Holy Spirit is omnipotent. That means He has all power. The Bible also tells us that He is omnipresent. That means He is everywhere at the same time.

What should this mean to me? With the seventeenth-century Anglican bishop Jeremy Taylor, I can say, "It is impossible for that man to despair who remembers that his Helper is omnipotent."

Hope for Today

Are you feeling weakened or overwhelmed by your current circumstances? Remember that greater is He who is in you than he who is in the world. You have everything you need.

SUFFICIENT GRACE

"My grace is sufficient for you."
2 CORINTHIANS 12:9

The prayer of Jesus in the Garden of Gethsemane is perhaps the greatest, most moving prayer ever uttered. In it our Lord asked that the cup of crucifixion, which was about to be thrust upon Him, might be taken away. But then, in the very next breath He said, "Nevertheless, not as I will, but as You will" (Matthew 26:39). What a prayer! What strength! What power!

When the apostle Paul asked God to remove his "thorn in the flesh," God did not remove it, saying instead, "My grace is sufficient for you." Rather than complain or become angry at God, Paul joyfully submitted to God's will. He discovered that God's grace truly was sufficient, even in the midst of pain.

Christ desires to be with you in whatever crisis you may find yourself. Call upon His name. See if He will not do as He promised He would. He may not make your problems go away, but He will give you the power to deal with them and to overcome them by His grace.

HOPE FOR TODAY

If we only pray for the removal of problems, we will often be disappointed.
If we pray for God's presence in the midst of our problems, we will always
receive what we have asked.

CHANGED FOR LIFE

We . . . are being transformed into the same image from glory to glory.

2 CORINTHIANS 3:18

You can scrub a pig, sprinkle Chanel No. 5 on him, put a ribbon around his neck, and take him into your living room. But when you turn him loose, he will jump into the first mud puddle he sees because his nature has never been changed. He is still a pig.

We constantly try to reform ourselves. Stores are filled with self-help books claiming to hold the secret to personal reformation. But such efforts are only temporary at best. A deeper transformation is needed—a transformation of the heart.

And it is possible! The Bible teaches that when we come to Christ, we are spiritually born again. God's Spirit comes to live within us and change us. Our motives change, our objectives change, our dispositions change, and our eternal destiny changes.

No, it doesn't happen all at once. We will spend the rest of our lives learning what it means to follow Christ. But it begins now, as we open our hearts to Him. Is your life "being transformed . . . from glory to glory"?

HOPE FOR TODAY

In Christ, we don't have to be who we were yesterday. We don't have to cling to anger, bitterness, or regret. In Christ, we are not cleaned-up versions of our old selves; we are made brand-new.

MAKING GOOD DECISIONS

Then the king . . . rejected the advice of the elders.
2 CHRONICLES 10:13

Tragically, many people are the victims of their own bad decisions. Faced with choices every day, they turn their backs on what is right or what is best and decide instead on what is wrong or what will bring them harm. Only afterward do they realize that bad decisions always result in bad consequences.

King Rehoboam stubbornly rejected the wise advice of his nation's elders and instead followed those who told him only what he wanted to hear. As a result, conflict broke out and the nation divided. The Bible warns, "Whatever a man sows, that he will also reap" (Galatians 6:7).

Life is filled with decisions—some minor, but some life changing. How will you make them? The most important thing I can tell you is this: Seek God's will in every decision. Pray. Turn to the Scriptures. Seek the advice of godly friends. Ask the Holy Spirit to guide you. God loves you, and His way is always best.

HOPE FOR TODAY

No decision is too big or too small to turn over to God. He will guide your every step (Proverbs 16:9) if you let Him. Study His Word and pray so that you're not led astray.

WHAT GOD CALLS WISDOM

He Himself is our peace, who . . . has broken down the middle wall of separation.

EPHESIANS 2:14

Some time ago a university professor was quoted as saying, "There are two things that will never be solved—the problems of race and war." Perhaps he was right; only time will tell.

Admittedly, however, the Bible gives us little reason for optimism about any lasting solution to these problems. The reason? Both racism and war have their origin in the pride and covetousness of the human heart. Until our hearts are changed, we will fall back into the same destructive sins.

That doesn't mean we throw up our hands in despair and refuse to do anything about war or racism—not at all. The Bible calls Christ the "Prince of Peace" (Isaiah 9:6). He shattered the prejudices of His day by reaching out to those of another race, and He expects no less of us.

The object of the Cross is not only pardon for our sins, it is also a changed life. Ask God to help you be an instrument of His love to those around you.

HOPE FOR TODAY

As long as there is sin, there will be strife and contention. Even so, peace is still a goal for believers. The psalmist said that we are to "seek peace and pursue it" (Psalm 34:14). With whom do you need to seek peace today?

TRUST AND OBEY

Blessed is the man
who makes the LORD his trust.
PSALM 40:4 NIV

Some years ago someone gave my little boy a dollar. He brought it to me and said, "Daddy, keep this for me." But in a few minutes he came back and said, "Daddy, I'd better keep my own dollar." He tucked it in his pocket and went out to play. In a few minutes he came back with tears in his eyes, saying, "Daddy, I lost my dollar. Help me find it."

How often we commit our burdens to the Lord and then fail to trust Him by taking matters into our own hands. Then, when we have messed things up, we pray, "Oh, Lord, help me, I'm in trouble."

The choice is yours. Do you want to trust your life in God's "pocket" or keep it in your own? The Bible's promise is true: "Blessed is the man who makes the LORD his trust."

HOPE FOR TODAY

We can trust our heavenly Father with every aspect of our lives. He is able to bear every burden and protect what is precious. We will never regret entrusting our lives to His care.

THE TRANSFER IS COMPLETE

He made Him . . . to be sin for us, that we might
become the righteousness of God in Him.

2 CORINTHIANS 5:21

When we come to Christ, the Bible says He imparts His righteousness to us. Once we were sinners in God's eyes; now He sees us as righteous because of Christ.

How could this happen? In ourselves we aren't righteous. As the Bible says, "There is none righteous, no, not one" (Romans 3:10). But when we accept Christ, the filthy rags of our sin are replaced by the glorious robe of Christ's righteousness. Our sins were transferred to Him—and His righteousness was transferred to us.

Did we deserve it? No. Did we earn it? No. It is all because of grace—all because of God's undeserved favor toward us in Christ. We can never win God's favor by our deeds, no matter how good we are. Only Christ can save us. Thank God that you now stand before Him, clothed in the perfect righteousness of Christ!

HOPE FOR TODAY

How is it that we can boldly approach the throne of grace when we have all fallen short (Romans 3:23)? We can do so because when God looks upon a believer, He sees us through the righteousness of His Son.

PEACE, PERFECT PEACE

"Peace I leave with you, My peace I give to you."
JOHN 14:27

Worry," said Vance Havner, "is like sitting in a rocking chair. It will give you something to do, but it won't get you anywhere." Worry and anxiety have hounded the human race since the beginning of time, and modern man with all his innovations has not found the cure for the plague of worry.

What is the answer? Imagine in your mind a ferocious ocean storm beating against a rocky shore. The lightning flashes, the thunder roars, the waves lash the rocks. But then imagine that you see a crevice in the rocky cliff—and inside is a little bird, its head serenely tucked under its wing, fast asleep. It knows the rock will protect it, and thus it sleeps in peace.

God promised Moses, "I will put you in the cleft of the rock, and will cover you with My hand" (Exodus 33:22). That is God's promise to us. Christ is our Rock, and we are secure in His hands forever. The storm rages, but our hearts are at rest.

HOPE FOR TODAY

God tells His people not to worry. Worrying never worked anything out; nothing has ever come to be or not because a person worried. You can rest easy when you know that God is at work.

KEEP HEAVEN IN VIEW

We are afflicted in every way, but not crushed.

2 CORINTHIANS 4:8 NRSV

I have found in my travels that those who keep Heaven in view remain serene and cheerful in the darkest day. If the glories of Heaven were more real to us, if we lived less for material things and more for things eternal and spiritual, we would be less easily disturbed by this present life.

This is not escapism, as some would argue. If anything, a firm faith in the future should make us more responsible in the present. All around us are people who never give a moment's thought to Heaven or eternity. How will they learn of the future if we don't tell them in the present? The real escapism, I would contend, is refusing to face the future that God has prepared for us.

In these days of darkness and upheaval and uncertainty, the trusting and forward-looking Christian remains optimistic and joyful, knowing that Christ someday must rule, and that "if we endure, we shall also reign with Him" (2 Timothy 2: 12).

HOPE FOR TODAY

Whether today is filled with pleasure or pain, we must see it for what it is: temporary. Earthly happiness and heartache pale in comparison with the treasures that await us in glory.

JULY

"What man of you, having a hundred sheep, if he loses one of them, does not leave the ninety-nine in the wilderness, and go after the one which is lost until he finds it?"

LUKE 15:4

A CLEAN SLATE

Create in me a clean heart, O God,
And renew a steadfast spirit within me.
PSALM 51:10

Did you ever have the experience in school of erasing an entire whiteboard? When the slate has been wiped clean, it is as if nothing at all had ever been written on it.

This is what God does for us when we come to Him, confessing our sin and trusting Christ as our Savior and Lord. First John 1:9 says, "If we confess our sins, He is faithful and just to forgive us our sins, and to cleanse us from all unrighteousness." Note what He promises to do: forgive and cleanse. The slate is wiped clean! Only God can do that. We can't do it ourselves.

How many times in your life have you wished you could start all over again with a clean slate, with a new life? Resolve right now to allow God to wipe your slate clean by confessing your sins and letting Him give you a brand-new start.

HOPE FOR TODAY

It's popular to repurpose things. While you may give an old dresser new life as a desk, many will still see a dresser. When God forgives you, there is no trace of who you used to be; you're brand new!

THE CALL OF CHRIST

The wisdom of this world is foolishness with God.

1 CORINTHIANS 3:19

Some may contend that the way for the church to make the world a better place is to become like it. But whenever the church does this, it ends up compromising its spiritual authority and losing its influence. Instead of changing the world, the world changes it.

God doesn't want us to isolate ourselves. In praying for His disciples, Jesus said, "As You sent Me into the world, I also have sent them into the world" (John 17:18). If we isolate ourselves from others, we have no impact and demonstrate a lack of love.

But neither does God want us to become like the unbelieving world. We are to be separate, refusing to adopt its motives, attitudes, and patterns of behavior. The Bible warns, "All that is in the world—the lust of the flesh, the lust of the eyes, and the pride of life—is not of the Father but is of the world" (1 John 2:16). Let Christ fill your life, and there won't be room for the world.

HOPE FOR TODAY

Jesus never hid from the world. The unclean, diseased, and ostracized were never turned away from His presence. The key for believers today is simply to spend time in the Word *before* spending time in the world.

THE LIGHT OF SALVATION

Whoever confesses that Jesus is the Son of God, God abides in him.
1 JOHN 4:15

Only when we comprehend the great price God was willing to pay for our redemption do we begin to realize that something is horribly wrong with the human race. It must have a Savior, or it is doomed!

Sin cost God His very best. Is it any wonder the angels veiled their faces and were silent in their consternation as they witnessed the outworking of God's plan? How inconceivable it must have seemed to them, when they considered the fearful depravity of sin, that Jesus should shoulder it all.

But they were soon to unveil their faces and offer their praises again. A light was kindled that day at Calvary—"the light of the gospel of the glory of Christ, who is the image of God" (2 Corinthians 4:4). The Cross blazed with the glory of God as the most terrible darkness was shattered by the light of salvation. Satan's depraved legions were defeated; they could no longer keep humanity in darkness and defeat.

Has the light of the gospel shone in your heart? And is it shining through you to others?

HOPE FOR TODAY

As believers, we sometimes grow casual toward the Cross. We forget that it should have been us bearing the shame and facing God's wrath. Ask God to rekindle a fire within you for sharing the gospel.

A STATUE OF LIBERTY

"If the Son makes you free, you shall be free indeed."
JOHN 8:36

During the national observance of the one hundredth anniversary of the Statue of Liberty in New York Harbor, I was struck by the great emphasis on the number of immigrants who had often left everything behind. Coming to America with nothing but the clothes on their backs, they risked their lives for something they valued more highly than everything they had left behind: freedom. They did not take their adopted country's hard-won freedom for granted—and neither must we.

Their experience is a picture of what we must do when we come to Christ. We must forsake our allegiance to this world, leave behind all that it offers, and become citizens of a new kingdom—the kingdom of God. His statue of liberty is in the form of the Cross.

The statue in New York Harbor lifts her lamp "beside the golden door." The statue of liberty on that hill outside Jerusalem lights the way into eternal life.

HOPE FOR TODAY

No one braves the treacherous journey to America in order to live as they would in their homeland. Likewise, Christ did not leave glory and suffer an agonizing death so that you could live in anything less than absolute freedom.

THE KNOWLEDGE OF GOD

Oh, the depth of the riches both of the
wisdom and knowledge of God!
ROMANS 11:33

It was the mystery of lightning (so the story goes) that prompted Benjamin Franklin to attach a key to the tail of a kite during a thunderstorm, to prove the relationship between lightning and electricity. We have always tried to understand the world around us; it is one of the things that sets us apart from the animals.

Some of the mysteries of the past have been figured out by science. Others still puzzle us. This fact remains: all of the garnered wisdom of the ages is only a scratch on the surface of humanity's search for the knowledge of the universe.

This inability to comprehend fully the mysteries of God's creation does not in any way cast doubt on the Christian faith. On the contrary, it enhances our belief. We do not understand the intricate patterns of the stars in their courses, but we know that He who created them does, and that just as surely as He guides them, He is charting a safe course for us.

The next time you look into the heavens at night, remember the words of the psalmist: "The heavens declare the glory of God" (Psalm 19:1).

HOPE FOR TODAY

There comes a point in the journey of faith when you become okay not knowing what you're not meant to know. We continually seek to know God more, knowing that He can't be fully known this side of Heaven.

A GLORIOUS GRANDSTAND

Since we are surrounded by so great a cloud of
witnesses, let us lay aside every weight.

HEBREWS 12:1

I f the angels rejoice over one sinner who repents (Luke 15:10), then the angelic hosts are numbered among the spectators in the heavenly grandstands. They are included among those who are referred to as "so great a cloud of witnesses" (Hebrews 12:1); and they never miss any of the details of our earthly pilgrimages.

Nor does our God—Father, Son, and Holy Spirit—overlook what goes on here. As the Bible says, "All things are . . . open to the eyes of Him to whom we must give account" (Hebrews 4:13).

In his book *Though I Walk Through the Valley*, Dr. Vance Havner told of an old preacher who worked into the night on a sermon for his small congregation. His wife inquired why he spent so much time on a message he would give to so few. To this the minister replied, "You forget, my dear, how large my audience will be!" Dr. Havner added, "Nothing is trivial here if heaven looks on. We shall play a better game if, 'seeing we are encompassed,' we remember who is in the grandstand!"

HOPE FOR TODAY

Nothing about our lives is trivial when God Himself looks on. No activity is too mundane for the heavenly host to observe. How would you go about your daily tasks if you believed this to be true?

THE DAY IS AT HAND

Put on the armor of light.

ROMANS 13:12 NASB

I once read about a sundial on which was inscribed the cryptic message, "It is later than you think." Travelers would often pause to meditate on the meaning of that phrase. Its author undoubtedly wanted to remind others of the shortness and uncertainty of life.

We Christians have a sundial—the Word of God. From Genesis to Revelation it bears its warning: "It is later than you think." Writing to the Christians of his day, Paul said, "It is already the hour for you to awaken from sleep; for now salvation is nearer to us than when we believed. The night is almost gone, and the day is at hand. Let us therefore lay aside the deeds of darkness and put on the armor of light" (Romans 13:11–12 NASB).

Learn to live each day as if it were your last. Someday it will be.

HOPE FOR TODAY

Think about the last twenty-four hours. Did you love your neighbor well? Seek peace? Make disciples? Would you consider the hours well spent if they were your last before meeting Christ face to face?

GOD FEELS WHAT WE FEEL

Through the LORD's mercies we are not consumed,
Because His compassions fail not.

LAMENTATIONS 3:22

When I was a small boy, I thought of God as an old man with a long white beard. After all, hadn't Michelangelo and other artists painted Him that way? Perhaps in my childish mind, I thought He resembled an old man in other ways also—somewhat feeble and harmless, not quite in touch with me and my problems.

Later, as I read the Bible, I realized that God is a spirit. He does not have a body, nor is He confined to one place (as a physical being would be). At the same time, He has the attributes of a person: He thinks, He speaks, He communicates, He loves, He becomes angry, He grieves. Because God is a person, He feels what we feel.

No matter what we face, He understands what we are going through. He even understands our temptations, for Christ "has been tempted in every way, just as we are—yet . . . without sin" (Hebrews 4:15 NIV). And that is why you can bring anything—anything—to Him in prayer, confident that He will understand.

HOPE FOR TODAY

Do you feel like no one understands your pain, comprehends your loss, or knows the temptations you battle? God sent His Son to earth, wrapped in human flesh, to identify with the suffering of human nature. Trust Him to help you overcome the battles you encounter.

A THIRST FOR RIGHTEOUSNESS

"Blessed are those who hunger and thirst for righteousness."
MATTHEW 5:6

God is the only source of true happiness, because He offers those intangibles that we mistakenly believe can be found on earth: contentment, security, peace, and hope for the future. None of these can be found in a job, a human relationship, money, power, or position. They are God's alone to give.

How hard it is for us to believe this, however! This is understandable if we haven't given our lives to Christ; then, the Bible says, our spiritual eyes are blind, unable to see God's truth until the Holy Spirit opens them. But blindness can happen to believers also when we fall into the pattern of the world, vainly pursuing happiness in the same ways the world does.

That is why the Lord Jesus, in His Sermon on the Mount, told us where ultimate happiness lies: "Blessed are those who hunger and thirst for righteousness, for they shall be filled" (Matthew 5:6). This is God's promise—and it is true.

Riches . . . or righteousness? Which will be your goal?

HOPE FOR TODAY

It's a hard lesson to learn: the world always delivers less than it promises. God, on the other hand, has never failed to keep His Word. Seek righteousness and discover the blessed life.

PEACEMAKERS

"Blessed are the peacemakers,
For they shall be called sons of God."
MATTHEW 5:9

To have peace with God and to have the peace of God in our hearts is not enough. This vertical relationship must have a horizontal outworking, or our faith is in vain. Jesus said that we were to love the Lord with all our hearts and our neighbors as ourselves.

This dual love for God and others is like the positive and negative poles of a battery—unless both connections are made, we have no power. A personal faith is normally useless unless it has a social application. (A notable exception would seem to be the thief on the cross, who repented only moments before his death—and yet countless people have been touched over the centuries by his example of faith.)

If we have peace with God and the peace of God, we will become peacemakers. We will not only strive to be at peace with our neighbors, but we will be leading them to discover the source of true peace in Christ. Is the peace of Christ in your life overflowing to others?

HOPE FOR TODAY

What would it look like to have the peace of Christ in your life? Perhaps you would choose grace instead of the grudge you've been holding. Do an honest evaluation and seek peace in every area of your life.

I AM THE TRUTH

"You shall know the truth, and the truth shall make you free."
JOHN 8:32

Many today say there is no such thing as absolute truth. From philosophers to pop musicians, the word goes out that truth is only what you want it to be, and what is true for you isn't necessarily true for anyone else.

But Jesus Christ is absolute truth. Dozens of times He declares, "I tell you the truth." In one of His boldest and most uncompromising statements He affirmed, "I am the way, the truth, and the life" (John 14:6). The apostle John stated, "Grace and truth came through Jesus Christ" (John 1:17). James said that God "chose to give us birth through the word of truth" (James 1:18 NIV).

Do not be misled by the moral and spiritual relativity of our age. God has revealed His truth to us—in His written Word, the Bible, and in the living Word, Jesus Christ. And because Jesus is absolute truth, you can depend on Him absolutely!

HOPE FOR TODAY

There have been those who have attempted to rewrite history books. Scientific theories have been proven false. Scripture has stood the test of time; there is comfort in knowing that generations have turned to the same truths found within its pages.

CRUCIFIED WITH CHRIST

Be imitators of God as dear children.

EPHESIANS 5:1

The story is told of a man who glanced at the obituary column in his local newspaper. To his surprise he saw his own name, indicating that he had just died. At first he laughed about it. But soon the telephone began to ring. Stunned friends and acquaintances called to inquire and to offer their sympathy.

Finally, in irritation, he called the newspaper editor and angrily reported that even though he had been reported dead in the obituary column, he was very much alive. The editor was apologetic and embarrassed. Then in a flash of inspiration, he said, "Don't worry, sir! I'll make it right tomorrow—I'll put your name in the births column."

This may sound like merely a humorous incident, but it is also a spiritual parable. Not until we have allowed our old selves to be nailed to the Cross and to die can our new selves be born again and emerge to grow up into the likeness of Christ. The Bible is marvelously true: "And you He made alive, who were dead in trespasses and sins. . . . Therefore be imitators of God as dear children" (Ephesians 2:1; 5:1).

HOPE FOR TODAY

As children of God, we can both obey His commands and copy His behavior, knowing we have been raised to imitate our heavenly Father.

GOD PROMISES PROTECTION

"I will never leave you nor forsake you."
HEBREWS 13:5

Never doubt that you are in the midst of a battle—a spiritual battle with Satan, who will do everything he can to discourage and defeat you. Never underestimate his determination or misunderstand his intentions.

God wants to teach us how to defend ourselves against sin and Satan. Satan, the ultimate bully, attacks us at our weakest points and wants to defeat us so that we will not be effective for God.

God offers spiritual training to build us up inside in much the same way that physical exercise can build us up on the outside. He has also provided all the resources we need to defend ourselves and keep Satan at bay. These include the Bible, prayer, faith, righteous living, and the Holy Spirit within us.

But, like physical training, we must be diligent in their application. God has not promised to shield us from trouble, but He has promised to protect us in the midst of trouble. Most of all, never forget that because of Christ's death and resurrection, Satan is already a defeated foe—and someday the war will be over.

HOPE FOR TODAY

Satan loves to be underestimated. He would love for believers to view him as a harmless cartoon character. Scripture paints a very different picture. We must be on guard for the enemy who seeks to devour.

BEYOND THE STARRY SKY

We are looking for the city that is to come.

HEBREWS 13:14 NRSV

Paul looked forward to death with great anticipation. He said, "For to me, to live is Christ, and to die is gain" (Philippians 1:21). Death for him was not an enemy to be feared, but a reality to be welcomed, in God's time. For Paul death was the joyous gateway to new life—the life of Heaven.

Without the resurrection of Christ, we could have no hope for the future. The Bible promises that someday we are going to stand face-to-face with the resurrected Christ. All our questions will be answered, and all our sorrows and fears will vanish. An old gospel hymn puts it well:

> *Face to face with Christ my Savior,*
> *Face to face, what will it be?*
> *When with rapture I behold Him,*
> *Jesus Christ who died for me?*
> *Face to face I shall behold Him,*
> *Far beyond the starry sky;*
> *Face to face in all His glory*
> *I shall see Him by and by.*
> —CARRIE E. BRECK

HOPE FOR TODAY

Death, for a Christian, is not an end. It's a celebration, a chance to see loved ones, heroes of the faith, and Jesus. To die truly is gain.

THE BLESSING OF BURDENS

The LORD has comforted His people,
and will have compassion on His suffering ones.
ISAIAH 49:13 NRSV

C omfort and prosperity have never enriched the world as much as adversity. Out of pain and problems have come the sweetest songs, the most poignant poems, the most gripping stories, and the most inspiring lives.

Yet it is hard to think about this when troubles overwhelm us or uncertainty and fear grip our hearts. Our problems are real, and it is difficult in the heat of the moment to think of anything else.

In my travels over the years, I have often visited Switzerland and gone soaring above the countryside on chair lifts high in the Alps. Looking down we can see almost a carpet of wild flowers, some of the most beautiful in the world. Only a few months before, those plants were buried under heavy snow. Yet that snow prepared the way for their growth—providing them with water, and even insulating them from the winter winds. Our burdens can be like that snow, preparing the way for something beautiful once the winter is past.

HOPE FOR TODAY

When have you felt closer to the Lord: times of prosperity or times of pain? Scripture says that God is close to the broken-hearted. Whatever your trial, ask God to make His presence known in the midst of it.

ONLY ONE WAY

Whoever desires, let him take the water of life freely.

REVELATION 22:17

A driver stopped to ask the way to a certain street. When told, he asked doubtfully, "Is that the best way?" The man replied, "That is the only way."

There is only one way of salvation—and that is Christ. Jesus said, "No one comes to the Father except through Me" (John 14:6). Peter declared, "There is no other name under heaven given among men by which we must be saved" (Acts 4:12).

Is this arrogance or intolerance? No—and Christians must never be guilty of those attitudes. We are saved solely by God's grace; we do not deserve it. But Christ was God's appointed means of salvation. Only Christ died for our sins; only Christ rose from the dead.

God's offer of forgiveness and new life still stands. If you have never done so, turn to Christ today. And if you do know Him, pray today for someone you know who does not yet believe, and ask God to help you tell that person of His salvation.

HOPE FOR TODAY

Jesus offering Himself as the only way to God is pure grace. We don't have to figure it out on our own; we don't have to attempt other ways and fail. Do you want God? Jesus says, "I'm the way."

COMMITTED LOVE

Perfect love casts out fear.

1 JOHN 4:18 NIV

When I understand something of Christ's love for me as a sinner, I respond with love for Christ—and that love includes feelings and emotions.

But emotions come and go, and we must not allow them to mislead us. God loves me, whether I "feel" it or not. Christians who gauge their relationship with Christ only by their feelings seldom have a stable spiritual life.

What makes the difference? It can be summarized in one word: commitment. Feelings come and go, but commitment stays. (The same should be true in a marriage.) We who have committed our lives to Christ may feel joy, gratitude, love, and so on. But even when we don't have those feelings, our commitment keeps us true to Christ.

This commitment not only keeps us faithful to Christ when we don't feel like it; it also keeps away negative emotions such as doubt and fear. John Witherspoon, the only cleric to sign the Declaration of Independence, once said, "It is only the fear of God that can deliver us from the fear of man."

HOPE FOR TODAY

When Christ chose the Cross, He was forever committing Himself to us. Let's choose, on the front end, to be equally committed to Him no matter what trials or tragedies may come.

A Higher Destiny

The way of the LORD is strength for the upright.

Because God is the giver and source of life, He has a legitimate claim upon our lives. He is our heavenly Father, and He has the right to expect us to be His loyal and loving children. Because I am His child, He also longs to have fellowship with me.

The story of the prodigal son (which you can read in Luke 15:11–32) is a revelation of God's desire for human fellowship. He yearns over His children who have wandered far from Him and longs for them to come home and be near to Him.

All through the Bible we see God's patience and perseverance as He pursues misguided and obstinate men and women—men and women who were born to a high destiny as His sons and daughters, but who strayed from His side. From Genesis to Revelation, God is constantly saying, "Return to Me, and I will return to you."

No matter how far you have strayed, God still loves you, and He wants to welcome you home—forever.

Hope for Today

During times of tragedy, many cry out for Jesus to return. But, for those with loved ones who don't know Him, each day that Jesus tarries is an act of grace. Pray for the prodigals in your life today.

THE BIBLE IS TRUE

Forever, O LORD,
Your word is settled in heaven.
PSALM 119:89

As we survey the world scene with Bible in hand, we know we do not worship an absentee God. He is standing in the shadows of history, still working to bring His plans to completion.

Therefore we are not disturbed by the pictures of chaos, violence, bloodshed, and war that fill our television screens and flood our newspapers. We know these are the consequences of humanity's evil and sin, caused by our rebellion against God. Every headline, every news report confirms what the prophet Jeremiah said centuries ago: "The heart is deceitful above all things, and desperately wicked; who can know it?" (Jeremiah 17:9).

But never forget: God will speak history's final word. Every day the world moves closer to the time when Christ will return, Satan will be defeated, and God's perfect plan will be fulfilled.

No matter how foreboding the future, the Christian knows the end of the story—and it is glorious! Don't lose heart. The best is yet to be!

HOPE FOR TODAY
Multiple news outlets and social media cause us to be inundated with all the evils of the world. Satan would like us to feel as if the world is out of control, but that isn't true. God has not relinquished control of His creation.

VALUABLE TO GOD

He who trusts in his riches will fall,
But the righteous will flourish like foliage.

PROVERBS 11:28

A certain rich man died and the question was asked at his funeral, "How much did he leave?"

"He left it all," came the reply.

Often, I hear someone introduced this way: "This is Bob, and he works for . . . ," as if where a person works or what a person does determines his or her value. (I have noticed it is usually only the well-to-do or those who are thought of as "successful" who are introduced this way.)

Yet God does not judge us by our success. He loves each person the same. Your value and mine do not come from what we do, the clothes we wear, the house we live in, or the type of car we drive. Our value comes from the fact that God made us and loves us, and Christ died for us. Our value comes from the fact that He adopted us into His family, and we are now His children forever.

Don't depend on possessions or position for your identity. Get your identity from Christ, for you are of infinite worth to Him!

HOPE FOR TODAY

How do you identify yourself? Is it based on something that can change in a moment: marital status, job, or material possessions? Seek your identity in the unchanging love of God.

Victory in Jesus

Thanks be to God, who gives us the victory through our Lord Jesus Christ.
1 Corinthians 15:57 NRSV

Haydn, the great musician, was once asked why his church music was so cheerful. He replied, "When I think upon God, my heart is so full of joy that the notes dance and leap, as it were, from my pen, and since God has given me a cheerful heart, it will be pardoned me that I serve Him with a cheerful spirit."

Haydn had discovered the secret to lasting joy: "I think on God." Looking at our circumstances won't bring us lasting joy. It may even make us depressed or angry. But when we "think on God"—when we turn our minds and hearts to His power and His love for us—we can't help but be joyful. Paul said, "Set your mind on things above, not on things on the earth" (Colossians 3:2). Discouragement flees in the face of joy.

Every day brings battles and temptations. But the strength we need for conquering them comes from Christ. We can do like the little girl who said that when the devil came knocking with a temptation, she just sent Jesus to the door!

Hope for Today

Jesus promises fullness of joy to those in His presence. When fear, discouragement, or loneliness begin to creep in, there is one logical place to run. Draw near to Jesus, and allow His joy to overflow within you.

LOOK TO GOD

"Lift up your heads, because your redemption draws near."
LUKE 21:28

If you've ever flown in an airplane, you know that your perspective of the earth is far different from what it was when you were on the ground. Pictures of the earth that have been taken from the moon and from space show an earth that looks much different from what we see down here.

This is the kind of perspective God wants to give us concerning our lives. As we look to God, instead of to ourselves and our circumstances, our perspectives change.

Don't get bogged down in the circumstances of life. At the moment we see only our immediate problems and burdens, but God sees the whole. He sees not only the present but the future as well. He wants to lift us above ourselves. He wants us to see everything in light of His plans. The psalmist said, "The LORD will perfect that which concerns me" (Psalm 138:8).

Don't get bogged down. Keep your eyes on God, for He sees the whole picture, and He knows what is best for you. You can trust Him, because He loves you.

HOPE FOR TODAY

It's easy to become preoccupied with trying to understand why certain situations happen or how they can be used for something good. Choose, instead, to focus on Who is working behind the scenes; it is the only detail that matters.

A Solid Foundation

The Lord is my rock and my fortress and my deliverer.
2 Samuel 22:2

My children used to sing a song in Sunday school classes: "The wise man built his house upon the rock." A wise man does build his house upon the Rock—the Lord Jesus Christ and His Word—for nothing built of or on any other substance will stand the test of time.

In big cities I often see wrecking balls destroying old structures to make way for new ones. Some of these "old structures" in America are less than a hundred years old. In Europe, buildings several centuries old are common. But even these buildings will eventually be destroyed, by a natural disaster if not by man.

Only what is built on the solid foundation of Christ will last. Jesus said, "Everyone who hears these words of mine and puts them into practice is like a wise man who built his house on the rock" (Matthew 7:24 NIV). Are you listening to God's Word and putting it into practice every day?

Hope for Today

Have you ever lost something valuable to theft or natural disaster? It's sometimes hard to come back from that kind of loss. But a life built on Christ can never be shaken; joy, peace, and salvation are eternally secure.

A GENTLE KINDNESS

The Lord's servant must not be quarrelsome but kindly to every one.

2 TIMOTHY 2:24 NRSV

Jesus was a gentle and compassionate person. When He came into the world, there were few hospitals, few places of refuge for the poor, few homes for orphans. There were no hospitals to treat the mentally ill, no shelters for the homeless. In comparison to today, it was a cruel world.

Christ changed all that. He healed the sick, fed the hungry, and opened the eyes of the blind. He commanded His disciples, "Love your neighbor as yourself" (Matthew 19:19) and taught them to observe what we have come to call the Golden Rule: "In everything, do to others what you would have them do to you" (Matthew 7:12 NIV). Wherever true Christianity has gone, Jesus' followers have performed acts of kindness, love, and gentleness.

Do others see Christ's gentleness and compassion in you?

HOPE FOR TODAY

God's people are to be kind to everyone. That neighbor who doesn't keep his yard like you would prefer? That coworker who sees things a little differently? Who needs to see kindness in you today?

OVERCOMING TRIBULATION

"You will have tribulation; but be of good cheer, I have overcome the world."
JOHN 16:33

When trials come, we sometimes act as if God is on vacation. We question God: *Why is this happening to me? What did I do to deserve this? Why am I going through this difficult circumstance? What's wrong with You, God?!*

But such complaining is shortsighted and wrong. God is far higher than we are, so who are we to say He is wrong, or tell Him what He ought to be doing? As God reminded Job, "Where were you when I laid the foundations of the earth?" (Job 38:4). Such complaining also shows a lack of faith; we are doubting God's wisdom and His love for us.

Read the promises of Scripture for the answer. Jesus said, "In the world you will have tribulation." He didn't say that you could have tribulation or that if you aren't a good person, tribulation will come your way. Jesus flatly stated you will have tribulation. It is as certain as growing older.

But the wonderful promise of Christ is that while you will have trials and tribulations, "Be of good cheer, I have overcome the world."

HOPE FOR TODAY

God never attempts to trick us like a doctor who says, "This won't hurt a bit." Don't be surprised or anxious at troubles; God hasn't dropped the ball. Everything is going just as He said it would and will also end as victoriously as He said it would.

JOY ON THE JOURNEY

The joy of the LORD is your strength.

NEHEMIAH 8:10

Some people have a warped idea of living the Christian life. Seeing talented, successful Christians, they attempt to imitate them. For them, the grass on the other side of the fence is always greener. But when they discover that their own gifts are different or their contributions are more modest (or even invisible), they collapse in discouragement and overlook genuine opportunities that are open to them. They have forgotten that they are here to serve Christ, not themselves.

Be like the apostle Paul and say, "None of these things move me" (Acts 20:24). Few men suffered as Paul did, yet he learned how to live above his circumstances—even in a prison cell. You can do the same. The key is to realize you are here to serve Christ, not yourself.

God does not promise us an easy life, free of troubles, trials, difficulties, and temptations. He never promises that life will be perfect. He does not call His children to a playground, but to a battleground. In the midst of it all, when we serve Christ, we truly discover that "the joy of the LORD is [our] strength."

HOPE FOR TODAY

Everyone has a cross to bear, and they're all different. Someone else's cross may only seem lighter because someone else is carrying it! Whatever you're facing, the joy of the Lord is all the strength you need.

A VICTORIOUS CHRISTIAN

The Spirit also helps in our weaknesses.

ROMANS 8:26

We need to rely constantly on the Holy Spirit. We need to remember that Christ dwells in us through the Holy Spirit. Our bodies are the dwelling place of the Third Person of the Trinity.

Why don't we rely on Him as we should? We don't realize how weak we are. We don't realize how strong our enemy is. We may even doubt if God is really going to help us. Or we think we can do it all ourselves—or that we must.

But we should ask Him to do it all and to take over in our lives. We should tell Him how weak, helpless, unstable, and unreliable we are. It is important that we stand aside and let Him take over in all our choices and decisions. We know that the Holy Spirit prays for us (Romans 8:26), and what a comfort that should be to the weakest of us.

A victorious Christian is one who, in spite of worries, inner conflicts, and tensions, is confident that God is in control and will be victorious in the end. Whatever our difficulties, whatever our circumstances, we must remember, as Corrie ten Boom used to say, "Jesus is victor!"

HOPE FOR TODAY

There will not be much victory for one who lives by "if it's gonna be, it's up to me." By ourselves, we are no match for Satan and his minions. With Christ, however, the victory is guaranteed.

FREE TO CHOOSE

Choose this day whom you will serve.

JOSHUA 24:15 NRSV

Repeatedly in the Bible, both nations and individuals had to make decisions affecting their futures—and so do we. Sometimes they made wrong choices and suffered the consequences as a result.

When we face decisions, we need to remember that God hasn't left us in the dark, nor is He uninterested. God loves us, and He wants what is best for us. He has a perfect path in life for us, and He wants us to choose it instead of the wrong paths Satan would tempt us to follow.

Even when our way seems unclear, God gives us light. He gives us His Word, the Bible—and many of our decisions would be much easier if we only knew its moral and spiritual principles. He also gives us wisdom (sometimes through other people) to understand our situation, and He gives us the Holy Spirit to guide us.

Never make a decision without committing it to God and seeking His will. He promises to guide you—and He will.

HOPE FOR TODAY

Are you facing a decision or situation where you just don't know what to do? Don't panic; spend some time in prayer, reading God's Word and being still. God knows exactly what to do, and He will show you.

SIMPLE TRUST

Trust in the LORD with all your heart,
And lean not on your own understanding.

PROVERBS 3:5

There will always be secrets and motives of God that lie beyond our grasp. God knows everything; we do not. Only in Heaven will we understand God's ways more fully. As Paul said, "Now I know in part, but then I shall know just as I also am known" (1 Corinthians 13:12).

But based upon what we do know about God's character, demonstrated supremely in the Cross, we can trust that God is doing what is best for us. God says in His Word, "I know the plans I have for you . . . plans to prosper you and not to harm you, plans to give you hope and a future" (Jeremiah 29:11 NIV).

As Corrie ten Boom once explained, "Picture a piece of embroidery placed between you and God, with the right side up toward God. Man sees the loose, frayed ends; but God sees the pattern."

God is in control. Whatever comes into our lives, we can confidently say, "We know that all things work together for good to those who love God, to those who are the called according to His purpose" (Romans 8:28).

HOPE FOR TODAY

Lord, I confess that there is much I don't understand, but I know that You love me. Because of that love, I can trust You in every trial and will follow wherever You lead me.

THE LIGHT OF LIFE

Your faith and hope are in God.
1 PETER 1:21 NIV

We get so used to this world that we lose sight of the next. We get so used to the darkness and chaos of this world's suffering and violence that we lose sight of the brightness of Him who alone could say, "I am the light of the world. He who follows Me shall not walk in darkness, but have the light of life" (John 8:12).

He alone is "the Lamb of God, who takes away the sin of the world!" (John 1:29). He alone is the Hope of the hopeless, the Savior of the lost, the Guide of the wandering. He alone is "the radiance of God's glory and the exact representation of his being, sustaining all things by his powerful word" (Hebrews 1:3 NIV).

Today world leaders struggle with almost insurmountable problems—and they always will. But in the midst of this world's persistent darkness, never lose sight of Jesus. He alone is the hope of the world—and He is your hope as well.

HOPE FOR TODAY

Jesus has always brought light to places of darkness. Fear, guilt, and shame flourish in the dark; the dark is no place for God's people. Ask Jesus to shine His light into every area of your life.

EFFECTIVE PRAYER

"Before they call, I will answer;
And while they are still speaking, I will hear."
ISAIAH 65:24

John Knox spent much time in prayer, and the church in Scotland burst into new life. John Wesley prayed long and often, and the Methodist movement was born. Martin Luther prayed earnestly, and the Reformation exploded across Europe.

Why was prayer so important to these spiritual giants of the past? Because they knew they were up against almost overwhelming forces of spiritual opposition. They also knew the urgency of the gospel message, and they understood that prayer is an essential weapon in advancing the gospel to the ends of the earth. Like Paul, they knew that "the weapons of our warfare are not carnal but mighty in God for pulling down strongholds" (2 Corinthians 10:4). Is our situation any different today?

God desires that we Christians be concerned and burdened for a lost world. If we pray this kind of prayer, an era of peace may come to the world and wickedness may be turned back. "The effective, fervent prayer of a righteous man avails much" (James 5:16).

HOPE FOR TODAY

How much time do you spend in prayer? Is it your first line of defense or a last resort? We would see mighty works of God in our families, churches, and communities if we took God at His Word and took prayer seriously.

August

But one and the same Spirit works all these things,
distributing to each one individually as He wills.

1 Corinthians 12:11

PRAYER RELEASES GOD'S POWER

Pray without ceasing.

1 THESSALONIANS 5:17

How many times have you heard someone say, "All I can do is pray"?

All I can do is pray?! You might as well say to a starving man, "All I can do is offer you food," or to a sick person, "All I can do is give you medicine that will make you well," or to a poor child, "All I can do is buy the toy you most want for your birthday."

Praying unlocks the doors of Heaven and releases the power of God. James 4:2 says, "You do not have because you do not ask." The Bible says, "Be anxious for -nothing, but in everything by prayer and supplication, with thanksgiving, let your requests be made known to God" (Philippians 4:6).

And we are to let God know not only our needs but also the needs of others. So often our prayers focus only on ourselves. But God wants to use us, through our prayers, to touch the lives of other people as well. For whom should you be praying this day?

HOPE FOR TODAY

It's an automatic response when we hear of someone's trial: "I'll be praying for you." How often do we walk away and never think of it again? How fervently would we pray if we truly believed it unleashed the power of God?

CHOOSE LIFE

I have set before you life and death, . . . therefore choose life.
DEUTERONOMY 30:19

Before the space shuttle program, American ships and helicopters would recover astronauts whose tiny space capsules had parachuted into the enormous sea. The astronauts would be lifted out of their capsule into a helicopter, which would then fly them to the safety of the ship.

I often thought, as I watched these scenes on television, how like God this operation was. God hovers over the entire world, seeking to pluck from sin immortal souls in danger of "drowning" in Hell. He tosses out a line to all those who are in trouble. Some grab on to God's line and freely receive the gift of His Son, Jesus Christ. They are pulled to safety and, eventually, taken to Heaven.

But others ignore the line, or even knock it away, believing they are not really in peril, or that they can make it to safety on their own. Tragically, they are lost not because God has rejected them, but because they have rejected God.

Don't make the wrong choice!

HOPE FOR TODAY
It is God's desire that none should perish (2 Peter 3:9). Who do you know adrift in a sea of sin? Share the lifeline of the gospel with them today.

CHRIST—OUR EXAMPLE

He learned obedience by the things which He suffered.
HEBREWS 5:8

The main reason Jesus died on the Cross was to save us from our sins. But the New Testament also stresses the importance of His suffering as an example for us.

The Greek word for example comes from ancient school life, and refers to something written down by the teacher so it could be followed and copied exactly by a child learning to write. Christ is our copybook. We look to Him as our teacher, and by His suffering He gave us an example to follow so we can learn how suffering is to be borne.

How did Jesus bear it? By not giving in to despair or doubt. By looking beyond His suffering and seeing the glory that was to come. By remembering that the Father was with Him and would use His suffering for good. We can do the same.

The author of Hebrews wrote, "Consider him who endured such opposition from sinful men, so that you will not grow weary and lose heart" (Hebrews 12:3 NIV). Yes, *consider* Him.

HOPE FOR TODAY

A woman once said, "I pray I remain faithful when it's my turn to suffer for Christ." We'll all have "our turn" at suffering; Paul said it has been granted to us not only to believe but to suffer for Him (Philippians 1:29). It's all grace.

PATIENCE AND PERFECTION

The testing of your faith produces patience.

JAMES 1:3

Patience isn't easy for most of us. If a plane is delayed a few minutes or something doesn't happen exactly when or how we expected it to, we get impatient and frustrated. I have heard of people who quit going to a particular church because the preacher didn't stop exactly on time! James said, "Be patient, then, brothers, until the Lord's coming. See how the farmer waits for the land to yield its valuable crop and how patient he is for the autumn and spring rains. You, too, be patient and stand firm, because the Lord's coming is near" (James 5:7–8 NIV).

Patience is not simply teeth-clenched endurance. It is an attitude of expectation. The farmer patiently watches his barren ground because he knows there will be results. He has patience in his labors because there will be products of his labor.

So it is in the spiritual realm. God knows the final product of what is happening to us, and He would have us link patience to our faith. Ask God for the gift of patience—and then use it.

HOPE FOR TODAY

Lord, I will wait with expectation—eager to see what You will do in my situation. I will not sulk or sit idly by. While You work behind the scenes, I will be at work in prayer.

PEACE ON EARTH?

He Himself is our peace.

EPHESIANS 2:14

For as long as I can remember, there have been innovative ideas for bringing peace to this earth. Organizations have been created, much money and time have been spent, treaties have been signed, books have been written—all in an effort to find a formula that would bring peace on earth and good will to men.

World War I was called "the war to end all wars," but it wasn't. Whether nations fight one another or not, there is "warfare" in the home: warfare between husband and wife, between parents and children, between brothers and sisters, between neighbors, between boss and employee.

What can be done? It sounds almost simplistic to say we need to turn to God—but that is the only lasting solution. Only God can remove the poisons of greed and hatred and jealousy in our hearts, and replace them with contentment and compassion and forgiveness. Only He can subdue the violence and anger that rage within us, and replace them with His peace and love.

Whatever wars rage in your life, lay them at the foot of the Cross and ask Jesus to give you His peace.

HOPE FOR TODAY

No matter how hard we seek peace in our homes, communities, and in our world, lasting peace only comes through Christ.

A HAPPY HOME

Children are a gift from the Lord;
they are a reward from him.
PSALM 127:3 TLB

Today there are more pressures on the home than perhaps at any other time in the history of the human race.

By necessity or by desire, more parents are working today than ever before. Many feel guilty about leaving their children in the care of others or having them return to an empty home while they are at work. But many women and men still devote more attention to their working life than they do to their family life. Is it any wonder, then, that so many homes are in trouble?

What achievement in life is equal to a happy home and rearing successful children who grow up to praise their parents? Every material goal, even if it is met, will pass away. But the heritage of children is timeless.

Our primary responsibility is to be sure our children grow up in homes where God is honored and the love of Christ reigns. Do your children sense that Christ is at the center of your home?

HOPE FOR TODAY

Parents often have earthly goals for children: good jobs, education, marriage, and so on. As parents, our main desire should be that they seek God and obey His will for their lives. That is the best lesson they can learn in our homes.

PRAY ABOUT YOUR PROBLEMS

Don't worry about anything; instead, pray about everything.
PHILIPPIANS 4:6 TLB

What do you do when you have a problem? Do you worry? Most of us do. But does worrying solve the problem? No, it does not. So if worry doesn't solve the problem, why worry?

The Bible's account about Hezekiah gives us an idea for problem solving: "Hezekiah received the letter from the hand of the messengers, and read it; and Hezekiah went up to the house of the LORD, and spread it before the LORD. Then Hezekiah prayed before the LORD" (2 Kings 19:14–15).

Instead of turning to God as a first resource, we so often turn to Him as a last resort. Follow Hezekiah's formula. Turn to God first with your problems, for only He is capable of handling them in a way that will be in your best interest—and according to His perfect will.

HOPE FOR TODAY

Pray before you panic. Did you receive bad news? Pray. Have a big decision to make? Pray. Is a loved one far from the Lord? Pray. Prayer is the greatest tool of the believer.

THE PROBLEM OF SUFFERING

I have kept His way and not turned aside.

JOB 23:11

Some scholars think Job may be the oldest book in the Bible. Whether that is true or not, it certainly deals with one of humanity's oldest questions: why does God allow suffering?

It isn't an easy issue, because it goes to the heart of our deepest questions about God. After all (the argument runs), how could a loving and gracious God allow suffering? To put it another way, if God lets us suffer, He must not love us. But that conclusion is false. God does love us—and the proof is the suffering He allowed His Son to endure on the Cross.

What, then, is the answer to this age-old question? The key is to understand the character of God. That is what Job discovered. No, God never gave him a logical, complete answer for his suffering. But through his experience Job came to realize that God could be trusted, because He is merciful and loving. And you can trust God too—not because He always gives us all the answers, but simply because He is God.

HOPE FOR TODAY

During a trial, it is tempting to ask why we are suffering. The answer doesn't lie in the *why* of our suffering. The answer lies in the *who* is with us in the midst of our pain.

JESUS' PRAYER PROGRAM

"Whatever you ask the Father in My name He will give you."
JOHN 16:23

One of the most amazing things in all the Scriptures is how much time Jesus spent in prayer. He had only three years of public ministry, yet He was never too hurried to spend hours in prayer. He prayed before every difficult task confronting Him. He prayed with regularity—not a day began or closed in which He did not unfold His soul before His Father.

How quickly and carelessly, by contrast, we pray. Snatches of memorized verses are hastily spoken in the morning; then we say good-bye to God for the rest of the day until we rush through a few closing petitions at night.

This is not the prayer program that Jesus outlined. Jesus pleaded long and repeatedly. It is recorded that He spent entire nights in fervent appeal. No one could have been busier—but He was never too busy for prayer.

What keeps you from making prayer a priority in your schedule?

HOPE FOR TODAY

Forgive me, Lord, for treating prayer like an option instead of a necessity. What could possibly be a better use of my time than intimate conversation with the God who created me? Speak, Lord. Your servant is listening.

TRUST AND TOIL

As the body without the spirit is dead, so faith without works is dead also.

JAMES 2:26

The Scriptures teach that a Christian is one who trusts Christ as Savior and obeys Him as Lord. That is the essence of Christian discipleship—believing and following.

The New Testament makes no separation between belief and obedience. They are linked together as one, because if you truly believe, you will truly follow. Trust makes us part of the kingdom, but our love for God and obedience to His will are the badges of our citizenship in that kingdom.

That is why the Christian life is a happy blend of trust and toil, resting and striving, receiving and doing. God does His part, and we must do ours. A farmer's crop is a gift from God—but it also requires hard work. God may give a person the gift of music—but it takes practice and discipline to make it come alive.

Is any area of your life "off-limits" to Christ? Believe—and obey.

HOPE FOR TODAY

"Trust and obey," the old hymn says, "for there's no other way to be happy in Jesus." Are you feeling unhappy or unfulfilled? Ask God to reveal any areas where you aren't fully trusting and obeying Him.

GOD, OUR FATHER

"I will be a Father to you,
And you shall be My sons and daughters."
2 CORINTHIANS 6:18

In the familiar story of the prodigal son, the young man was not satisfied to be in his father's house with all of his needs met. He wanted more. He believed the lie that something more exciting was in store for him away from his father.

Isn't this how we sometimes behave—even as Christians? We think that God is holding out on us, that there is something better than a close relationship with our heavenly Father, that the world offers us more excitement and fulfillment than God does.

But it isn't true. By thinking this way and then acting on it—whether or not we go as far away as the prodigal—we create our own desperate circumstances. Then we turn back to God, crying out for deliverance and forgiveness.

Fortunately, our heavenly Father always hears our cries. Full repentance is always answered by full forgiveness. But wouldn't it have been far better to have avoided the sin in the first place? Don't ever—*ever*—think that Satan's way is better than God's way. It *never* is.

HOPE FOR TODAY

Satan is always waiting for an opportune time to tempt us away from Jesus (see Luke 4:13). We must not neglect prayer, the study of God's Word, or fellowship with other believers, for these things will keep us near the cross.

THE HOPE OF HEAVEN

Precious in the sight of the LORD
Is the death of His saints.
PSALM 116:15

D eath is the one experience through which we all will pass. We may meet it with resignation, denial, or even without a moment's thought—but come it will.

But death for the believer is distinctly different from what it is for the unbeliever. For us, it isn't something to be feared or shunned, for we know death is but the shadowed threshold to the palace of God. No wonder Paul declared, "I desire to depart and be with Christ, which is better by far" (Philippians 1:23 NIV).

Sometimes God gives His departing saints glimpses of Heaven (partly, I believe, to encourage those of us who remain). Just before dying, my grandmother sat up in bed, smiled, and said, "I see Jesus, and He has His hand outstretched to me. And there is Ben, and he has both of his eyes and both of his legs." (Ben, my grandfather, had lost an eye and a leg at Gettysburg.)

Are you looking forward to that day when you will go to be with Christ, "which is better by far"?

HOPE FOR TODAY
Do you dread or fear death? God promises that the glories that await us far outshine anything we will be leaving behind.

235

EVERLASTING LOVE

"I have loved you with an everlasting love;
Therefore with lovingkindness I have drawn you."
JEREMIAH 31:3

Who can describe or measure the love of God? Our Bible is a revelation of the fact that God is love. When we preach His justice, it is justice tempered with love. When we preach His righteousness, it is righteousness founded on love. When we preach atonement for sin, it is atonement necessitated because of love, provided by love, finished by love.

When we preach the resurrection of Christ, we are preaching the miracle of love. When we preach the abiding presence of Christ, we are preaching the power of love. When we preach the return of Christ, we are preaching the fulfillment of love.

No matter what sin we have committed, no matter how black, dirty, shameful, or terrible it may be, God loves us. We may be at the very gate of Hell itself, but God loves us with an everlasting love. The proof? Jesus Christ, God's only Son, went to the Cross for us. "For God so loved the world that He gave His only begotten Son, that whoever believes in Him should not perish but have everlasting life" (John 3:16).

HOPE FOR TODAY

How many mistakes have you made and how many pits have you fallen into because you just wanted to be loved? The beautiful truth of the Cross is that you are loved more lavishly than you can even imagine.

THE WORK OF ANGELS

Bless the LORD, you His angels,
Who excel in strength, who do His word.
PSALM 103:20

It's natural to concentrate on what the angels do for us, these who are "sent to serve those who will inherit salvation" (Hebrews 1:14 NIV).

But the Bible indicates the angels do much more than that. Especially, we are told, the angels unite in constant praise to God, giving glory to His name and rejoicing in His holiness and perfection. "Bless the LORD, you His angels."

God gave Isaiah a vision of Heaven, where the angelic hosts proclaim, "Holy, holy, holy is the LORD of hosts; the whole earth is full of His glory!" (Isaiah 6:3). John saw "many angels around the throne . . . saying with a loud voice: 'Worthy is the Lamb who was slain'" (Revelation 5:11–12). Jesus said there is "rejoicing in the presence of the angels of God over one sinner who repents" (Luke 15:10 NIV).

Are these angels not examples to us? Shouldn't rejoicing and praise be hallmarks of our lives? Praise banishes darkness and brings us closer to God. Martin Luther once said, "Come, let us sing a psalm and drive away the devil!"

HOPE FOR TODAY

Would those around you describe you as a person of praise? How often are you found rejoicing? Let's take our lead from the angelic beings around the throne. Let joy and praise be evident in our lives.

FULL SURRENDER

"Whoever loses his life for My sake . . . will save it."
MARK 8:35

A police sergeant once asked me the secret of victorious Christian living. I told him there is no magic formula. But if any one word could describe it, it would be surrender.

You may ask, "How can I surrender my life?" It is surrendered in the same way that salvation comes to the sinner. There needs to be confession of sin and a complete yielding of every area of our lives, personalities, and wills to Jesus Christ—plus faith that Christ will accept that commitment.

It's not enough for us to be confirmed or to make a decision for Christ at an altar. We cannot walk successfully in the glow of that experience for the rest of our lives. Again and again we need to renew those vows and covenants with the Lord. We need to take inventory and have regular spiritual checkups.

Jesus said, "If anyone desires to come after Me, let him deny himself, and take up his cross daily, and follow Me" (Luke 9:23). Daily surrender—that's the key to daily victory.

HOPE FOR TODAY

God doesn't make it difficult to come to Him. Fighting takes far more energy than surrendering. How often do we experience pain and endure suffering because we have failed simply to surrender to the love of God?

FERVENT PRAYER

"If My people . . . will . . . pray and seek My face, . . . I will hear from heaven."

2 CHRONICLES 7:14

From one end of the Bible to the other, there is the record of those whose prayers were answered—men and women who turned the tide of history by prayer, who fervently prayed, and saw God answer.

Elijah prayed, and God sent fire from Heaven to consume the offering on the altar he had built in the presence of God's enemies. Elisha prayed, and the son of the Shunammite woman was raised from the dead. Hannah prayed, and God gave her a son, Samuel, who would bless God's people for decades.

Paul prayed, and dozens of churches were born in Asia Minor and Europe. Peter prayed, and Dorcas was raised to life, adding years of service for Jesus Christ.

These believers' prayers were the natural outflow of their deep inner faith. Their prayers were part of a greater whole: godly lives lived for God's glory. As the seventeenth-century theologian John Owen said, "He who prays as he ought, will endeavor to live as he prays."

HOPE FOR TODAY

Prayer journals are powerful tools. When you begin to see the fruit of your prayers, you will develop an insatiable desire to pray more. If you don't keep a journal, today is a great day to start.

TEACHER AND LORD

"You call me Teacher and Lord, and you say well, for so I am."
JOHN 13:13

I wonder if you've ever thought about the incredible number of messages that rain down on us every day: television ads, e-mails, phone calls, magazines, junk mail, videos, billboards, conversations. The list is almost endless.

How many of those shape our thinking? How many of them subtly convince us that the road to happiness is really paved with possessions, or beauty, or money, or fame, or any of a hundred other things? How many of them persuade us that the most important thing in life is financial success, or the esteem of others, or power, or sex? It's hard to resist the cumulative impact of so many messages.

But God says our thinking must be shaped by His truth. What this world calls valuable, God calls worthless. What this world scorns, God exalts. "My thoughts are not your thoughts, nor are your ways My ways" (Isaiah 55:8).

Jesus said, "You call Me Teacher and Lord, and you say well, for so I am." Is He your Teacher and Lord—or is the world?

HOPE FOR TODAY
The way to recognize a forgery is not to study the forgery but to be intimately acquainted with the truth. Satan will make subtle attempts to lead us astray with lying messages, but we will not be fooled if we are filled with God's truth.

HOPE FOR THE HEART

My heart is glad, and . . .
My flesh also will rest in hope.
PSALM 16:9

Perhaps the greatest psychological, spiritual, and medical need that all people have is the need for hope. Dr. McNair Wilson, a famous cardiologist, remarked in his autobiography, *Doctor's Progress*, "Hope is the medicine I use more than any other—hope can cure nearly anything."

Years ago Dr. Harold Wolff, who was professor of medicine at Cornell University Medical College and associate professor of psychiatry, said, "Hope, like faith and a purpose in life, is medicinal. This is not a statement of belief, but a conclusion proved by meticulously controlled scientific experiment."

When hope dies, despair will overwhelm us. Hope is both biologically and psychologically vital to us. Men and women must have hope—and true hope comes only from Christ. He gives us hope for the future as we turn in faith to Him—hope for eternity, and hope for right now.

HOPE FOR TODAY

Hoping in earthly things often leads to despair. Accomplishments don't bring the peace we had hoped. Relationships don't fulfill us the way we hoped. But, when we place our hope in Christ and the salvation He offers, that hope never disappoints (Romans 5:5).

LOVING COMPASSION

In this is love, not that we loved God, but that He loved us.
1 JOHN 4:10

The supreme happiness of life," Victor Hugo said, "is the conviction that we are loved." "Love is the first requirement for mental health," declared Sigmund Freud.

Unfortunately, many people go through life feeling unloved—and unlovable. Perhaps they were constantly criticized or ignored as children, or their family was torn by conflict. Perhaps they made bad choices about important issues in life—which only confirmed their belief that they were unworthy of love. This may be your experience.

But listen: I have good news! No matter the reason, your feelings aren't telling you the truth! God loves you, and if you begin to see yourself the way God sees you, your attitudes will begin to change. If He didn't love you, would Christ have been willing to die for you? But He did! The Bible says, "By this we know love, because He laid down His life for us" (1 John 3:16).

God loves you. Hammer that truth into your heart and mind every day. It will make all the difference.

HOPE FOR TODAY

God's Word is His love letter to each one of His children. By reading it, we are reminded that the high King of heaven left His throne, came to earth, and conquered the grave so that we might be set free from the chains of death and live with Him forever. That is true love.

242

FACING REJECTION

He is despised and rejected by men,
A Man of sorrows and acquainted with grief.

ISAIAH 53:3

Throughout His earthly life, Jesus was constantly exposed to personal criticism and rejection. At the beginning of His ministry, His own townsfolk at Nazareth tried to hurl Him down from the brow of a hill (Luke 4:29). The religious and political leaders constantly argued with Him and conspired to kill Him. Eventually He was arrested and brought to trial before Pilate and Herod. Even though He was guiltless of the accusations, He was denounced as an enemy of God and man and was sentenced to death.

How did Jesus respond to this criticism and rejection? First, with steadfastness. He did not tone down His message, nor did He stop doing what He knew was right. Second, with strength. Ahead of Him was the Cross—but He did not lose courage or shrink from what He knew was God's will. Third, with submission. When Herod prodded Jesus to defend Himself, "He answered him nothing" (Luke 23:9). Only one thing mattered: fulfilling God's purpose for His life.

How will we meet criticism?

HOPE FOR TODAY

In a time when compromise is the cry of the day, standing firm on truth will always bring criticism. We must, like Christ, remain steadfast, be strong in the Lord, and accept that the world will reject us as it did Him.

THE WAY OF MEEKNESS

"Blessed are the meek,
For they shall inherit the earth."
MATTHEW 5:5

No person is meek by nature. We insist on our own way (even if we are mild-mannered by nature), and if anyone blocks our path we react with hurt, anger, resentment, and even revenge.

Moses was meek, but he was not meek by nature. God worked meekness into his life over a forty-year period.

Peter was certainly not meek by nature. He was impetuous, saying and doing the first thing that came into his mind. But little by little, the Holy Spirit of God transformed Peter after the resurrection of Jesus.

Before his conversion, Paul was not meek. His job was to persecute Christians! Yet Paul wrote to the church at Galatia, "The fruit of the Spirit is . . . gentleness, goodness, . . . meekness" (Galatians 5:22–23 KJV).

It is our human nature to be proud and self-assertive, not meek. Only the Spirit of God can transform our lives through the new birth experience and then make us over again into the image of Christ. He is our example of true meekness.

HOPE FOR TODAY

Teach me, Lord, to live for the One and not number one. Help me overcome my human nature and yield to the Holy Spirit. I long to live in Your image.

THE REALITY OF HEAVEN

God will wipe away every tear from their eyes.

REVELATION 7:17

I n the midst of his suffering, Job said, "Man is born to trouble as surely as sparks fly upward" (Job 5:7 NIV). It is true. I have never met a person who did not have troubles of some kind. Fear and sickness rob us of happiness; broken relationships and shattered dreams destroy our peace.

But one of God's greatest promises is that all of these will be forgotten in Heaven, where "there shall be no more death, nor sorrow, nor crying. There shall be no more pain, for the former things have passed away" (Revelation 21:4).

This is the supreme reality of Heaven. Throughout eternity there will be an intimate relationship between Christ and His church. He will be the Lamb who is on the throne, and He shall lead His people to fountains of living waters.

With this great certainty and assurance, the future holds no terrors we cannot face. Beyond any crisis lies Heaven and the utopia of our dreams. Thus Christians should never be filled with fear, discouragement, or despondency. Ahead of us is Heaven!

HOPE FOR TODAY

The joys of this life pale in comparison to Heaven; the pains will no longer be remembered. Each day should be filled with the joy and anticipation of knowing we are one day closer to an eternity with Christ.

Truly Transformed

Present your bodies a living sacrifice. . . . And do not be conformed to this world.
Romans 12:1–2

Others can't see what goes on inside of you—your thoughts and emotions, your dreams and motives. Nor can they "see" your inner commitment to Christ.

All they can see is your body—and they will judge what is on the inside of you by what they see happening on the outside. A frown signals concern or disapproval; a smile signals gratitude or welcome; a clenched fist signals hostility or anger.

Do you see why Paul tells us to "present [our] bodies a living sacrifice"? The reason is simple: the way we use our bodies will signal to others what we really are on the inside. We may claim to follow Christ, but if our actions tell a different story, people have a right to question our claim. Our dress, our speech, our habits—all should honor Christ. We are to be "blameless and pure, children of God without fault in the midst of a crooked and depraved generation" (Philippians 2:15 NIV).

Do your outer actions signal your inner commitment to Christ?

Hope for Today

A preacher once said that many will be surprised at the people they see in Heaven. Based on your words and actions in recent days, would anyone be surprised to see you there?

PURE IN HEART

"Blessed are the pure in heart,
For they shall see God."
MATTHEW 5:8

Why does Jesus say we should be "pure in heart"? The reason is because our heart—our inner being—is the root of all our actions. From our hearts come our motives, our desires, our goals, our emotions. If our hearts aren't right, our actions won't be either.

Jesus put it this way: "From within, out of the heart of men, proceed evil thoughts, adulteries, fornications, murders, thefts, covetousness, wickedness, deceit, lewdness, an evil eye, blasphemy, pride, foolishness" (Mark 7:21–22). Not a very pretty picture!

But God wants to give us a pure heart—and He will. He does this first of all when we turn to Christ in repentance and faith, for "the blood of Jesus Christ His Son cleanses us from all sin" (1 John 1:7). But God also purifies our hearts day by day, as we submit to the Holy Spirit and—with His help—flee from evil and seek what is good. "Blessed are the pure in heart."

HOPE FOR TODAY

What we allow into our hearts affects every area of our lives. What we see, hear, and meditate on matters. Who we seek counsel from matters. Guard your heart above all else (Proverbs 4:23).

HE STILL SUSTAINS US

The eternal God is your refuge.

DEUTERONOMY 33:27

When we hear the word *suffering* we usually think of physical pain. But psychological suffering is just as real—and sometimes more devastating.

It may be an inner grief or sorrow you cannot express, even to your dearest friend or spouse. It may sap your strength or paralyze you with anxiety. It may harm your relationships, or even grip you so tightly that it becomes more than just a temporary problem, but a serious psychological illness.

Paul knew what it was to experience -psychological -suffering; he told the Corinthians he had written to them "out of much affliction and anguish of heart" (2 Corinthians 2:4). In the Garden of Gethsemane, Jesus, "being in agony, . . . prayed more earnestly" (Luke 22:44). After denying His Lord three times, Peter "went out and wept bitterly" (Luke 22:62).

But when such times come (and they come to us all), God still loves us. He does not abandon us. Remember: "The eternal God is your refuge, and underneath are the everlasting arms" (Deuteronomy 33:27).

HOPE FOR TODAY

People are sympathetic toward physical pain; friends rush in to offer support. Yet, we tend to feel abandoned in times of emotional pain. Jesus knows the unseen agony, and He has not left you alone.

GOD IS OUR STRENGTH

The LORD is my light and my salvation;
Whom shall I fear?
PSALM 27:1

It is a fact that the Lord is my light and my salvation. So why should I be afraid? Since the Lord fears nothing, why should we fear?

The Scripture also declares that God is a "very present help in trouble" (Psalm 46:1). If we can't trust the all-powerful, all-knowing, all-loving God of the universe to help us, where can we turn? But we can trust Him!

God is able, indeed He is anxious, to deliver us from all sorts of trouble. He wants to give us strength to overcome the temptation to sin that separates Him from those He loves. He wants to give us the courage to confront our problems (instead of avoiding them or denying them), and then to find the practical wisdom and help we need to deal with them.

What do you fear today? Failure? Rejection? An illness or physical danger? The uncertainty of the future? Whatever it is, ask God to help you turn it over to Him. "The LORD is my light and my salvation; whom shall I fear?"

HOPE FOR TODAY

God is poised and ready to come to the help of His children. There is no enemy too tough, no trial too big, no sin unforgivable. The only question is: Have you asked Him to help, or are you trying to go it on your own?

THE DIVINE "FIRE"

"I will give them a new heart and a new mind."
EZEKIEL 11:19 TEV

When a person comes in contact with the living God, he or she can never be the same again. This divine "fire" either draws or drives, saves or destroys, helps or hinders. Accepted and utilized, it becomes a boon and a blessing. Rejected, it becomes a bane and a curse.

One dying thief was drawn to the warmth of the Savior; he responded in faith and was saved. The other dying thief turned away and rejected God's compassion; he was lost forever.

God takes the weak and makes them strong. He takes the vile and makes them clean. He takes the worthless and makes them worthwhile. He takes the sinful and makes them pure.

With this in mind, Ezekiel said, "Thus saith the Lord God . . . I will give them a new heart and a new mind. I will take away their stubborn heart of stone and will give them an obedient heart" (Ezekiel 11:19 TEV).

No, you will never be the same once you know Christ. What difference will He make in your life today?

HOPE FOR TODAY

Which thief on the cross are you? One doubts and cries out, "If you were the Son of God, you would get me out of this trial." The other confesses, "Only the Son of God would enter this trial with me."

AN ATTITUDE OF GRATITUDE

Let the peace of Christ rule in your hearts. . . . And be thankful.

COLOSSIANS 3:15 NIV

Thankfulness isn't our usual response when something goes wrong. We may have a hundred good things for which to be thankful—but let one bad thing happen, and it's all we think about!

But the Bible says, "In everything give thanks" (1 Thessalonians 5:18). No matter what happens, we are to give thanks. Cultivate a spirit of thanksgiving in your life. Thank God for every blessing He gives you. Thank Him for Christ and what He has done for you. Even when things go wrong, thank Him that they aren't worse, and you are still in His hands.

Having an attitude of thankfulness in all of life's circumstances will help you react as old Matthew Henry did when he was mugged. He wrote in his diary, "Let me be thankful first because I was never robbed before; second, although they took my purse, they did not take my life; third, because although they took my all, it was not much; and fourth, because it was I who was robbed, not I who robbed."

I wonder if I could be that thankful!

HOPE FOR TODAY

If we would have eyes that recognize God's gifts, we would see that the blessings far outweigh the burdens. Take time and write down every gift today holds, from sunrise to sunset.

Perfect Peace

The love of God has been poured out in our hearts
by the Holy Spirit who was given to us.
Romans 5:5

Years ago when I traveled to Europe to preach, I liked to travel by sea. I enjoyed the five days of relative quiet on the ship.

On one of my voyages Captain Anderson of the United States took me down to see the ship's gyroscope. He said, "When the sea is rough, the gyroscope helps to keep the ship on an even keel. Though the waves may reach tremendous proportions, the gyroscope helps to stabilize the vessel and maintain a high degree of equilibrium."

As I listened, I thought how like the gyroscope is the Holy Spirit in our hearts. Let the storms of life break over our heads. Let the enemy, Satan, come in like a flood. Let the waves of sorrow, suffering, temptation, and testing be unleashed upon us. Our souls will be kept on an even keel and in perfect peace when the Holy Spirit dwells in our hearts. He comforts us with God's abiding presence, and assures us that God's promises are true.

Hope for Today

The person who doubts is tossed about by every storm that comes (James 1:6). The person of faith, come what may, simply carries on. The Holy Spirit makes all the difference in how we handle life's trials.

DIAMONDS IN THE DARK

Blessed is the man who fears the LORD,
Who delights greatly in His commandments.
PSALM 112:1

We Christians should stand out like sparkling diamonds against a dark velvet background. We should be more wholesome than anyone else. We should be poised, cultured, courteous, gracious—but firm in the things we do and do not do. We should laugh and be radiant; but we should refuse to allow the unbelieving world to pull us down to its level.

Christ meant for His followers to be different—and if we are truly following Him, we will be. But merely being different is not enough. We are to be the cleanest, the most holy, the kindest, the most unselfish, the friendliest, the most courteous, the most industrious, the most thoughtful, the truest, and the most loving people on earth. The Bible says, "Those who are wise will shine like the brightness of the heavens, and those who lead many to righteousness, like the stars for ever and ever" (Daniel 12:3 NIV).

Dr. Albert Schweitzer, the great missionary doctor and statesman, once said, "To be glad instruments of God's love in this imperfect world is the service to which man is called."

HOPE FOR TODAY

So many people are afraid to be different, and, yet different is exactly what this world needs from us. Do you want to see change? Be different.

REST FOR GOD'S PEOPLE

There remains therefore a rest for the people of God.
HEBREWS 4:9

We are the most entertained generation in history. Television sets pull in thousands of channels. Professional sports teams and pop music groups take in (and spend) billions of dollars. Millions of people own second and third homes for vacations. Our children are upset if they don't get the latest computer games for Christmas.

I believe this frantic search for entertainment is a symptom of something deeper. Some have suggested we are the most bored generation in history—and perhaps they are right. Down inside is an empty place in our hearts—a restlessness, a desire for inner peace and tranquility—that will not go away. The irony is, the more we try to satisfy it, the less content we become.

Only Christ can fill that empty space in our hearts, and He will do so as we open our lives to Him. But God's Word also points us to the future—to Heaven, where our restless hearts will be at peace. "There remains, therefore, a rest for the people of God."

HOPE FOR TODAY

Our lives are filled to the brim with things that serve to distract us from God. Like Martha, we are consumed with distractions while in the very presence of the Lord. Seek to have a Mary heart that chooses the better portion.

September

Through the Lord's mercies we are not consumed,
Because His compassions fail not.
They are new every morning;
Great is Your faithfulness.

LAMENTATIONS 3:22–23

A TIME APART

The eyes of the LORD are on the righteous,
And His ears are open to their prayers.

1 PETER 3:12

Many people want to work for God, but they don't want to spend time with God. They are content with busyness instead of calmness, walking quietly in the presence of a Friend.

God calls us to work for Him, of course; there is no place in the Christian life for laziness or a lack of diligence. But God also calls us to Himself. He calls us to "come with me by yourselves to a quiet place" (Mark 6:31 NIV).

Jesus, we read, "having risen a long while before daylight . . . went out and departed to a solitary place; and there He prayed" (Mark 1:35). If the Son of God needed time alone with His Father, how much more do we?

It is not easy to shut out the world, set aside a few minutes by yourself, and spend time in God's Word and prayer. But it is essential if we are to grow in our relationship with God and be strengthened for the battles ahead. Don't delay. Begin now to spend time alone with God every day.

HOPE FOR TODAY

We can serve and miss the Savior. Are we volunteering our time but neglecting our prayer life? Do we serve in the community while our Bibles gather dust? We will be most effective when we are filled with the Spirit.

OUR STUBBORN WILLS

Repent therefore and be converted.
ACTS 3:19

Becoming a Christian is a once-for-all event in which we repent of our sins and cast ourselves on Christ alone for our salvation. When we are converted, God takes us "out of darkness into His marvelous light" (1 Peter 2:9).

But being a Christian is a daily, ongoing experience. It is a lifelong process of daily repentance and faith, of turning from sin and seeking to live for Christ, in the power of the Holy Spirit. That is where our wills come in. Although we have been converted and God has come to live in us, our old nature is still "alive and kicking." Our stubborn wills still demand to put self first instead of Christ. It isn't easy to bring our stubborn wills into submission to Christ, but when we do, it is as if a misplaced vertebra has snapped back into place. Instead of the stress and tension of a life out of harmony with God, we discover the serenity of His presence.

Who will control your will today? You—or Christ?

HOPE FOR TODAY
Each morning, we must choose to die to self again. We hand the reigns over to Christ and give Him complete control. Some days, it's easy; some days, it's not. But it's always best.

WE NEED MERCY

The LORD is good;
His mercy is everlasting.
PSALM 100:5

Many Christians do not see God in all of His wholeness. We glibly quote John 3:16—but we forget this verse: "He who does not believe has been judged already" (v. 18 NASB).

Yes, God is loving and compassionate. But He is also absolutely holy and pure, and because of that He is the Judge who will someday bring His full wrath to bear on those who refuse to repent.

All too often we are more afraid of physical pain than of moral wrong. The Cross is the proof that holiness is a principle for which God would die. God cannot clear the guilty until atonement is made. But that is what happened at the Cross.

Do not take sin lightly. Do not tolerate sin in your life, saying, "Oh well, God will forgive me anyway." Sin is an offense to almighty God, and while He will have mercy on us when we repent, He also is the Judge, and "everything is uncovered and laid bare before the eyes of him to whom we must give account" (Hebrews 4:13 NIV).

HOPE FOR TODAY

We can't fully appreciate the mercy we've received until we come to terms with the truth: only the Cross could combat our sin nature.

GOD CONTROLS THE CLOCK

There is laid up for me the crown of righteousness.

2 TIMOTHY 4:8

Many people are asking, "Where is history heading?" A careful student of the Bible will see that God controls the clock of destiny. Amidst the world's confusion, God's omnipotent hand moves, working out His unchanging plan and purpose.

Not that we always see His hand at work. As the old English hymn writer William Cowper put it, "God moves in a mysterious way, His wonders to perform." God is not absent. By His providence He sustains us, and behind the scenes He is working to bring about His divine purpose.

What is that purpose? Paul put it this way: "That . . . He might gather together in one all things in Christ, both which are in heaven and which are on earth" (Ephesians 1:10). Someday Satan's rule will be ended, and Christ will reign as Lord over all creation. Someday all the sin and rebellion of this corrupted universe will be destroyed, and Christ's kingdom of righteousness and peace will rule forever.

Don't be discouraged by what you see in the headlines every day. God is at work, and someday Christ will rule.

HOPE FOR TODAY

Many will be surprised at the way it all plays out; God's people will not. We know that this world and everything in it will pass away. Let's live in a way that let's Christ know that we're expecting Him.

HOME AT LAST

"Behold, I make all things new."
REVELATION 21:5

Heaven is a place so beautiful that when the apostle John caught a glimpse of it, the only thing to which he could liken it was a young woman on the crowning day of her life: her wedding day. He said that the holy city was like "a bride beautifully dressed for her husband" (Revelation 21:2 NIV).

Artists have tried to paint pictures of Heaven, but even the most impressive image falls far short of the reality. Under the inspiration of the Holy Spirit, John could only hint at the splendor we shall see someday: "It shone with the glory of God, and its brilliance was like that of a very precious jewel, like a jasper, clear as crystal" (Revelation 21:11 NIV).

Yet the Bible's emphasis is not on Heaven's beauty but on Heaven's joy. The Bible teaches that Heaven will be a home that is happy because there will be nothing in it to hinder happiness. "And there shall by no means enter it anything that defiles. . . . But the throne of God and of the Lamb shall be in it" (Revelation 21:27; 22:3).

HOPE FOR TODAY

What currently hinders your happiness? What stands in the way of peace and contentment? You can be certain that, whatever stands in your way, will not be present in Heaven.

COMPASSION AND LOVE

Beloved, if God so loved us, we also ought to love one another.

1 JOHN 4:11

Charles Allen once made this statement: "Some people seem to have such a passion for righteousness that they have no room left for compassion for those who have failed."

I pray that would never be true of us. God, our Father, has shown us such great kindness and gentle mercy. May we ever reach out to the lost in compassion and love to bring them gently to Jesus Christ. Jesus, "when He saw the multitudes, . . . was moved with compassion for them, because they were weary and scattered, like sheep having no shepherd" (Matthew 9:36).

Let me share these lines from an unknown poet:

> Just to be tender, just to be true,
> Just to be glad the whole day through,
> Just to be merciful, just to be mild,
> Just to be trustful as a child:
> Just to be gentle and kind and sweet,
> Just to be helpful with willing feet, . . .
> Just to let love be our daily key,
> That is God's will for you and me.

HOPE FOR TODAY
Lord, may I never forget the depths to which You reached to rescue me.

GOD HATES SIN

I acknowledged my sin to You,
And my iniquity I have not hidden.
PSALM 32:5

We live in an age when sin is winked at and where God is treated as one who is indulgent, softhearted, and understanding—tolerant of those who break His commandments. People today find it difficult to believe that God hates anything, including sin. The image many people have of Him is of a rather senile old grandfather who shakes his head in amusement when his grandchildren misbehave.

But I will tell you that God has not forgotten about sin, though some may pretend it doesn't exist. God hates sin. Why? Because He loves us, and He knows the terrible devastation sin brings to us.

Sin is like a deadly cancer, inexorably leaving suffering and death in its wake. Left unforgiven, sin also sends men and women into an eternity apart from God—into hell. God hates sin, because He hates what it does to us! Confess your sin today. Don't wait. Receive God's forgiveness and restoration so that you might be of use to Him and enjoy His love forever.

HOPE FOR TODAY
Some wish to live with an "I'm okay, you're okay" attitude. We think this is kindness, but it is the opposite. It is cruel to sit back and knowingly watch another person rush headlong into an eternity without God.

COMPLETE CONSECRATION

"Whoever desires to come after Me, let him deny himself."
MARK 8:34

Today Christ is calling Christians to cleansing—to dedication—to conse-cration—to full surrender. If you are a Christian and have been suffering defeat or living outside the will of God, I beg you to surrender every area of your life to Christ.

Only surrendered Christians will make an impact on our world. The world does not need any more lukewarm Christians, or lazy Christians, or quarrel-some Christians, or doubting Christians, or prideful Christians. The Bible says, "A double minded man is unstable in all his ways" (James 1:8 KJV). What keeps you from fully surrendering your life to the King of kings and the Lord of lords?

Your response will make the difference between success and failure in your spiritual life. It will make the difference between your needing help and your being able to help others. It will revolutionize your habits, your prayer life, your Bible reading, your giving, your testimony, and your church relationships. This is the Christian's hour of decision!

HOPE FOR TODAY
God is very clear about how He feels about mediocre Christians (Revelation 3:16). Lukewarm faith is grotesque to the One who sacrificed His only Son to have us as His own. Ask God to set your soul ablaze!

PEACE IN THE STORM

May the God of hope fill you with all joy and peace.
ROMANS 15:13

A wonderful old hymn says, "He gives us peace in the midst of a storm." In life we face all kinds of storms. We usually think of the personal "storms" that come our way—financial worries, problems in our marriage or family, illness, the betrayal of a friend, and so forth. But we face other kinds of storms that also threaten to engulf us: storms of materialism, storms of secularism, storms of moral degeneracy, storms of injustice, terrorism, and war.

Do you remember the violent storm that came upon Jesus and His disciples one night on the Sea of Galilee? His disciples grew panicky—but Jesus stayed fast asleep. He was at peace because He knew God was in control. He was at peace also because He was sovereign over the storm, and He knew it would vanish at His words: "Peace, be still!" (Mark 4:39).

Jesus' words still calm the turmoil in our lives. Is some storm making you fearful today? Stay close to Jesus, for His Word brings peace.

HOPE FOR TODAY
Jesus can calm any storm, conquer any foe, and meet any need. Let the waves roll and the winds blow; we have the water-walking, dead-man-raising, death-defeating Savior in our boat.

REACH FOR HIS HAND

The Lord, He is the One who goes before you. He will be with you.

DEUTERONOMY 31:8

Once many years ago when I was going through a dark period, I prayed and prayed, but the heavens seemed to be brass. I felt as though God had disappeared and I was alone with my trial and burden. It was a dark night for my soul.

I wrote my mother about the experience and will never forget her reply: "Son, there are many times when God withdraws to test your faith. He wants you to trust Him in the darkness. Now, Son, reach up by faith in the fog and you will find that His hand will be there." In tears I knelt by my bed and experienced an overwhelming sense of God's presence.

Whether or not we feel God's presence when our way seems dark, by faith we know He is there. You can stake your life on His promise: "I will never leave you nor forsake you" (Hebrews 13:5).

HOPE FOR TODAY

Has your way grown dark? Are you tempted to panic? Don't retreat. Reach out. Choose faith over fear; God has not left you alone. You are securely held in the palm of His hand.

THINGS THAT CANNOT BE SHAKEN

We are receiving a kingdom which cannot be shaken.
HEBREWS 12:28

This date of September 11 will be engraved on the memories of people everywhere for generations to come. On that terrible day when terrorists commandeered several passenger planes and killed thousands of innocent people in New York and Washington D.C., we began to realize the true depths of evil in the human heart, and the uncertainty and fragility of life itself.

What lessons would God teach us from such an appalling tragedy? I confess I don't know the full answer. Many people, I know, for the first time faced the shallowness and emptiness of their lives, and turned to God as a result. Millions came together to pray.

But one lesson God would teach us all is this: our only lasting hope is in Him. Life has always been uncertain; September 11 only made it clearer. Where will you turn for your security? Put your life in Christ's hands, for only He offers us "a kingdom which cannot be shaken."

HOPE FOR TODAY

We live as if tomorrow is a guarantee, but it's not. What if today was all we had left? Will what we have on the agenda serve to further God's eternal kingdom, or our own shakeable one?

ANGELS WATCHING

We should live soberly, righteously, and godly in the present age.
TITUS 2:12

God's command to live righteous and godly lives should sober us, for the Bible tells us that our lives are Heaven's primary concern. Paul said, "I solemnly charge you in the presence of God and of Christ Jesus and of the chosen angels, that you guard and keep [these rules]" (1 Timothy 5:21 AMP).

Think of it: even the angels of Heaven are constantly watching how we live as Christians! Is it merely curiosity on their part, idly wondering if we will fail or prove faithful? No. They know the hour is urgent and that what we do is important. Eternal issues are at stake, and we are in the midst of a cosmic struggle.

Don't think it doesn't matter how you live; it does! It matters to God, and it matters to His holy angels. It also matters to those around you. Jesus said, "Let your light so shine before men, that they may see your good works and glorify your Father in heaven" (Matthew 5:16).

HOPE FOR TODAY

Imagine all the host of Heaven watching with bated breath wondering what you will do next. Your life matters, and the choices you make matter. Nothing about you is inconsequential. Live with purpose.

ABUNDANT PARDON

Blessed is he whose transgression is forgiven,
Whose sin is covered.
PSALM 32:1

The story is told about a sensitive boy in the eighteenth century who joined the British Army, but when the shots began to fly, he deserted. Years later he became a great astronomer, discovering a new planet. King George sent for him. He went, fearful the king would order his execution for being a deserter. Instead the astronomer was given an envelope—and inside was a royal pardon. The king said, "Now we can talk, and you shall come up and live at Windsor Castle." He was Sir William Herschel.

Herschel was guilty and deserved condemnation. But King George had mercy on him, and even made him a member of the royal household. This is what God promises us. We are guilty and helpless. But God loves us, and "he saved us, not because of righteous things we had done, but because of his mercy" (Titus 3:5 NIV). Never forget: "God did not send His Son into the world to condemn the world, but that the world through Him might be saved" (John 3:17).

HOPE FOR TODAY

The enemy wants us to believe that what we've done is beyond the reach of God's grace, but he's a liar. Jesus' blood reaches the darkest corners and flows into the deepest pit. His grace is enough.

THE PROPER PROPORTION

Do not love the world or the things in the world.

1 JOHN 2:15

Christians are warned not to love the world—but what is worldliness? Some have misunderstood it.

Worldliness is an attitude, a spirit, an atmosphere that permeates the whole of human society. It is an attitude that puts self first and ignores God and His commandments. Its horizon is this present world, and it never gives a thought to God or to eternity. It exhibits itself in a thousand different ways—in habits, in selfish pleasures, in a grasping for material things, in driving ambition, in exalting oneself at the expense of others.

We must avoid everything God has labeled sinful; of that there can be no doubt. But some elements of daily life aren't necessarily sinful in themselves; they only become sinful if they are abused. Pleasure isn't always wrong—unless it is abused. Ambition is an essential part of true character—but if abused it can destroy us.

Be on guard, lest a spirit of worldliness creep into your life. The Bible warns, "Do not love the world or the things in the world."

HOPE FOR TODAY

Is there anything attempting to take the place of God in your life? That thing will begin consuming more of your time, energy, and thoughts. May the meditations of your heart be acceptable in His sight.

GOD VALUES FAITH

How precious also are Your thoughts to me, O God!
How great is the sum of them.
PSALM 139:17

How happy would a parent be if his child constantly questioned him whether his or her needs would be met? The parent would feel frustrated and sad, perhaps even angry that the child did not trust him.

The Bible has scores of references telling us how much it pleases God for us to trust Him for our every need. The Roman soldier expressed great faith when he told Jesus just to "say the word" and his servant would be healed (Matthew 8:8). Jesus told His disciples, "Look at the birds . . . they neither sow nor reap nor gather into barns; yet your heavenly Father feeds them. Are you not of more value than they?" (Matthew 6:26).

God values our trust in Him above every other character quality. And how do we develop trust? By spending time in God's presence, through prayer, worship, and by reading His Word. We develop trust also as we step out in faith and discover He really can be trusted. Are you trusting Him for every need in your life?

HOPE FOR TODAY

Do not worry. Do not fear. Do not doubt. Do not be anxious. It's phrased a number of ways, but God's instruction is the same: just trust Him. He is able and He is willing to handle whatever comes your way.

KEPT BY THE SPIRIT

We know that He abides in us, by the Spirit whom He has given us.

1 JOHN 3:24

A boat doesn't sink because it is in the water; it sinks because the water gets into it.

In the same way, Christians don't fail to live as they should because they are in the world; they fail because the world has gotten into them. We don't fail to produce the fruit of the Holy Spirit because we live in a sea of corruption; we fail because the sea of corruption has gotten into us.

It can happen almost without our realizing it. At one time we were dedicated to Christ, surrendered to the will of God. But little by little the chilling waters of the world crept in. We became preoccupied with the things of this world rather than the things of Christ.

Most ocean-going ships have pumps running constantly, sucking out any water that might have leaked into the hull. Similarly, we need to keep the "pumps" of repentance running. We need to plug the holes with the truth of God's Word. Don't let the world sink your ship!

HOPE FOR TODAY

We are faced with the choice multiple times a day: the Word or the world. The choice isn't always good versus bad; Satan is far more subtle. Ask God to give you the wisdom to discern what is good and what is best.

PERFECT PEACE

May the God of hope fill you with all joy and peace.
ROMANS 15:13

I know that modern living taxes the faith of the strongest Christians, but none of us should doubt the ability of God to give us grace sufficient for our trials, even amid the stresses of this century. We Christians are to trust that God is still on the throne. He is a sovereign God, working out things according to His own plan.

Some section hands on a British railroad found a thrush's nest under the rail and the hen peacefully sitting on the eggs, undisturbed by the roar of the fast trains above and around her. What a picture of perfect trust! The Bible says, "You will keep him in perfect peace, whose mind is stayed on You" (Isaiah 26:3).

Believe me, God's grace is more than adequate for these times. Even as I grow older, I am learning, day by day, to keep my mind centered on Christ. When we do, the worries and anxieties and concerns of the world pass away and nothing but "perfect peace" is left in the human heart.

HOPE FOR TODAY

When God's love fills a heart, it occupies every single part of it with the fruit of His Spirit. His perfect peace leaves no room for fear in the heart of the believer (1 John 4:18).

PRAY WITHOUT CEASING

"Men always ought to pray and not lose heart."

LUKE 18:1

A prayer does not have to be eloquent or contain the language and terms of a theologian. In fact, sometimes our simplest, most heartfelt prayers are the most pleasing to God.

When you made your decision for Christ, you became a child of God, adopted by Him into His family forever. Now you have the wonderful privilege of coming directly into His presence and addressing God as your Father. In the beginning you may not be fluent, but it's important to begin. My late wife had a notebook she had kept of our children as they were beginning to talk. She treasured these first attempts, mistakes and all. She said, "I wouldn't take anything for that book."

When Paul said we should "pray without ceasing" (1 Thessalonians 5:17), he chose a term used in his day to describe a persistent cough. Repeatedly, throughout our day, we should be turning quickly to God to praise and thank Him, and to ask for His help. God is interested in everything we do, and nothing is too great or too insignificant to share with Him.

HOPE FOR TODAY

Do you struggle with knowing what to say when you pray? Paul told his readers to offer thanks and present their requests (Philippians 4:6.) Acknowledge your sin and shortcomings. Thank God for His grace, gifts, and guidance. Trust Him, knowing that He loves you with an everlasting love.

CHRIST IS COMING AGAIN

*Looking for the blessed hope and glorious appearing
of our . . . Savior Jesus Christ.*

TITUS 2:13

One of the best ways to get rid of discouragement is to remember that Christ is coming again. What is happening in your life right now is not going to last forever!

The most thrilling, glorious truth in all the world is the second coming of Jesus Christ. When we look about today and see pessimism on every side, we should remember that the Bible is the only book in the world that reliably predicts the future. The Bible is more modern than tomorrow's news report. It says the consummation of all things shall be the coming again of Jesus Christ to this earth.

This truth gives us hope—but it should also sober us and make us more diligent. After all, we do not know when Christ will return. Jesus Himself said, "Of that day and hour no one knows, not even the angels of heaven, but My Father only" (Matthew 24:36). Believing in the return of Christ doesn't make us less concerned about this world; it makes us more concerned, because we know time may be short. Now is the time to live for Christ and witness for Him.

HOPE FOR TODAY

Believers happily anticipate Christ's return because it signals the end of our earthly struggles. Knowing that He could return at any time should also instill in us an urgency to share the gospel with those around us. Who, in your life, needs to hear the good news of the Cross today?

THE STAFF OF LIFE

Your word I have hidden in my heart,
That I might not sin against you.
PSALM 119:11

The Bible isn't just another great book. It is God's Word, given by God to tell us about Himself.

Peter declared, "We did not follow cunningly devised fables . . . for prophecy never came by the will of man, but holy men of God spoke as they were moved by the Holy Spirit" (2 Peter 1:16, 21). Paul stressed, "All Scripture is given by inspiration of God, and is profitable for doctrine, for reproof, for correction, for instruction in righteousness" (2 Timothy 3:16).

I have known many outstanding leaders who made the Bible their guide. The late Herbert J. Taylor, businessman and former president of Rotary International, told me he began each day by reading the Sermon on the Mount aloud.

Let the Bible be your firm foundation. Let it be the staff of life that nourishes your soul. Let it be the sword of the Spirit that cuts away sin. Many years ago I heard these words: "Sin will keep you from God's Word—or God's Word will keep you from sin!"

HOPE FOR TODAY

The Bible has wisdom for every situation you encounter, every decision you must make, and every moral dilemma you face. God's Word has an answer to all of life's questions.

GOD OF ALL COMFORT

Because he himself suffered when he was tempted, he
is able to help those who are being tempted.

HEBREWS 2:18 NIV

Once when I was in my late teens, I was in love with a girl. It might have been puppy love, but it was real to me, the puppy! We became tentatively engaged to be married, even though we were both much too young. However, she felt that the Lord was leading her to another young man—one of my best friends.

I suffered a broken heart, and I remember going to a clergyman friend of mine to seek his help. He turned me to 2 Corinthians 1:3–4: "Blessed be the God and Father of our Lord Jesus Christ . . . who comforts us in all our tribulation, that we may be able to comfort those who are in any trouble, with the comfort with which we ourselves are comforted by God."

From those words of the apostle I gained comfort. But there is more to it than that. This passage from Paul suggests a new insight into suffering. Briefly put, it is this: not only are we comforted in our trials, but our trials can equip us to comfort others. Has God taught you something through your trials that could help someone else today?

HOPE FOR TODAY

Some don't want to discuss their trials because it brings up bad memories or causes embarrassment. But God calls us to share our stories. We never know who in the trenches needs to hear it.

SEARCHING FOR HOPE

"In the world you will have tribulation; but be of good cheer, I have overcome the world."

JOHN 16:33

Once when I referred to the future that God is planning, a university student asked me, "Isn't this a form of escapism?" I said, "In a sense, yes; and before the devil gets through with this world, we are all going to be looking for exit signs!"

As Christians we look beyond this world to God's promise of "new heavens and a new earth in which righteousness dwells" (2 Peter 3:13). But in the meantime, the world remains mired in the same heartaches and injustices it has suffered since the fall—and Jesus said we shouldn't be surprised: "In the world you will have tribulation."

Some people mistakenly think that if they become Christians, God will take away all their problems. It just isn't so. Sin still dwells within us, and Satan is still at work.

But that isn't the full story! Jesus added, "But be of good cheer, I have overcome the world." Notice: He not only will overcome the world—He already has!

HOPE FOR TODAY

No matter how bad things get in this world, we don't need to desperately seek to escape. The day is already appointed for Christ to return, and at the proper time, He will appear. Stand tall; your King is coming.

GOD'S WORD

Desire the pure milk of the word, that you may grow thereby.
1 PETER 2:2

Just as our bodies need food, so our souls need spiritual food. Without it we become malnourished and weak, susceptible to every temptation and unable to do the work God calls us to do.

Where do we find this spiritual food? In the Bible, the Word of God. The Bible reveals Christ, the Bread of Life and the Water of Life. If we fail to partake of this spiritual nourishment, we will lose our spiritual vitality.

People in some parts of our world do not enjoy the freedom we have to read the Bible. But most of us cannot hide behind that excuse. The problem for most of us is not getting a Bible, but using a Bible—actually picking it up and reading it.

Don't be content to skim through a chapter, merely to satisfy your conscience or because of some long-established habit. Rather, read the Bible as if your life depended on it. Meditate on it, memorize it, hide it in your heart so it permeates your whole being. A small portion well digested is of far greater spiritual value than a lengthy passage hurriedly scanned.

HOPE FOR TODAY

There are countless blogs, books, conferences, and speakers that can give useful knowledge about Scripture. None of it, though, can ever take the place of opening the pages of God's Word for ourselves.

GOD'S REVELATION

Forever, O LORD,
Your word is settled in heaven.
PSALM 119:89

What does revelation mean? It means that something that has been hidden is now made known. If it isn't revealed, it remains hidden.

Some people see God that way—hidden and unknown. Such a view assumes God doesn't want to be known or even that God is incapable of being known because "God" is just a vague impersonal force, like gravity.

But God has revealed Himself. He is not hidden! He has spoken to us, and if we will listen, we can not only discover what He is like, but we also can come to know Him in a personal way.

God has two textbooks. One is the textbook of nature. By looking at the world, we can learn something about its Creator.

The other is the textbook of revelation, the Bible. It is more than an ancient record of events; it is God's Word, given to us by the inspiration of the Holy Spirit to guide our lives. God has spoken—and He still speaks. Are you listening?

HOPE FOR TODAY

It is God's desire that all would come to know Him and to be saved. Praise Him that He doesn't hide Himself from anyone. Through His written Word and through His creation, God is still reaching out to each of us in a personal way.

TREASURE THAT LASTS

"Lay up for yourselves treasures in heaven."
MATTHEW 6:20

Some time ago two old friends were dying. The one was rich, and the other poor. The rich man was outside of Christ, but the poor man was a strong believer. One day the rich man was talking to another of his friends. "When I die," he said, "I shall have to leave my riches. When he dies, he will go to his riches."

Thus, in just a couple of sentences, the rich man summed up the contrast between them. The man worth everything, in reality, had nothing; the man with nothing, in reality, had everything.

These two men are a vivid illustration of what Jesus said to His disciples: "Do not lay up for yourselves treasures on earth . . . but lay up for yourselves treasures in heaven. . . . For where your treasure is, there your heart will be also" (Matthew 6:19–21).

Does that mean we must renounce everything we own? No, not unless God clearly commands us to do so. But it does mean that we should commit everything we have—including our lives—to Christ, and put His will above everything else.

HOPE FOR TODAY

We take nothing with us into eternity. Let's spend our time, resources, and energy on laying up treasures in heaven. We will never regret anything done or given for the cause of Christ.

FAITH IN GOD

Faith is the substance of things hoped for.

HEBREWS 11:1

Faith must have an object. We don't simply have faith; we have faith in something or someone. Faith in "faith" is meaningless.

For the Christian there is only one object for faith: the living God. Anything less is insubstantial, unreal, even deceptive. Our faith is in the God who created this world and who came down to earth in the person of His Son, Jesus Christ. We put our faith in Christ because He alone is the Savior. The Bible says, "Through Him [you] believe in God, who raised Him from the dead and gave Him glory, so that your faith and hope are in God" (1 Peter 1:21).

People today put their faith in all kinds of ideas and beliefs, from astrology and alleged "spirit guides" to science and humanism. But only Christ reveals God to us, and only He can bridge the gap between us and God—a gap caused by sin. Do not be deceived or misled. Only Christ is worthy of your faith.

HOPE FOR TODAY

Have you ever put faith in something or someone only to discover that your faith was misplaced? It's happened to many over the years, but it doesn't have to be that way. A faith correctly placed does not disappoint (Romans 5:5).

OUR GREAT ASSURANCE

Let us draw near with a true heart in full assurance of faith.
HEBREWS 10:22

Disregard your feelings when you come to Christ. You aren't saved by your feelings; you are saved by Christ. Feelings come and go, but Christ remains.

Only the facts matter—the fact that Jesus Christ died for your sins and rose again; the fact that if you have committed your life to Him, He has promised to forgive you and save you. The Bible says, "God has given us eternal life, and this life is in His Son. He who has the Son has life" (1 John 5:11–12).

That is God's promise to you—and He cannot lie. Your feelings will lie to you—and Satan may even use them to convince you that God has abandoned you or that you have lost your salvation. But remember: "There is no truth in [Satan]. When he lies, he speaks his native language, for he is a liar and the father of lies" (John 8:44 NIV).

How wonderful to know our faith is based on God's truth and not our feelings!

HOPE FOR TODAY
The enemy will attempt to make it complicated, but it's actually very simple: Satan is incapable of telling the truth (John 8:44), and God is unable to lie (Titus 1:2). In times of doubt, you only need to know what God says on the matter.

TO DIE IS GAIN

To me, to live is Christ and to die is gain.
PHILIPPIANS 1:21 NIV

M ost of us know what it means to be stunned by the sudden passing of a dedicated friend, a godly pastor, a devout missionary, or a saintly mother. We have stood at the open grave with hot tears running down our cheeks and have asked in utter bewilderment, "Why, O God? Why?" We know the impact these people made, and we can't help but think of the good they might have continued to do, had they lived longer.

The death of the righteous is no accident. Do you think that God—whose watchful vigil notes the sparrow's fall and who knows the number of hairs on our heads—would turn His back on one of His children in the hour of peril? With Him there are no accidents, no tragedies, and no catastrophes as far as His children are concerned.

It was Sir Walter Scott who asked, "Is death the last sleep? No, it is the final awakening." That is true for every believer in Christ. Even when grief overwhelms us or confusion assails us, we still can trust God's all-knowing love.

HOPE FOR TODAY

When we are grieving the loss of a loved one, we are not alone. Our heavenly Father understands our sadness. However, we can find joy if we remember He has a wonderful eternity planned for each believer.

SAFE AND SECURE

He became the author of eternal salvation to all who obey Him.

HEBREWS 5:9

With the exception of Jesus, no one in the Bible probably endured more scorn than Noah. Told to build an ark to escape God's judgment, we read that "Noah did; according to all that God commanded him" (Genesis 6:22).

Can you imagine what his neighbors said? Can you picture them shaking their heads and laughing, calling him a fool and murmuring he must be out of his mind? Can you envision them angrily rejecting his warnings of coming judgment and returning to their idolatrous ways (for 2 Peter 2:5 calls Noah "a preacher of righteousness")?

But when the flood came, only Noah and his family were saved. For those who scorned his pleas, it was too late.

You and I are called to proclaim a message that often seems foolish to an unbelieving world—the message of the Cross. Will everyone accept it? No. Will some mock us? Yes. But never stop sharing the gospel, for it is still "the power of God for the salvation of everyone who believes" (Romans 1:16 NIV).

HOPE FOR TODAY

Is there someone you've neglected to share your faith with because you feared their response? If you care about them at all, you will risk it. Great will be your reward in Heaven (Matthew 5:12).

DISPEL DISCOURAGEMENT

Wait on the LORD; be of good courage,
And He shall strengthen your heart.

PSALM 27:14

The root of discouragement is unbelief. Perhaps you are discouraged because you think that you aren't making enough money (and you aren't convinced God can supply your needs). Or you are frustrated in your job (and you refuse to believe God can help you be content). Or maybe you are worried about health problems (and you don't even stop to consider that your life is in God's hands).

Discouragement is a large cloud that, like all clouds, obscures the warmth and joy of the sun. In the case of spiritual discouragement, the cloud eclipses the Son of God, the Lord Jesus in our lives. Discouragement is Satan's device to thwart the work of God in our lives. Discouragement blinds our eyes to the mercy of God and makes us perceive only the unfavorable circumstances.

There is only one way to dispel discouragement, and it is not by our own strength or ingenuity. It is by turning in faith to God, believing that He loves us and is in control of the future. The Bible says, "Wait on the LORD . . . and He shall strengthen your heart."

HOPE FOR TODAY

Focus on circumstances, and God seems distant. Focus on Christ, and problems seem to fade away.

OCTOBER

No temptation has overtaken you except such as is common to man; but God is faithful, who will not allow you to be tempted beyond what you are able.

1 CORINTHIANS 10:13

TRIUMPH OVER TRAGEDY

Every good gift and every perfect gift is from above,
and comes down from the Father of lights.
JAMES 1:17

The key to understanding tragedy is to understand its source. Death and pain and every other tragedy came into this world because of sin. When Adam and Eve sinned in the garden of Eden, they weren't just doing something God had told them not to do. It was a blatant, open act of rebellion—in thought, word, and deed—against the God who had made them and had supplied their every need. It was saying God was a liar and believing Satan instead. It was yielding to the temptation to "be like God" (Genesis 3:5).

Every graveyard, every hospital, every prison, every courtroom is a witness to the terrible legacy of that rebellion. No, I don't fully understand why God allows evil to happen. But evil happens because we live in an evil world. Never underestimate the devastating effects of sin.

What was sin's greatest tragedy? It was the Cross—for had it not been for sin, Jesus would never have had to die. But Christ triumphed over tragedy—and so can we, because of Him.

HOPE FOR TODAY

Forgive me, Father, for doubting the goodness and sufficiency of Your gifts. May I never seek anything except what comes from Your hands. Thank You for the most perfect of Your gifts: Your Son.

POOR IN SPIRIT

While we were still sinners, Christ died for us.

ROMANS 5:8

One of the hardest truths for some people to accept is that there is absolutely nothing they can do to win their salvation.

No matter how generous . . . how honest . . . how compassionate they are—it is never enough. God is holy, and His standard is perfection. If we think we are good enough, it simply proves our pride.

Only when we see ourselves as God sees us—sinners, guilty before Him—will we realize our need of a Savior. C. H. Spurgeon said, "The first link between my soul and Christ is not my goodness but my badness, not my merit but my misery, not my riches but my need."

But the amazing thing is this: in spite of our sin, God still loves us. He loves us so much that Christ died on the Cross for us. All we can do is believe and receive—believe Christ died for us and by faith receive Him into our lives. No, you can't win your salvation—but Christ has won it for you!

HOPE FOR TODAY

Who ever heard of a love story where Someone so pure and perfect loved someone so wretched? The scandalous nature of the Cross is that, while we were still sinners, Christ died for us (Romans 5:8).

ANSWERED PRAYER

Let us . . . come boldly to the throne of grace, that we may obtain mercy.
HEBREWS 4:16

Frequently people say to me, "God answered my prayer!" Usually they mean God granted them whatever they had requested, either for themselves or for others.

God always answers the prayers of His children—but His answer isn't always "Yes." Sometimes His answer is "No," or "Wait"—and they are answers just as much as "Yes."

Think of Paul, pleading with God to remove his "thorn in the flesh" (probably a painful illness). But God's answer was "No" (see 2 Corinthians 12:7–10). God had something better—a path leading him into deeper dependence on God and His grace. Or think of Jesus, praying as He faced the agony of the Cross: "If it is possible, let this cup pass from Me" (Matthew 26:39). But God's answer was "No"—because there was no other way for our salvation to be won.

God knows far better than we do what is best for us. Thank God even when He says "No" or "Wait." His answer is always perfect.

HOPE FOR TODAY

I long to have a faith that rejoices as much in a "no" as in a "yes," knowing my God has heard my cry and loves me enough to do what is best and not what feels good to me in the moment.

GOD'S PLANS ARE BEST

As for God, His way is perfect.
PSALM 18:30

Things didn't always work out the way Paul planned.

Expecting to preach in Asia Minor, "they were forbidden by the Holy Spirit" (Acts 16:6). Looking forward to instructing the new converts in Philippi, Paul and his companion instead found themselves thrown into prison (see Acts 16:11–24). Encouraged by the response to the gospel in Thessalonica, he was suddenly assailed by a mob and accused of having "turned the world upside down" (Acts 17:6). As a result he was forced to flee.

But in every instance God was in control! Paul was forbidden to preach in Asia Minor—because God was opening the door to Europe. Paul found himself in jail—and as a result the Philippian jailer and his family were converted. Paul had to flee Thessalonica—and Berea, the next town, "received the word with all readiness" (Acts 17:11).

Things don't always work out the way we plan. But if we commit our way to Christ and walk in obedience to Him, we discover His plans are always better.

HOPE FOR TODAY

We may never know what would have happened if, in a certain situation, we got "our way." We *can* know that His way is perfect, and ours is not, and we can rest in that. Not my will, but Thine.

MATERIALISM

"You cannot serve God and mammon."

LUKE 16:13

The Bible strictly forbids idolatry. One of the Ten Commandments declares, "You shall not make for yourself a carved image; . . . you shall not bow down to them nor serve them" (Exodus 20:4–5).

But almost anything can become an idol—something we worship and serve in place of God. It might be success, or pleasure, or possessions, or money, or anything else we let control our lives. They aren't necessarily wrong in themselves, but they become idols when we make them the most important things in life.

The Bible rejects idols for at least two reasons. First, idols are false. They cannot save us or change our lives for the better. Second, idols cut us off from God. We substitute them for God—and as a result, we turn our backs on Him and never come to know Him and love Him as we should.

Has any idol taken God's rightful place in your life? Don't let it happen. God has commanded, "You shall have no other gods before Me" (Exodus 20:3).

HOPE FOR TODAY

An idol lies, and it never satisfies. It steals your worship and offers nothing in return. Worship the Lord and only Him. He has proven His love for you in a way no false god ever could.

STRANGERS IN THE WORLD

I urge you, as aliens and strangers in the world, to abstain from sinful desires.

1 PETER 2:11 NIV

Aliens from other countries are rarely shown the "welcome mat." They are often accepted reluctantly or with a tongue-in-cheek attitude. They may even find themselves victims of discrimination, rejection, or intolerance.

The Bible says that we Christians are "aliens and strangers in the world." Our citizenship is in Heaven, which is our real home. As long as we live on this earth, we don't quite fit in. Our customs are different, our goals are different, our ways of living are different, and our concerns are different.

And as Christ's followers (instead of followers of this world), we may find ourselves scorned, rejected, or even persecuted. If so, we shouldn't be surprised. Jesus warned, "If they persecuted Me, they will also persecute you" (John 15:20).

But never forget: you are a citizen of the kingdom of God. And someday you will be home!

HOPE FOR TODAY

If we are strangers in the world and are meant to stand out, what does it say about us if we blend right in? Shouldn't we be concerned if we feel comfortable and at home?

YIELDED TO GOD

Know ye not, that to whom ye yield yourselves
servants to obey, his servants ye are?

ROMANS 6:16 KJV

Eric Liddell, the missionary and great runner whose story is told in the film *Chariots of Fire,* has been described as "ridiculously humble in victory, utterly generous in defeat." That's a good definition of what it means to be meek. Eric Liddell was fiercely competitive, determined to use his God-given abilities to the fullest. But his meekness, kindness, and gentle spirit won the admiration even of those he defeated.

Meekness involves being yielded. The word *yield* has two meanings. The first is negative, and the second is positive. On one hand it means "to relinquish, to abandon"; on the other hand, it also means "to give." This second definition is in line with Jesus' words: "He who loses [or gives] his life . . . will find it" (Matthew 10:39).

Those who submit to the will of God do not fight back at life. They learn the secret of yielding—of relinquishing and abandoning—their own lives and wills to Christ. And then He gives back to them a life that is far richer and fuller than anything they could ever have imagined.

HOPE FOR TODAY

We'll never regret yielding to the will of God. We trust Him with our lives, knowing that anything of value we lose will be restored (Joel 2:25). There is freedom in yielding that can't be found in fighting for control.

GOD'S MESSAGE

"He who hears My word, and believes Him who sent Me, has eternal life."

JOHN 5:24 NASB

I know little about nuclear fission or uranium and other elements used in making nuclear explosives. Yet I believe in the atomic bomb, and so do you. But how can we believe that it exists if we don't understand it or have any scientific knowledge about the way it works?

The answer is obvious. Others understand nuclear fission, even if we don't, and others have seen what happens when a nuclear reaction takes place, even if we haven't. We read what they say, and we accept it as the testimony of reliable witnesses.

I spend much of my time perusing the pages of a book—the Bible. In it I discover that centuries ago God acted and spoke, and reliable witnesses have written it down. God even guided them as they wrote, so that now I read the very words of God Himself.

I may not understand everything there is to know about God—but I know Him and trust Him, because I read of Him in the Bible. Most of all, I know He came down to this earth in the person of His Son, and "grace and truth came through Jesus Christ" (John 1:17).

HOPE FOR TODAY

Advanced degrees are nice, and the ability to read Greek and Hebrew is impressive. Yet, over the years, many of the most moving testimonies have been from those who claimed the promise: "because the Bible tells me so."

SURROUNDED WITH SONG

You shall surround me with songs of deliverance.

PSALM 32:7

Someone has said that when faith is strong, troubles become trifles.

That doesn't mean our troubles aren't real, or that we act as if they didn't exist. God takes them seriously—so seriously that He sent Jesus Christ into the world to deal with their root cause, which is sin.

But just as Jesus triumphed over death, so He helps us triumph over trouble. Even in the midst of troubles, the Bible says, "I will turn their mourning to joy" (Jeremiah 31:13).

How does it happen? By looking in faith to God. He has not abandoned us, and He has plans for our future. He can even give us an optimistic spirit—somewhat like the Englishman I heard about during World War II who stood looking at the deep hole in the ground where his bombed-out home had once stood. "I always did want a basement, I did," he said. "Now I can jolly well build another house like I always wanted!"

HOPE FOR TODAY

Have you watched someone experience unspeakable loss and learn to smile again? Did you endure something you thought you would never survive and, yet, here you are? Only God brings beauty from ashes.

THE CLOUDS OF LIFE

The Lord went before them by day in a pillar of cloud to lead the way.

EXODUS 13:21

Clouds will come. They are part of life. But by God's grace we need not be depressed by them. Just as clouds can protect us from the brightness of the sun, life's clouds can reveal the glory of God, and from their lofty height God speaks to us.

Like the children of Israel, we are travelers to the promised land. As they traveled through the wilderness, the Bible says, "The Lord went before them by day in a pillar of cloud to lead the way."

Perhaps, like them, you are passing through a wilderness right now. It may be the wilderness of a broken marriage, or a financial reversal, or a major disappointment, or a threatening illness. It may even be a wilderness of doubt or sin.

But God is with you in the wilderness, and He goes before you to encourage and guide you. He brought the children of Israel through the wilderness—and He will bring you through yours as well, as you look in faith to Him. Never forget: "He is the living God, and steadfast forever" (Daniel 6:26).

HOPE FOR TODAY

The children of Israel knew that the presence of God was in the cloud, and they only moved when it moved. We can view our clouds the same way; God is still with us, and we wait for Him to move.

Redeemed by Love

You were redeemed . . . with the precious blood of Christ.
1 Peter 1:18–19 niv

The word *redeem* means "to buy back"—to recover by paying a price. The word *redeemed* can be illustrated by the ancient world through the position of a slave who had been captured in battle or enticed into serving one who was not his legal master. His real master, however, intent on recovering his slave's service and love, would buy him back—redeem him from the enemy—at great personal cost.

That is what God did for us. Captured by Satan and enticed into his service, we were slaves of sin, without any hope of deliverance. But God still loved us, and He was determined to restore us to His household. By His death on the Cross, Jesus paid the price for our deliverance, a price far greater than our true value. He did it solely because He loved us. Now we have been redeemed!

Hope for Today

An object is only worth what someone is willing to pay for it. God looked down from Heaven, saw us stained with sin and trying to cover ourselves, and was willing to sacrifice His Son to redeem us.

DETERMINED DISCIPLES

"If you abide in My word, you are My disciples indeed."

JOHN 8:31

A *disciple* in Jesus' time was someone who followed a teacher or philosopher. A disciple was both a learner and a follower—believing the teacher's message and then putting it into practice.

Jesus gave the word *disciple* added meaning, however, because His disciples also went out to tell others about Him. A disciple of Jesus, therefore, is someone who has committed his or her life to Jesus, and seeks each day to learn, to follow, and to share Him with others. Does this describe you?

No, the first disciples weren't perfect, and neither are we. Like them, we need to learn more and follow more, and share more. But all of us who belong to Christ are called to be disciples. Unlike the original disciples, we can't physically spend time with Jesus, but we can learn from Him by reading His Word. We can follow Him by obeying His will. And we can share Him with a world that desperately needs to be saved.

HOPE FOR TODAY

What have you done today to learn more about God? Are you following Him more today than yesterday? What are you doing to share Him with others? The answers will reveal your devotion to being a disciple.

AN ALTERED ATTITUDE

Return to the LORD your God,
For He is gracious and merciful.
JOEL 2:13

From time to time I have had people pour out their hearts to me because their sins had been discovered and they were in serious trouble. They wept bitterly because they had devastated their marriage or ruined their reputation.

But later someone would tell me they were back in the same situation. They had not learned from their experience, and seemed determined to bring even more chaos into their lives.

What was the problem? The problem was lack of repentance. Their tears were tears of self-pity—but not of repentance. True repentance is a turning from sin—a conscious, deliberate decision to leave sin behind—and a conscious turning to God, with a commitment to follow His will.

Repentance is only one part of our response to Christ (and even the strength to repent comes from God). But it is an essential part, for without it we cannot claim Christ is our Lord. The Bible says, "Godly sorrow brings repentance that leads to salvation and leaves no regret" (2 Corinthians 7:10 NIV).

HOPE FOR TODAY

Are you living in regret or repentance? To turn away from our sins is not enough; we must also turn to the Lord. Only He can create a new heart within us and give us the strength to live differently.

TRIUMPH THROUGH TRUST

Neither death nor life, . . . nor things present nor things to come, . . . shall be able to separate us from the love of God.

ROMANS 8:38–39

There are two ways to respond to adversity: discouragement or trust.

The problem with giving in to discouragement is that it only makes things worse, for with it may come bitterness, anger, jealousy, revenge, and so forth. We may even try to escape through drugs or alcohol. But do any of these solve the problem? No!

God has a better way—the way of trust. Sometimes He may show us that we were in the wrong. When that is the case, we need to confess it, repent, and seek His forgiveness. Sometimes, however, we can only accept what is happening and ask God to help us endure it and triumph over it.

One of the best ways to overcome adversity, I've found, is to praise God right in the middle of the turmoil. Turning to God's Word will also encourage us; many of the psalms, for example, were written in the midst of suffering and adversity. Follow the psalmist's example: "Bless the LORD, O my soul, and forget not all His benefits" (Psalm 103:2).

HOPE FOR TODAY

It's easy to praise after the fact when we receive the healing, the restored relationship, and the financial windfall. It is a true and mature faith that praises God in the midst of the trial and trusts Him even before the outcome is revealed.

AN UPSIDE-DOWN WORLD

God is not ashamed to be called their God.

HEBREWS 11:16

We live in an upside-down world. People hate when they should love, quarrel when they should be friendly, fight when they should be peaceful, wound when they should heal, steal when they should share, do wrong when they should do right.

I once saw a toy clown with a weight in its head. No matter how it was placed, it invariably assumed an upside-down position. It could be placed on its feet or on its side and when let go it flipped back on its head.

The clown illustrates why the disciples seemed to be misfits to the world. To an upside-down person, a right-side-up person seems upside down. To the nonbeliever, the true Christian is an oddity and an abnormality.

Yet this isn't the whole picture, for all around us are people who sense something is wrong with their topsy-turvy lives, and they yearn to be right side up. Will you pray for them and ask God to help you point them to life's only solid foundation—Jesus Christ?

HOPE FOR TODAY

We can never make a person right-side up any more than we can right ourselves. Only God can cause a person to see that he or she is, indeed, upside down, but we can point him or her in the right direction.

HOPE FROM GOD'S WORD

The grass withers, the flower fades,
But the word of our God stands forever.
ISAIAH 40:8

Amissionary in China who was imprisoned by the Japanese during World War II managed to take a forbidden Gospel of John with her into prison. She carefully hid it, and each night when she went to bed, she pulled the covers over her head and memorized one verse. She did this until the day she was freed.

When the prisoners were released, most of them shuffled out, but the missionary was so chipper someone said she must have been brainwashed. A *Life* magazine reporter who had interviewed her said, "She's been brainwashed for sure. God washed her brain."

I urge you not only to read God's Word but to memorize it. You may find it hard at first, but as you repeat a verse or a group of verses over and over to yourself, you will find they begin to take root in your soul. The psalmist declared, "Your word I have hidden in my heart, that I might not sin against You" (Psalm 119:11). Then when adversity or troubles arise, those verses will come back and give you hope.

Is God's Word stored up in your heart and mind for the future?

HOPE FOR TODAY
God's Word is alive and active and it is a powerful sword in times of battle. Spend time daily reading the Bible, meditating on it, and memorizing Scripture. It is through these times of training that we implant God's Word in our hearts. When the enemy strikes, it is too late to learn how to wield the sword.

LOVE AND MARRIAGE

He who loves his wife loves himself.
EPHESIANS 5:28

There are three elements to a successful marriage. The first is love—not just an emotional feeling or a physical attraction, but a deep commitment to put the other person first.

The apostle Paul defined love beautifully in 1 Corinthians 13. Read it and you will know how God defines love. Men are to love their wives as Christ loved the church. What woman wouldn't respond to such a selfless expression of love?

Maturity is the second ingredient in a successful marriage. Too many are getting a divorce at the first sign of trouble. Maturity means a willingness to act responsibly and not take the easy way out.

Third, faith must be an ingredient for a marriage to be successful. Marriage is difficult enough these days with all of life's pressures, but without Christ at the center of a marriage and a home, it becomes even more difficult. It takes three to make a great marriage: you, your spouse, and Christ. I have seldom seen a marriage fail when the husband and wife pray and worship God together.

HOPE FOR TODAY

A godly marriage is a powerful thing. Perhaps, you don't have an earthly example to follow. If that's the case, read and study how Christ loves the church and follow His example.

GOD WANTS OUR FELLOWSHIP

Come near to God and he will come near to you.

JAMES 4:8 NIV

What a blessed promise and provision this is! It means each of us can come close to God, with the assurance He will come close to us—so close that we become conscious of His presence. This is the greatest experience we can know.

But for most of us this isn't easy. Life presents us with too many distractions, and the last thing we have time for is to be alone with God. Children, work, television, the Internet, even church activities drain away our time.

Maybe you will have to readjust your priorities. Maybe you will have to say no to certain activities or demands. Whatever it takes, make time to be alone with God.

Remember: He wants your fellowship, and He has done everything possible to make it a reality. He has forgiven your sins, at the cost of His own dear Son. He has given you His Word, and the priceless privilege of prayer and worship.

He will come near to you, if you will come near to Him.

HOPE FOR TODAY

The God who created the universe desires your presence; take that in for a moment. He's always ready to speak to you. He is always glad that you came. Go to Him often and obey His every Word.

TEACHER AND GUIDE

"When He, the Spirit of truth, has come, He will guide you into all truth."
JOHN 16:13

The moment you receive Jesus Christ as Savior and Lord, the Holy Spirit takes up residence in your heart. Right now He lives within you! The Bible says, "If anyone does not have the Spirit of Christ, he is not His" (Romans 8:9).

The Holy Spirit helps us in life's struggles, and we must never forget that. But the Holy Spirit also plays two other important roles we must not overlook.

First, He convicts us of sin. The Bible says, "He will convict the world of sin, and of righteousness, and of judgment" (John 16:8). While this verse focuses on His convicting power among unbelievers, the Holy Spirit also convicts believers when we sin.

The second role of the Holy Spirit is as a teacher. The Bible says, "He will guide you into all truth." Just as surely as the Holy Spirit inspired the writers of the Bible, so He will instruct us as we meditate on God's Word.

Are you a willing student of the Holy Spirit?

HOPE FOR TODAY

As believers, we should rely on God's Holy Spirit. What an amazing teacher and trusted guide! Learn to listen and follow His guidance throughout the day.

MOVED WITH COMPASSION

You, O Lord, are a God full of compassion . . .
abundant in mercy and truth.

PSALM 86:15

The word *compassion* comes from two Latin words meaning "to suffer with." What better picture to describe God's compassion for us?

Suffering is the common lot of the human race. We see pictures on television of people ravaged by war or famine, and our hearts are touched (as they should be). But all around us are people who suffer in others ways: loneliness, fear, rejection, disability, grief, poverty, discrimination, addiction, or a multitude of other problems.

But God has compassion on us—He suffers with us. He knows what we are going through, and He cares. The greatest act of compassion in the history of the human race was the Cross, for there Christ suffered for us. He endured sin's penalty so we would not have to endure it ourselves.

Now Jesus calls us to have compassion on others, for His sake—to suffer with them, and to point them to the One who suffered for them. The Bible says, "Be sympathetic, love as brothers, be compassionate and humble" (1 Peter 3:8 NIV).

HOPE FOR TODAY

Give me a heart so moved with compassion, Lord, that I am unable to sit idly by. Show me how to love well, to serve selflessly, and to point others to the One who can meet their every need.

"COME HOME"

Our citizenship is in heaven, from which we also eagerly wait for the Savior.
PHILIPPIANS 3:20

Once there was a widow and her son who lived in a miserable attic. Years before, she had married against her parents' wishes and had gone with her husband to live in a foreign land.

He had proved irresponsible and unfaithful, and after a few years he died without having made any provision for her and the child. It was with the utmost difficulty that she managed to scrape together the bare necessities of life.

One day the postman knocked at the attic door. The mother recognized the handwriting on the letter he brought and with trembling fingers broke the seal. There was a check and a slip of paper with just two words: "Come home."

Someday a similar experience will be ours—an experience shared by all who know Christ. We do not know when the call will come. It may be when we are in the midst of our work. It may be after weeks or months of illness. But someday a loving hand will be laid upon our shoulder and this brief message will be given: "Come home."

HOPE FOR TODAY

Can you imagine more beautiful words, after a long journey through a foreign land, than the Father saying, "Come home"? It will happen for those who belong to Him.

IT WAS LOVE

"I have loved you with an everlasting love;
Therefore with lovingkindness I have drawn you."

JEREMIAH 31:3

Many people have difficulty believing God is a God of love. "How could He be," they ask, "when the world is filled with so much suffering and evil?" It is not an easy issue—but if you really want to know the reality of God's love, look at the Cross.

It was divine love that made Christ endure the Cross, despising the shame.

It was love that restrained Him when He was falsely accused of blasphemy and led to Golgotha to die with common thieves. He raised not a hand against His enemies. It was love that kept Him from calling legions of angels to come to His defense.

It was love that made Him, in a moment of agonizing pain, pause and give hope to a repentant sinner who cried, "Lord, remember me when You come into Your kingdom" (Luke 23:42).

It was love that caused Jesus to lift His voice and pray, "Father, forgive them, for they do not know what they do" (Luke 23:34). Does God love us? Yes—and the proof is the Cross.

HOPE FOR TODAY

God showed His love in a way that could never be questioned. Whatever comes our way, we can look to the Cross and know without a doubt that our heavenly Father loves us. The answer to "How do I know?" will always be the Cross.

A CLEAR CONSCIENCE

The blood of Christ . . . [will] cleanse our consciences.
HEBREWS 9:14 NIV

Each of us has a conscience that sits as a judge over our every thought, word, and deed. It can be sensitive, undeveloped, or distorted, depending upon the way we have used or abused it.

The human conscience is defiled by sin, says the Bible—and that is one reason it is not a reliable guide by itself. Our conscience needs to be cleansed by the purifying work of the Holy Spirit, and honed and sharpened by the truth of the Word of God. Satan can even twist our consciences if they are not yielded to Christ and convince us that wrong is really right.

But in spite of its frailty, our conscience is still important, and God still uses it to warn us of danger. All of us have experienced the backlash of guilt after a transgression.

Is God speaking to you about something that is not right in your life? Something you may be doing although you know it dishonors Christ? Don't ignore that voice or think it doesn't matter. Face your sin, confess it, put it right, and never touch it again.

HOPE FOR TODAY

Thank You, God, for the gift of a conscience that warns me when I'm straying into dangerous territory. May I always be obedient and allow the Holy Spirit to guide me according to Your will.

RESTING FAITH

The testing of your faith produces patience.

JAMES 1:3

Dwight L. Moody was fond of pointing out that there are three kinds of faith in Jesus Christ: struggling faith, which is like a man floundering and fearful in deep water; clinging faith, which is like a man hanging to the side of a boat; and resting faith, which finds a man safe inside the boat—strong and secure enough to reach out his hand to help someone else.

Notice that each man had faith. Each knew the boat was his only hope. But only one had a resting faith. Only one had discovered he could actually be in the boat—where all he had to do was rest.

This is the kind of faith God wants us to have—a faith that trusts Him totally. But sometimes we discover its reality only after we have endured a struggling or clinging faith. Sometimes we only realize we can get in the boat when the storm rages and we cry out to God with new faith. Then our Savior graciously extends His hand and says, "Come to Me . . . and I will give you rest" (Matthew 11:28).

HOPE FOR TODAY

Are you in the boat with a resting faith? Then look around you. Use what you know to be true of God to help strengthen someone else's faith. There's always room for more in the boat.

DOING GOD'S WILL

Doing the will of God from the heart.
EPHESIANS 6:6

We are admonished to seek out the will of the Lord. In Ephesians 5:17 we read, "Therefore do not be unwise, but understand what the will of the Lord is."

Some people, however, misunderstand the will of God. They think it must be a harsh, joyless thing, intended to make us miserable. But listen: God's will comes from God's love.

If you love someone, will you want to make him miserable? Will you go out of your way to punish him if he doesn't do exactly what you tell him to? No, of course not—not if you really love him.

The same is true with God. God loves you, and because He loves you, He cares about what happens to you. He loves you too much to let you wander aimlessly through life, without meaning or purpose. The Bible says, "You will show me the path of life; in Your presence is fullness of joy" (Psalm 16:11).

Covet God's will for your life more than anything else. To know God's will—and to do it—is life's greatest joy.

HOPE FOR TODAY
A Christian will never experience true contentment or peace outside of God's will. We experience the most joy not when we are living in material abundance but when we are living in obedience to the Lord.

ONE SURE GUIDE

Your word is a lamp to my feet
And a light to my path.
PSALM 119:105

As Christians, we have only one authority, one compass: the Word of God. In the midst of a thousand different voices, all claiming their own authority and clamoring for our allegiance, only one Voice will tell us the truth. That Voice? The written Word of God, given to us by God to tell us what we are to believe and how we are to live. As the psalmist said, "The entrance of Your words gives light" (Psalm 119:130).

In a letter to a friend, Abraham Lincoln said, "I am profitably engaged in reading the Bible. Take all of this Book upon reason that you can and the balance upon faith, and you will live and die a better man."

Coleridge said he believed the Bible to be the Word of God because, as he put it, "it finds me."

"If you want encouragement," John Bunyan wrote, "entertain the promises."

Martin Luther said, "In Scriptures, even the little daisy becomes a meadow."

The Bible is our one sure guide in an unsure world. Is it your guide?

HOPE FOR TODAY

What are you using to find your way? Some follow public opinion or what feels good in the moment. Jesus says, "Follow Me," and we have the Word of God to light the way.

THE ARK OF SALVATION

By faith Noah, . . . became an heir of the righteousness which comes by faith.
HEBREWS 11:7 RSV

God warned the people of Noah's day, "My Spirit shall not strive with man forever" (Genesis 6:3). They laughed at Noah, mocked his words, and went about their usual business and pleasures without ever dreaming he might be right. God was speaking—but they ignored Him. Eventually God's patience gave out—and by then it was too late.

Outside the ark men and women struggled for their lives, clutching at pieces of driftwood, until the pitiless hand of death reached up and drew them down beneath those cruel waves. All were lost. Every soul outside the ark perished. They had had their chance, but tossed it away.

You cannot come to Christ unless the Spirit of God brings you. But what if you ignore His warnings? Then you are in the gravest danger, for someday God will no longer be calling to you. Then it will be too late. Come to Christ while there is still time. Christ, God's greater Ark, stands ready to welcome you to safety today.

Are you in the Ark?

HOPE FOR TODAY

Can you imagine anything more heartbreaking than a man who never quite decides it's time to hear from God? It will be a reality for too many people. Pray fervently for the lost to heed His call.

GOD IS NEVER LATE

The LORD is your keeper;
The LORD is your shade at your right hand.
PSALM 121:5

In order for a tree or any plant to grow and bear fruit, its seed must first be planted in the ground and die. In order for spiritual fruit to appear in our lives, we must first be planted in the Word of God and then die to self. In the face of chastening, adversity, discipline, and affliction, God's Word nourishes our lives and fruit begins to appear. But it doesn't happen overnight. It takes time and patience.

Joseph would never have been of use to God had he not been sold into slavery by brothers who hated him, and then wrongly accused by Potiphar, who put him in prison. Even after he had told Pharaoh's cupbearer he would be restored to the king's court and asked him to tell Pharaoh of his unjust imprisonment, Joseph had to wait two more years for release from prison.

As we wait upon the Lord, He may sometimes seem slow in coming to help us, but He never comes too late. His timing is always perfect.

HOPE FOR TODAY
Are you in a season of waiting? Don't let it be a wasted season. Study God's Word so that your roots grow deep, and spend time in prayer so that you recognize His voice when it's time to move.

CITIZENS OF HEAVEN

"Because I live, you will live also."
JOHN 14:19

People spend billions of dollars every year on cosmetics, health spas, physical fitness machines, and concoctions claiming to make them live longer or slow down the aging process. But age will overtake even the most beautiful or physically fit people in the world, and eventually they will die—as will we.

But someday we who know Christ will have perfect bodies—bodies that will never age or experience pain. Someday our dead bodies will be "raised in glory" (1 Corinthians 15:43), and we will be like Christ in His resurrection body.

Can I imagine what that will be like? Not fully. But I do know this: the resurrected body of Jesus is the pattern or design for our new bodies. "For our citizenship is in heaven, from which we also eagerly wait for the Savior, the Lord Jesus Christ, who will transform our lowly body that it may be conformed to His glorious body" (Philippians 3:20–21).

What a future we have in Christ!

HOPE FOR TODAY
Won't it be wonderful to have a body that does not grow old or experience pain? In heaven, the beauty of this world will pale in comparison to the glory of heaven.

FINDING FULFILLMENT

"Let your soul delight itself in abundance."

ISAIAH 55:2

When Satan tried to trap Jesus at the beginning of His ministry, he used the same temptations he uses today.

One trap was the lure of things. Jesus had fasted for forty days, and Satan tried to take advantage of His hunger by urging Him to use His supernatural power to turn stones into bread. But Jesus replied, "Man shall not live by bread alone, but by every word that proceeds from the mouth of God" (Matthew 4:4). Not from Satan's mouth, but from God's!

Bread is important—but it isn't all-important, as Satan was suggesting. Pleasure and recreation have their place—but they mustn't have first place. Money is necessary, but money must serve us; we are not to serve it.

Isaiah said, "Listen carefully to Me . . . and let your soul delight itself in abundance" (Isaiah 55:2). Yes, delight in abundance—the abundance God gives you, both material and spiritual. Especially delight in the abundance of joy that comes from His presence. Satan will always offer you substitutes. Refuse them!

HOPE FOR TODAY

What substitutions have you been tempted to accept? Ask God to give you the wisdom to recognize a poor substitute or a quick fix and the self-control to wait for what is best.

THE HIGHEST CALLING

"Whoever of you does not forsake all that he has cannot be My disciple."
LUKE 14:33

When the Standard Oil Company was looking for a representative in the Far East, they approached a missionary and offered him $10,000. He turned down the offer. They raised it to $25,000, and he turned it down again. They raised it to $50,000, and he rejected it once more.

"What's wrong?" they asked.

He replied, "Your price is all right, but your job is too small." God had called him to be a missionary, and anything else was not worthy of his consideration.

What should we be for Jesus Christ? Most Christians are not called to be missionaries or preachers, but they are called to follow Christ. They are called to be faithful wherever He puts them—in the school, in the home, in the factory or office, in the neighborhood and nation. They are called to be controlled by the Spirit and to bear the fruit of the Spirit. They are called to be Christ's ambassadors wherever God puts them.

Nothing less than God's call is worthy of our consideration.

HOPE FOR TODAY

God's calling is noble whether He calls you to parenthood, a million-dollar company, or the mission field. The determining factor in a position's worth is not the monetary pay but whether or not it's within God's will. What's God's call on your life?

NOVEMBER

*And the L*ORD*, He is the One who goes before you. He will be with you, He will not leave you nor forsake you; do not fear nor be dismayed.*

DEUTERONOMY 31:8

PRAYER PARTNERS WITH GOD

The Spirit Himself makes intercession for us with
groanings which cannot be uttered.

ROMANS 8:26

Have you ever faced a situation that was so overwhelming or so confusing you didn't even know how to pray about it? Have you ever been so overcome with grief or burdened by heartache you couldn't put your emotions into words—much less pray about them?

What a comfort these words should be: "The Spirit helps us in our weakness. We do not know what we ought to pray for, but the Spirit himself intercedes for us . . . in accordance with God's will" (Romans 8:26–27 NIV).

Think of it: even when we don't know how to pray, the Spirit knows our needs, and He brings the deepest cries of our hearts before the throne of God. In ways we will never understand this side of eternity, God the Holy Spirit pleads for us before God the Father.

Turn to God in every situation—even when you don't feel like it. The Spirit is interceding for you, in accordance with God's will.

HOPE FOR TODAY

Have you ever gone through a trial and felt an unexplainable peace that you were certain meant that someone was praying? How amazing to think that someone may just be the Holy Spirit Himself!

TRUE HAPPINESS

Happy is the man who has the God of Jacob as his helper.
PSALM 146:5 TLB

Sometimes I almost wish Thomas Jefferson had not inserted those words in the American Declaration of Independence about "the pursuit of happiness."

He was correct, of course; God has given us the "right" (or at least the freedom) to pursue happiness. The problem is that millions think this must be the primary purpose of life, and they spend their lives frantically pursuing it. In the end, however, their search ends in disillusionment.

Happiness is a by-product of something greater, not an end in itself. Happiness cannot be pursued and caught, any more than one can pursue a sunny day, put it in a bottle, and then bring it out on a rainy day to enjoy again.

True happiness comes from a different pursuit—the pursuit of God. He has promised, "You will seek Me and find Me, when you search for Me with all your heart" (Jeremiah 29:13). That promise is true—because God also pursues us. He even sent His Son into the world to pursue us and bring us to Heaven.

Only God gives true happiness.

HOPE FOR TODAY

It's not unreasonable to desire happiness; it's just that we're often mistaken in how to achieve it. The person who longs to be happy is, in reality, a person desperate for God Himself.

FAMILIES OF FAITH

Through wisdom a house is built,
And by understanding it is established.
PROVERBS 24:3

The family is the most important institution in the world. It was God's idea in the first place. It was not the invention of sociologists or economists or government bureaucrats who decided it would make society operate more smoothly. Families existed before cities and governments, before written languages, nations, temples, and churches.

In the home, character and integrity are formed, values are made clear, and goals are set. These last a lifetime. And if they aren't formed correctly, that, too, will result in patterns—bad patterns—that last a lifetime, if God doesn't intervene.

Today, Satan is attacking the family as never before. But what are our defenses against such attacks?

As always, our best defense is the Word of God. Read the Bible together as a family. Have family devotions. Pray for one another daily by name. Be on guard against the forces that tend to pull families apart today. And most of all, commit your marriage to Christ, and make Him the center of your home—and your life.

HOPE FOR TODAY

With every new invention and technological advancement, time and attention are being taken away from the family. This lack of togetherness weakens the foundation and faith of the family unit. What is the state of your family?

THE UNCERTAINTY OF LIFE

Teach us to number our days,
That we may gain a heart of wisdom.
PSALM 90:12

We are not the masters of our fate. We think we control our lives—but we don't. In an instant life can radically change—a car accident, a heart attack, a child's raging fever. Frustrated researchers conquer one deadly virus, only to discover one even more lethal.

The psalmist pointed out our basic dilemma: "The length of our days is seventy years—or eighty, if we have the strength; yet their span is but trouble and sorrow, for they quickly pass, and we fly away" (Psalm 90:10 NIV). Even if we live to a ripe old age, he said, we seldom know peace.

No book is more realistic about the human situation than the Bible. It won't let us get by with frothy platitudes or unsupported optimism. But it also gives us hope. It tells us that Christ can change our lives, and that He has prepared a perfect place for us in Heaven.

Even your next breath is a gift from God. Don't take life for granted, but "gain a heart of wisdom."

HOPE FOR TODAY

Many people look back with regret and remorse at the years that slipped away from them. The psalmist said that it's a wise person who understands that time is fleeting and expresses gratitude for every breath.

SATISFYING THE SOUL

Direct me in the path of your commands,
for there I find delight.
PSALM 119:35 NIV

The Bible teaches that a person is more than just a body—each of us is actually a living soul! Our souls are created in the image of God. God Himself has implanted His own nature within us!

Just as our bodies have certain characteristics and appetites, so do our souls. The characteristics of the soul include intelligence, emotions, and will. The human soul or spirit longs for peace, contentment, and happiness. Most of all, the soul has an appetite for God—a yearning to be reconciled to its Creator and to have fellowship with Him forever.

In our world, we give most of our attention to satisfying the appetites of the body and practically none to the soul. Consequently we are one-sided. We become fat physically and materially, while spiritually we are lean, weak, and anemic.

The soul actually demands as much attention as the body. It demands fellowship and communion with God. It demands worship, quietness, and meditation. Nothing but God ever completely satisfies, because the soul was made for God. Don't starve your soul.

HOPE FOR TODAY

When was the last time you intentionally denied yourself food, drink, or rest? Be sure to tend to your soul's needs just as attentively.

THE WEAPONS OF FAITH

This is the victory that overcomes the world, our faith.

1 JOHN 5:4 RSV

One of Satan's sly devices is to divert our minds from the help God offers us in our struggles against evil, telling us we have to fight the battle alone. But God knows we need His help.

The Bible warns, "Be sober, be vigilant; because your adversary the devil walks about like a roaring lion, seeking whom he may devour" (1 Peter 5:8). What would you do if you met a lion? You'd probably run, and you'd probably grab any weapon you could to fend it off if it attacked.

And that is true in our struggles against evil. When evil and temptation stalk us, our first response should be to flee. And when they still attack, we should use every weapon we have to drive them away. The good news is this: God has provided the weapons! His Word, His angels, His Spirit, the encouragement and prayers of our brothers and sisters in Christ—these and more are "weapons" God provides.

We aren't in this battle alone—so why act like it?

HOPE FOR TODAY

Jesus spent time with His Father frequently during His earthly ministry. This dedication to prayer gave Him the strength He would need to endure temptation, betrayal, and physical suffering. Believers would be wise to follow His example.

WHAT IS JOY?

The joy of the LORD is your strength.
NEHEMIAH 8:10

Some people think Christians should always be smiling and happy, and something is wrong if they aren't.

But this isn't necessarily true. Jesus stood outside the tomb of His friend Lazarus, and we read that "Jesus wept" (John 11:35). As He approached Jerusalem "He saw the city and wept" (Luke 19:41) because of its spiritual blindness and guilt. He knelt in the Garden of Gethsemane and was "in agony . . . [and] His sweat became like great drops of blood" (Luke 22:44).

Don't confuse happiness with joy. Happiness comes with happy circumstances; joy wells up deep inside our souls as we learn to trust Christ. Joy does not mean that we are never sad or that we never cry. Joy is a quiet confidence, a state of inner peace that comes from God.

Life's troubles may rob us of our happiness, but they can never rob us of the joy God gives us as we turn in faith to Him and seek His face.

HOPE FOR TODAY

The world doesn't need believers to put on our "happy faces" to prove our faith is real. True joy radiates from within and makes its presence known regardless of circumstances. Let's be more concerned with authenticity than appearances.

BOUNDLESS BLESSINGS

He gathers the lambs in his arms
and carries them close to his heart.
ISAIAH 40:11 NIV

The Old Testament gives a wonderful picture of God as our Shepherd. One psalm begins, "Hear us, O Shepherd of Israel, you who lead Joseph like a flock" (Psalm 80:1 NIV). The almighty Creator of the universe stoops to be the Shepherd of His people!

A shepherd protects his sheep, feeds them, and pursues them when they stray. At evening he brings them into the fold, secure against every enemy. Without the shepherd, the sheep would scatter and wander into danger.

In the best-known of all the psalms, David makes the relationship personal. "The LORD is my shepherd," he cries exultantly, "I shall lack nothing." He then tells of God's constant care, until that day when "I will dwell in the house of the LORD forever" (Psalm 23:6 NIV).

But the New Testament tells of another Shepherd—the Lord Jesus Christ: "I am the good shepherd. The good shepherd gives His life for the sheep" (John 10:11). He guides and protects us, and even gave His life so we will be safely in His fold forever.

HOPE FOR TODAY

The relationship between a shepherd and his sheep is special. The shepherd keeps watch in the night, protecting his sheep, and knows which ones are his. Our Shepherd is just as protective and caring of His sheep.

BANISHING WORRY

The LORD is near to all who call upon Him,
To all who call upon Him in truth.
PSALM 145:18

Think of the things you do not worry about. Perhaps you never worry about whether you will be able to get water out of the faucet in your kitchen, or maybe you do not worry about a tree falling on your house. You may be a worrier by nature, but even the worst worrier in the world doesn't worry about some things!

Now ask yourself why you do not worry about such things. Is it because, in the case of running water, it has always been there when you wanted it? Or that a tree has never fallen on your house before? Certainty breeds trust, doesn't it? (You may even live in a place where there are no tall trees.)

We can be just as certain and just as worry-free about God's love and protection. What is the evidence? It is the Cross, where God fully expressed His love for us. The Bible says, "He who did not spare his own Son, but gave him up for us all—how will he not also, along with him, graciously give us all things?" (Romans 8:32 NIV). God's love is certain. He has never gone back on a single promise, and He never will.

HOPE FOR TODAY

God has never gone back on a single promise—ever. He gave His own Son to die in our place. What more could He possibly do?

CREATED IN HIS IMAGE

If anyone is in Christ, he is a new creation.

2 CORINTHIANS 5:17

Is it not logical to believe that the only One who can re-create us is the One who created us in the first place? If your watch were out of order, you wouldn't take it to an electrician. If your car needed overhauling, you wouldn't take it to a plumber. If you needed an operation, you wouldn't go to a machine shop.

Our spiritual problems can only be solved by the God who originally created us. He created us in His own image and likeness, and He knows all about us.

Today by the grace of His Son, God can re-create us in the likeness of Jesus' resurrection. Through faith in Jesus Christ, we are re-created and become partakers of His life. Just as we were born again by the Spirit of God, so we grow and become more like Christ as the Spirit works in our lives.

"Therefore, if anyone is in Christ, he is a new creation; old things have passed away; behold, all things have become new" (2 Corinthians 5:17). Don't be chained to the past. You are a new creation in Christ!

HOPE FOR TODAY

In Christ, you get to live in freedom. You are no longer chained to the mistakes and regrets of your past. The bitterness, anger, and pain that belonged to the old you are gone. You're brand-new.

A Home in Heaven

You yourselves had [in heaven] a better and lasting possession.

Hebrews 10:34 AMP

Paul once wrote, "If only for this life we have hope in Christ, we are to be pitied more than all men" (1 Corinthians 15:19 NIV). If there is no life after death, no Heaven, no promise of a better world—then life is empty, hopeless, without meaning or purpose.

But this life is not all! Ahead is Heaven, and someday "we shall always be with the Lord" (1 Thessalonians 4:17). Someday we will go to a home where all is happiness, joy, and peace. How barren our lives would be if we didn't have this hope.

Knowing Heaven is real will make a difference in the way we live. For one thing, we won't become attached to the things of this world. We will say with Paul, "I have learned in whatever state I am, to be content" (Philippians 4:11).

But Heaven should also give us a burden for those who do not have this hope. Every day you meet people who do not know Christ. Will you tell them?

Hope for Today

Each day we live with the reality of a heavenly home that awaits us. Problems and pleasures both pale in comparison. The secret to contentment in this life is that there is a greater life to come.

A UNITED FAMILY

All your children shall be taught by the LORD,
And great shall be the peace of your children.

ISAIAH 54:13

The family is the basic unit of society. But from the very beginning, since man sinned against God, the family has been in trouble. The first crime we read about in the Bible occurred when Cain killed his brother, Abel. Instead of love, family life all too often became marked by conflict and tension.

For best results in marriage and in building a stable home, follow the instructions of the One who performed the first wedding in the garden of Eden. Those instructions are in the Bible. The reason the family is in critical condition today is that we have neglected God's rules for a successful home. We have put self in place of sacrifice. We have valued things more than we have valued people.

You can have the right kind of home. Your home can be united if it is now divided. The place to begin is on your knees, asking Christ for forgiveness and then asking God to give you a new love for each other—and for Him. Don't let your family drift apart, but with God's help resist the pressure and come together around the Cross.

HOPE FOR TODAY

The greatest commandments apply to the family as a whole just as they do to an individual believer. Love the Lord with all your might and your neighbor (spouse/child) as yourself. Families could be healed if we went back to the basics.

Cling and Hope

The Lord will be a shelter for His people.
Joel 3:16

The late British historian Arnold Toynbee shared his personal slogan with the world when he said, "Cling, and hope." With all the ideals we held a few years ago crumbling, he advised the human race to cling and hope.

But cling to what? Millions cling to the wreckage they have made of their lives, thinking they have nowhere else to turn. Others cling to false ideologies or deceptive cults. Still others cling to possessions, or relationships, or pleasures. Yes, cling, and hope—but what if you are clinging to something that is sinking?

However, thousands of people still find refuge from the storms of life by their living faith in a living God!

To turn to God in an hour such as this in the history of the world is not escapism. Multiplied thousands have found that faith in Christ is more than adequate for the pressures of this hour.

The true Christian does more than cling and hope. He knows that, with Christ, he is secure forever. Is your hope in Him?

Hope for Today

Hope in the Lord is not wishful thinking but confident expectation. We cling to what was accomplished on the Cross, and we place our hope in the One who has never let us down.

GOD IN HUMAN FORM

[Christ] has gone into heaven and is at the right hand of God.

1 PETER 3:22

What proofs did Jesus offer that He was truly God come in human form? First, there was the proof of His perfect life. He could ask, "Which of you convicts Me of sin?" (John 8:46)—and no one could answer.

Second, there was the evidence of His miraculous power. His power was the power of God Almighty.

Third, there was the evidence of fulfilled prophecy. Hundreds of years before His birth the prophets of the Old Testament spoke precisely of His death and resurrection.

Fourth, there was the evidence of His resurrection from the dead.

Fifth, there is the proof of changed lives. Christ alone, the divine Son of God, has power to change the human heart. And He does.

Faith in Christ is not a leap in the dark. It is based on the solid facts of Christ's life, death, and resurrection. Thank God we have a solid foundation in Him!

HOPE FOR TODAY

Jesus didn't attempt to disguise His identity. Those who believe He never claimed to be God are not familiar with Scripture because that is the very reason they crucified Him! Believers know whom they have believed.

"EVEN SO, COME!"

"Behold, I am coming quickly!"
REVELATION 22:7

What would you say about a person who had made a hundred promises to you and already kept ninety-nine of them? You probably would think he or she was honest enough to fulfill the last promise as well, wouldn't you?

Jesus Christ has fulfilled every promise He ever made, except one. He has not yet returned. Will He?

In both the Old and New Testaments there are references to the return of the Lord. Isaiah, for example, looked forward to the day when the Messiah's kingdom would be a reality: "Behold, I create new heavens and a new earth; and the former shall not be remembered or come to mind" (Isaiah 65:17).

John quoted Christ as saying, "I go to prepare a place for you. And . . . I will come again and receive you to Myself" (John 14:2–3). The entire book of Revelation tells of the glorious return of Christ. And we can say with the apostle John, who wrote that book, "Amen. Even so, come, Lord Jesus!" (Revelation 22:20).

Are you looking forward to His return? And are you seeking until that day to be His faithful servant?

HOPE FOR TODAY

Jesus is coming back and could arrive at any moment. It's not as if He may, possibly, perhaps return. He is on His way—somewhere between there and here. Are you prepared for His arrival?

DEALING WITH ETERNITY

I will see Your face in righteousness;
I shall be satisfied when I awake in your likeness.

PSALM 17:15

When English patriot Sir William Russell went to the scaffold in 1683, he took his watch out of his pocket and handed it to the physician who attended him in his death. "Would you kindly take my timepiece?" he asked. "I have no use for it. I am now dealing with eternity."

This world fades into insignificance in the light of eternity. All the things that preoccupy us are no longer important, and only one thing counts: our relationship with God.

But we should live every day in light of eternity! As Peter wrote in his last letter, "Since all these things will be dissolved, what manner of persons ought you to be in holy conduct and godliness? . . . Be diligent to be found by Him in peace, without spot and blameless" (2 Peter 3:11, 14).

How different would today be if you knew it would be your last one on earth before meeting God face-to-face? We should strive to live every day as if it were our last, for one day it will be!

HOPE FOR TODAY

Look at the people around you. Do you know where they stand with God? If today were your last chance to tell them of Christ, would you enter eternity knowing you fulfilled your duty to share the gospel?

WE WILL SEE HIM

Our days on earth are as a shadow.

1 CHRONICLES 29:15

C. S. Lewis once observed that this life is only "shadow lands" compared with the glory to come. Even life at its best is but a shadow of Heaven.

Does that mean we turn our backs on this world and have nothing to do with its delights? Not necessarily. Sometimes (as Lewis was suggesting) the good things God gives us are a foreshadowing, a hint of what is to come. We experience the joy of marriage, knowing it is the foretaste of an even greater joy: the heavenly marriage feast of the Lamb (Revelation 19:9). We enjoy the beauty of God's creation, knowing it is the foretaste of an even greater beauty: the glory of Heaven (Revelation 21:23).

Take delight in the good things God gives you. Don't be too preoccupied to "smell the roses"! The Bible reminds us, "Every good gift and every perfect gift is from above, and comes down from the Father of lights" (James 1:17). And every one of His good gifts should remind us of the glory to come!

HOPE FOR TODAY

God placed us in this world, and though it is a broken version of His original creation, there are still gifts to be found in it. Look for glimpses of the Creator, and anticipate the moment when we see Him as He is.

SWEET SLUMBER

I will both lie down in peace, and sleep;
For You alone, O LORD, make me dwell in safety.
PSALM 4:8

By any measure drug and alcohol dependence has become one of our greatest social problems. The issue isn't just illegal drugs; many people depend on alcohol or over-the-counter or prescription drugs just to face each day or to get to sleep at night.

I'm not a doctor, of course, and I fully realize that some drugs have a legitimate place under careful medical supervision. But in my experience far too many people turn first to drugs or alcohol instead of to God. Rather than face their problems and deal with them (with God's help), they use drugs or alcohol to escape.

But such "solutions" never work and in fact only make things worse. No wonder the book of Proverbs warns that alcohol "at the last . . . bites like a serpent, and stings like a viper" (Proverbs 23:32).

Don't let anything substitute for God. He loves you, and He wants to give you peace—the peace that comes from knowing Him. Jesus' promise to His followers is true: "I will give you rest" (Matthew 11:28).

HOPE FOR TODAY
No place, product, or person can bring us the peace and safety our souls desire. Only Jesus can satisfy our deepest longings.

SUNSHINE AND SHADOW

If you should suffer for righteousness' sake, you are blessed.
1 PETER 3:14

All the masterpieces of painting contain both light and shadow. By them the artist highlights certain features of his subject, and they provide contrast and harmony to reveal beauty or character.

A happy life is not one filled only with sunshine, but one that uses both light and shadow to produce beauty. Suffering or persecution can become a blessing because they can form a dark backdrop for the radiance of the Christian life. The greatest musicians as a rule are those who know how to bring song out of sadness. Fanny Crosby, her spirit aglow with faith in Christ, saw more with her sightless eyes than most of us do with normal vision. She gave us some of the great gospel songs that cheer our hearts and lives.

Paul and Silas sang a song of praise at midnight in a rat-infested jail in Philippi, their feet in stocks, their backs raw from the jailer's whip. But their patience in suffering and persecution led to the conversion of the heathen prison warden and his family.

Don't despise the shadows God brings into your life. He can use them to produce a masterpiece.

HOPE FOR TODAY

Kintsugi is the Japanese art of mending broken pottery by filling in the cracks with gold or silver. The mended piece is often more beautiful than the original. God takes our brokenness and makes something beautiful.

ABIDING PEACE

Fear not, for I am with you;
Be not dismayed, for I am your God."
ISAIAH 41:10

Whenever I think of God's faithfulness in the midst of suffering, I am reminded of my dear late friend Corrie ten Boom, the remarkable Dutch woman who (with her family) hid Jews from the Nazis. After being imprisoned in Ravensbruk, the infamous concentration camp, Corrie traveled the world telling her story of suffering, forgiveness, and joy.

For thirty-five years she never had a permanent home, but when she was eighty-five and in declining health, some friends provided her with a lovely house in California. It was a luxury she never dreamed she would have (and one she never would have pursued on her own).

One day her friend, the late movie director James Collier, was visiting. He said, "Corrie, hasn't God been good to give you this beautiful house?"

She replied firmly, "Jimmy, God was good when I was in Ravensbruk too!"

Most of us will never experience the horrors Corrie knew. But no matter what we face, we can depend on God's promise: "Fear not; for I am with you."

HOPE FOR TODAY

Satan wants us to judge God's faithfulness based on our circumstances. But Scripture is clear that God was with Joseph in the pit, in the prison cell, and in the palace. God is good all the time.

THANKFUL IN PRAYER

Devote yourselves to prayer, being watchful and thankful.
COLOSSIANS 4:2 NIV

Prayer isn't just asking God for something we want. Prayer should also include confession of our sin and praise to God for who He is and what He has done for us.

But prayer should have an additional element, and that is thanksgiving. Repeatedly the Bible commands us to give thanks. The psalmist said, "Oh, give thanks to the LORD, for He is good! For His mercy endures forever" (Psalm 107:1). Jesus only distributed the bread He had miraculously provided for the crowds after "he had given thanks" (Matthew 15:36 NIV). At the Last Supper with His disciples, before facing the horror of the Cross, Jesus "gave thanks" (Luke 22:17, 19).

It's easy to be thankful when God blesses us with something good—a swift recovery from an illness, for example, or an advancement at work. But the Bible says we should "give thanks in *all* circumstances, for this is God's will for [us] in Christ Jesus" (1 Thessalonians 5:18 NIV, italics mine).

Thankfulness drives away a sour or prideful spirit. Make it part of your prayers every day.

HOPE FOR TODAY

Thank You, Lord, for the many ways You watch over and guide me. Give me a heart that is quick to give thanks for the many blessings You bestow. Thank You most of all for the Cross that served to set me free.

THE GRACE OF GRATITUDE

It is good to give thanks to the LORD.

PSALM 92:1

The Pilgrim Fathers who landed at Plymouth in America in 1620 knew nothing of the bountiful prosperity that so many people enjoy today. During that first long winter, seven times as many graves were made for the dead as homes were built for the living. Seed, imported from England, failed to grow, and a ship that was to bring food and relief brought thirty-five more mouths to feed, but not an ounce of provisions. They caught fish, hunted wild fowl and venison. They had a little English meal and some Indian corn.

Yet their lives were marked by a spirit of constant thankfulness. On one occasion William Brewster, rising from a scanty Plymouth dinner of clams and water, gave thanks to God "for the abundance of the sea and the treasures hid in the sand."

According to today's standards, they had little; but they possessed a sense of great gratitude. Gratitude is one of the greatest Christian graces; ingratitude, one of the most vicious sins. Ask God to open your eyes to all the blessings He has bestowed on you, and to give you a fresh spirit of gratitude—not just at this season of the year, but always.

HOPE FOR TODAY

An ungrateful heart minimizes God's blessings and focuses on what is not provided. The grace of gratitude is that we no longer see what is lacking and, instead, are in awe that we've been given so much.

God's Holiness

Holy, holy, holy is the LORD of hosts;
The whole earth is full of His glory!
ISAIAH 6:3

The Bible teaches that God is absolutely holy and pure. From Genesis to Revelation, God reveals Himself as so holy He cannot even look on sin.

Christ cried from the Cross, "My God, My God, why have You forsaken Me?" (Mark 15:34). What a horrible moment, as the blackness of human sin—now laid upon Christ—caused the Father to turn away in disgust. In that moment Jesus endured the ultimate punishment for our sins—the punishment of being banished from the presence of His Father on our behalf.

If you were asked to list the things you are thankful for, what would you include? Perhaps your family, health, friends, church—and those wouldn't be wrong. We should be grateful for every gift God gives us.

But the greatest gift of all is God's gift of His Son, who endured the penalty we deserved for our sin so we could be reconciled to a holy God. Never take that gift for granted! "Thanks be to God for His indescribable gift!" (2 Corinthians 9:15).

HOPE FOR TODAY

Prior to His death on the Cross, Jesus never knew a single moment without the Father's presence. The most painful thing Jesus endured was sin's penalty of separation from the Father so that we would never have to experience it.

TRUE THANKSGIVING

Oh, give thanks to the LORD, for He is good!

PSALM 107:1

Separated from friends, unjustly accused, brutally treated—if any man had a right to complain it was this man, languishing almost forgotten in a harsh Roman prison. But instead of complaints, his lips rang with words of praise and thanksgiving!

This was the apostle Paul—a man who had learned the meaning of true thanksgiving, even in the midst of great adversity. Look carefully at what he wrote during that prison experience: "Sing and make music in your heart to the Lord, always giving thanks to God the Father for everything, in the name of our Lord Jesus Christ" (Ephesians 5:19–20 NIV).

Think of it! "Always giving thanks . . . for everything" no matter the circumstances. Paul's guards and fellow prisoners must have thought him crazy—but that didn't stop him. Thanksgiving for Paul was not a once-a-year celebration, but a daily reality that made him a joyful person in every situation. May that be true of us.

HOPE FOR TODAY

Because of what Christ has done, we, too, can sing songs of praise at midnight (Acts 16:25). No matter how dark the season or how painful the trial, God is still good and worthy of praise.

GOD'S LOVE

In this the love of God was made manifest . . . that
God sent his only Son into the world.

1 JOHN 4:9 RSV

From Genesis to Revelation, from earth's greatest tragedy to earth's greatest triumph, the dramatic story of humanity's lowest depths and God's highest heights can be couched in twenty-five beautiful words: "For God so loved the world that He gave His only begotten Son, that whoever believes in Him should not perish but have everlasting life" (John 3:16).

Many people misunderstand God's attribute of love. "God is love" does not mean that everything is sweet, beautiful, and happy, or that God's love could not possibly allow punishment for sin.

God's holiness demands that all sin be punished, but God's love provided a plan of redemption and salvation for a lost and sinful world. By that plan Jesus Christ came from Heaven to give His life as the final and perfect sacrifice for sin.

But we must respond. We must believe. We must commit our lives to Jesus Christ and trust Him as our Savior and Lord. Have you put your faith in Him? If so, everlasting life is yours!

HOPE FOR TODAY

God loves you so much that He sent His Son to save you. If you were the only person on earth, God would have still sent His Son to die so that you could be made right with Him. Will you respond to His call to eternal salvation by faith in Him?

WISDOM FROM ABOVE

The wisdom that is from above is first pure, then peaceable.

JAMES 3:17

Today there is more knowledge in the world than ever before. Computers or fiber optic cables can transmit information in a millisecond to any part of the globe. More facts have been discovered in the last one hundred years than all of the other centuries of human history combined. Yet that same time period also recorded the most devastating wars and the fiercest genocides in human history. We have never been further from solving our basic problems.

The Bible says there are two kinds of wisdom in the world. First, there is wisdom that is given by God, a wisdom that views life in terms of eternity. Of this wisdom, the Scripture says, "The wisdom that is from above is first pure, then peaceable, gentle, willing to yield, full of mercy and good fruits, without partiality and without hypocrisy" (James 3:17).

The second is the "wisdom of the world." This wisdom excludes God and His moral standards from human decisions, and seeks to solve society's problems apart from Him. But where has it gotten us? Which kind of wisdom will you choose?

HOPE FOR TODAY

There are people who show great wisdom who don't have a college degree; the opposite is also true. True wisdom comes from God. Let's be certain that we are making decisions based on the right kind of wisdom.

Traveling to Heaven

The Lord will . . . preserve me for His heavenly kingdom.
2 Timothy 4:18

Preparing for Heaven is much like going on a journey. First, you must decide you want to go there. Next, you must purchase your ticket.

But wait! How will you purchase it? Can you buy it by being a good person? Or going to church or acting religious? Or giving money or volunteering your time to help others? The Bible says none of these will suffice, because the ticket to Heaven is expensive—far too expensive for any human being to afford.

Does that mean we can never go there? No—and the reason is because Someone else has already purchased the ticket for us. That person was Jesus Christ, and the price He paid was His own blood, shed on the Cross for us.

Now He offers us the ticket to Heaven free and fully paid! Why refuse it? Why try some other way? Jesus' invitation is still open: "Come! Whoever is thirsty, let him come; and whoever wishes, let him take the free gift of the water of life" (Revelation 22:17 NIV).

Hope for Today
Steadfast love, forgiveness of sin, entry into Heaven, and an eternity with God—Jesus offers it all to every person. All we have to do is humble ourselves and come.

GIVING TO GOD

Honor the LORD with your possessions,
And with the firstfruits of all your increase.

PROVERBS 3:9

God doesn't need our money to get His work done. He is sovereign and can do it without our help. Yet He has arranged it so that His work often depends on our generosity.

At least two things happen when we give. First, when we give with the right attitude, God reminds us that what we have isn't really ours. He gave us everything we have, and it actually belongs to Him. King David prayed, "All things come from You, and of Your own we have given You" (1 Chronicles 29:14). We need to learn that truth.

Second, when we give, we help meet the needs of others whom God also loves. By giving to others we testify to God's love for them, and we point them to the greatest gift of all—God's gift of His Son for our salvation.

Someone has said that our lives should resemble channels, not reservoirs. A reservoir stores water; a channel distributes it. God wants us to be channels of blessing to others. Are you?

HOPE FOR TODAY

The truth is that God could do His work with more efficiency and less drama all on His own. It's pure grace that He offers us the opportunity to partner with Him in growing His kingdom.

A Heavenly Address

"I am going there to prepare a place for you."

John 14:2 NIV

I live in a place high on a mountain in a log cabin in North Carolina. I may travel all over the world, but I know that when I come home, I will return to a precise location. It will still be there at the end of my journey, and I always look forward to coming home!

In saying that He was going to prepare a place for us, Jesus was telling us that when we die, we are going to a precise location. We do not evaporate or disappear. In fact, He said, "In My Father's house are many mansions" (John 14:2). We are going to have a place in Heaven if we have trusted Christ as our Savior—and not only a place, but a mansion!

When we as Christians die, we go straight into the presence of Christ—straight to that place, straight to that mansion in Heaven to spend eternity with God. We are simply changing our address!

Hope for Today

Have you ever shown up early or unexpected to someone's house? It's awkward, right? On the other hand, when someone greets you at the door and has the guest room ready, it feels remarkable. When you arrive in Heaven, all the heavenly host will be expecting you.

GOD'S TRUTH

You are my hiding place . . . ;
I hope in Your word.
PSALM 119:114

God's Word never changes. Jesus said, "I tell you the truth, until heaven and earth disappear, not the smallest letter, not the least stroke of a pen, will by any means disappear from the Law" (Matthew 5:18 NIV). Jesus also declared, "Heaven and earth will pass away, but My words will by no means pass away" (Matthew 24:35).

This isn't because God is an inflexible or insensitive tyrant. It is because He knows what is best for us. He knows how we function, and He knows the pitfalls and dangers we face. If He didn't love us, He wouldn't try to guide us in the right path. But He does!

Only God's Word can help us avoid moral and spiritual danger, and lead us in the right way. The psalmist testified, "Your word is a lamp to my feet and a light to my path. . . . The entrance of Your words gives light" (Psalm 119:105, 130).

Let God's Word shape and guide you. God loves you too much to leave you in the dark!

HOPE FOR TODAY

There is security in knowing that God's Word never changes. What is true today will be true a thousand years from now. There is no surprise ending.

December

*Trust in the L*ORD *with all your heart,*
And lean not on your own understanding;
In all your ways acknowledge Him,
And He shall direct your paths.

PROVERBS 3:5–6

INFINITE GRACE

Grace and truth came through Jesus Christ.
JOHN 1:17

The word *grace* means more than just God's kindness or gentleness toward us, or even His mercy. It means His undeserved favor. It means God owes nothing to us, and we deserve nothing from Him. When the Bible says, "By grace you have been saved" (Ephesians 2:5), it means our salvation was totally unmerited. It came solely because of God's grace.

The motive of grace is the infinite, compassionate love of a merciful God, but the work of grace was Christ's death on the Cross. When I imagine Christ hanging from the Cross, the spikes in His hands, the crown of thorns on His brow, His blood draining from His body, the soldiers mocking Him—then I begin to see the depth of God's grace. Then I know that nothing can equal the infinite love of God for a sinful world.

But God's grace is also exhibited when we humbly bow before Christ in repentance and faith, for then we find forgiveness. Thank God for His grace, for without it we would have no hope!

HOPE FOR TODAY

Many good people will end up in hell because good will never be good enough. Would Christ have come to die if being good could get a person by? God gave us more than we could hope to deserve when He gave His Son.

SIN'S DEADLY HERITAGE

The creation itself will be liberated from its bondage to decay.

ROMANS 8:21 NIV

Recently some computers in our office were attacked by a major computer virus. Thinking they were opening a legitimate e-mail, the staff suddenly found their computers running amuck, unable to function as they were designed to do. Only a major reprogramming of their corrupted hard drives, I was told, restored them to usefulness.

I couldn't help but compare this to another virus—the "virus" of sin. God created our first parents perfect and without sin, their every need met and their relationship with God unblemished. But then they rebelled against God, sin entered the world—and since that day, the human heart has been infected with the deadly "virus" of sin. Our fellowship with God was destroyed, we became morally weak and corrupt, and even all creation was affected.

But Christ came to conquer the "virus" of sin! When He enters our lives, He begins to remake us from within. The "virus" no longer has absolute control. And someday God will remove the "virus" of sin forever, and all creation will be renewed.

HOPE FOR TODAY

Deep down inside we know: this world is not as it should be, and neither are we. There's a constant struggle between the desires of our flesh and the longings of our souls. One day, all will be restored.

FROM TIME TO ETERNITY

We give thanks to God . . . because of the hope which is laid up for you in heaven.
COLOSSIANS 1:3, 5

Once I stood in London to watch Queen Elizabeth return from an overseas trip. I saw the parade of dignitaries, the marching bands, the crack troops, the waving flags. I saw all the splendor that accompanies the homecoming of a queen.

However, that was nothing compared to the homecoming of a true believer. At that moment of death, the believer enters Heaven itself, carried upward by the angels to the glorious welcome awaiting the redeemed (Luke 16:22).

From our human viewpoint death is always tinged with sadness. It is not wrong to mourn the loss of a loved one; Jesus wept at the grave of His friend Lazarus (John 11:35).

But the Christian should never consider the death of a fellow believer as a tragedy. Paul said we should not "grieve like the rest of men, who have no hope" (1 Thessalonians 4:13 NIV). Yes, we have hope! The way to Heaven may lie through the valley of the shadow of death, but the angels accompany us all the way—and beyond is Heaven, our glorious home.

HOPE FOR TODAY

When a loved one who is a believer passes away, it makes us loosen our grip on earth and long for Heaven a little more. It is not a good-bye, but a "see you there."

PEACE IN PAIN

So walk in Him rooted and built up in Him.
COLOSSIANS 2:6–7

Not far from my home in North Carolina is Mount Mitchell, the highest point in the eastern United States. On its ridges are old trees that have been stunted and gnarled by the hostile climate and the sparse, rocky soil.

But local craftsmen have told me that when one of these trees finally dies, its wood is highly prized—and the reason is because it is so strong. The tree resisted those fierce alpine winds for decades, and they strengthened it.

What happens when the winds of adversity blow in your life? Do they flatten you, knock you down, stop your growth? Or, like those trees, do you grow stronger?

What makes the difference? The trees that survive, I am told, are those with the deepest roots. The roots are like an anchor helping them survive the storms, and they also draw up the soil's nutrients, helping the trees grow stronger.

Make sure your soul is firmly planted in Christ, so you may be "rooted and built up in Him and established in the faith" (Colossians 2:7).

HOPE FOR TODAY

If you've walked with God for any length of time, chances are that you've weathered some storms together. Keep your faith rooted in the truths of His Word and you won't fear the winds that blow.

TWICE BORN

"Unless one is born again, he cannot see the kingdom of God."
JOHN 3:3

We cannot fully explain the mystery of physical birth, but we accept its wonder, and we accept the fact of new life. What is it, then, that keeps us from accepting the reality and wonder of spiritual rebirth—of being "born again"? To those who have experienced it or seen it happen in others, it is just as real as physical birth.

Just as surely as God implants the life cell in the tiny seed that produces the mighty oak . . . as surely as He instills the heartbeat in the life of the tiny infant yet unborn . . . as surely as He puts motion into the planets, stars, and heavenly bodies—so He implants His divine life in the hearts of those who earnestly seek Him through Christ.

This is not conjecture; it is fact. But has it happened to you? If not, you are not only unfit for the kingdom of God—you are cheating yourself out of the greatest, most revolutionary experience known to any human being. By a simple prayer of faith, ask Christ into your life right now. He will come in, and you will be born again!

HOPE FOR TODAY

There are many things in life that we can't explain but we still experience and enjoy. The way God can remove a heart of stone and replace it with a heart of flesh (Ezekiel 36:26) is one of those things.

The Joy of Christmas

When they saw the star, they rejoiced with exceedingly great joy.

MATTHEW 2:10

Every year people write me saying how much they dread Christmas. Often their complaint stems from how busy they will be, or how much money they will spend.

Did those wise men who journeyed hundreds of miles across the desert to seek out the infant Jesus ever feel that way? After all, it took months to make the arduous trip, and they had gone to great expense to provide gifts of gold, frankincense, and myrrh for the new child.

I doubt it. In fact, as their journey neared its end, we read they had "exceedingly great joy." What made the difference? Their focus was totally on Jesus, the One who would be called "Immanuel, . . . God with us" (Matthew 1:23).

Don't let this Christmas season overwhelm you. Don't feel you have to do everything, or go into debt just to impress other people. Focus instead on Jesus. Take time every day to read the prophecies of His coming and the wonderful story of His birth. Make this Christmas one of "exceedingly great joy"!

Hope for Today

When you're tempted to count the shopping days remaining, go over your gift list for the hundredth time, or stress over where to have Christmas dinner, choose instead to focus on the joy that accompanied that first Christmas.

GOD SEES ALL

Great is our Lord, and mighty in power;
His understanding is infinite.
PSALM 147:5

Some years ago a friend of mine was standing on top of a mountain in North Carolina. The roads in those days were filled with curves, and it was difficult to see very far ahead. This man saw two cars heading toward each other. He realized they couldn't see each other. A third car pulled up and began to pass one of the cars, although there wasn't enough space to see the other car approaching around the bend. My friend shouted a warning, but the drivers couldn't hear, and there was a fatal crash.

This is how God looks upon us in His omniscience. He sees what has happened, what is happening, and what will happen. He also sees us when we foolishly think we can get by with breaking His moral laws, or we act out of sinful pride or lust or anger. Like the man on that mountain, He shouts His warnings at us—but we are too busy or too stubborn to listen.

God sees the whole picture. He knows what is best for us, and He knows what will destroy us. Don't think your way is better than His, but listen to His Word—and obey.

HOPE FOR TODAY
You know the path I take, Lord. Your Word is a light to that path, illuminating my way so that I may walk in Your footsteps.

TRAINING OUR CHILDREN

Train up a child in the way he should go,
And when he is old he will not depart from it.

PROVERBS 22:6

Children need to know right and wrong, and the best place to learn it is at home. If they don't learn it there, they may end up without any moral and spiritual anchor.

Children also want their parents to care enough for them to be strict. Parents who refuse to discipline their children are actually sending a signal saying they don't care what happens to them. The Bible says, "He who loves [his son] disciplines him promptly" (Proverbs 13:24).

The Bible also says to train our children in God's ways "precept upon precept, line upon line . . . here a little, there a little" (Isaiah 28:10). In other words, when a child is about to become a teenager, we can't suddenly say, "I've ignored it so far, but now I'll cram religion and morals into my child." It must start the very moment he or she has any understanding.

But what we do is as important as what we say, for children usually acquire their parents' characteristics and habits. What are our children (and grandchildren) learning from us?

HOPE FOR TODAY

Children don't need perfect parents; they need parents who point them to the perfect Savior. They need to see the fruit of Spirit in our lives and a faith that matures over the years.

THE PERIL OF PREOCCUPATION

Behold, God is great, and we do not know Him.
JOB 36:26

One evening in Jerusalem, I looked out my hotel window and saw the lights of Bethlehem in the distance. I thought about the response of the innkeeper when Mary and Joseph wanted to find a room where the child could be born. The innkeeper was not hostile; he was not opposed to them. But his inn was crowded, his hands were full, and his mind was preoccupied.

Perhaps he told them, "I wish I could help you, but I must keep my priorities. After all, this is a business, and this coming child is no real concern of mine. But I'm not a hard-hearted man. Over there is the stable. You are welcome to use it if you care to. That is the best I can do. Now I must get back to my work. My guests need me."

And this is the answer that millions give today. It is the answer of preoccupation—not fierce opposition, not furious hatred, but a lack of concern about spiritual things. Some of us are simply too preoccupied with other things to welcome Christ into our lives. Don't let that happen to you!

HOPE FOR TODAY

Many people that first Christmas evening in Bethlehem had Christ in their midst and were too distracted (Luke 10:40) or too consumed with themselves (Luke 7:46) to realize it or fully appreciate it. How many of us take for granted the presence of God in our lives?

Our Journey to God

He is able to keep what I have committed to Him until that Day.

2 Timothy 1:12

The Bible speaks of death as a departure. When Paul approached the valley of the shadow of death, he did not shudder with fear; rather, he announced with a note of triumph, "The time of my departure is at hand" (2 Timothy 4:6).

The word *departure* in Paul's time literally meant to pull up anchor and set sail. Everything that happens prior to death is a preparation for the journey. Just as a ship would be loaded with provisions and the voyage carefully mapped before its departure, so our time on this earth should be spent carefully preparing for our journey into eternity.

Many times in past years, I have said farewell to my late wife and children as I departed for a distant destination. Separation always brings a tinge of sadness, but there is the high hope that we shall meet again.

Such is the hope of every believing Christian as we stand at the grave of a loved one who has departed to be with the Lord. We say goodbye, but only until that new day dawns and we are together with the Lord.

Hope for Today

As believers, we are all journeying to the same destination. Some may arrive sooner, while others may take a longer route, but we will all meet up together, and it will seem as if we were never apart.

GOD SENT HIS SON

In Him dwells all the fullness of the Godhead bodily.

COLOSSIANS 2:9

On that first Christmas night in Bethlehem, "God was manifested in the flesh" (1 Timothy 3:16). This manifestation was in the person of Jesus Christ.

What an incredible truth! Think of it: the God of the universe came down from Heaven that first Christmas night and took human form! As the words of the familiar Christmas carol declare, "Veiled in flesh the Godhead see; hail th' incarnate Deity."

If you want to know what God is like, then take a long look at Jesus Christ—because He was God in human flesh. In Jesus were displayed not only the perfections that had been exhibited in the creation—such as wisdom, power, and majesty—but also such perfections as justice, mercy, grace, and love. "The Word was God. . . . And the Word became flesh and dwelt among us" (John 1:1, 14).

To His disciples Jesus said, "You believe in God, believe also in Me" (John 14:1). This sequence of faith is inevitable. If we believe in what God made and what God said, we will believe in the One whom God sent.

HOPE FOR TODAY

Many religions will claim to worship the same God as Christians while denying the deity of Christ. We know that they are in error because those who don't know Jesus don't know the Father (John 8:19).

THE ANTHEM OF HIS NAME

God also has . . . given Him the name which is above every name.

PHILIPPIANS 2:9

More than two thousand years ago, on a night the world has come to call Christmas, a young Jewish maiden went through the experience countless mothers had before her: she brought forth a child.

But this birth was like no other in the history of the human race. For one thing, this child had no human father. As the angel had promised, "The Holy Spirit will come upon you, and the power of the Highest will overshadow you" (Luke 1:35). In humble obedience the Virgin Mary responded, "Let it be to me according to your word" (Luke 1:38).

But this birth also was like no other because of the One who was born. This was no ordinary child. This was the unique Son of God, sent from Heaven to save us from our sins.

Amid the glitter and busyness of the season, don't lose sight of the miracle of that first Christmas. With the wise men, let us fall down and worship Him (Matthew 2:11).

HOPE FOR TODAY

Christ came with a mission; the cradle was always about the Cross. God came in the flesh to save His people, and nothing was going to stop Him. If that doesn't inspire awe, then we don't understand Christmas.

The Night of Light

"I am the light of the world. He who follows Me shall not walk in darkness."
John 8:12

This month the birthday of Jesus Christ will be celebrated all over the world. It will be celebrated in various ways, in many languages, by people of all races. For a few hours many in the world will stop talking of satellites, rockets, and war. For a few hours they will talk of peace on earth and good will toward men. People will exchange their gifts and talk about the Prince of Peace.

Imagine the scene in Bethlehem two thousand years ago. It was the night of nights, and yet it had begun as every other night had before it.

But it was to become the greatest, most significant night of history. This was the night when light would conquer darkness and bring in the day when there would be no more night. This was the night when those who lived in darkness would see a great light. This was the night God brought into the world the One who is "the light of the world."

May Jesus' light shine in your life this Christmas season!

Hope for Today

The birth of Christ was best announced at night; what better time to introduce the Light of the World? Don't despair when your world grows dark, for that is the perfect time for the Light of the World to shine.

OUR LOVING, COMPASSIONATE GOD

"I am the bread of life."
JOHN 6:35

Jesus came to the world so we could know, once and for all, that God is concerned about the way we live, the way we believe, and the way we die.

God could have told us in other ways, of course—and He had, throughout the pages of the Old Testament and in the lives of His people. By His written Word He declared His love for us.

But Jesus was the Living Word. By His life, death, and resurrection, Jesus demonstrated God's love in a way we could never deny. Paul wrote, "But God demonstrates His own love toward us, in that while we were still sinners, Christ died for us" (Romans 5:8).

Every time Jesus fed the hungry, He was saying, "I am the bread of life." Every time He healed a suffering person, He was saying, "It hurts Me to see you in pain." Every move He made, every miracle He performed, every word He spoke was for the purpose of reconciling a lost world to the loving, compassionate God.

HOPE FOR TODAY

God's Word is powerful; by it He spoke into existence all that was created. Yet, with our eternal destination at stake, He cared enough to come to earth, lay down His life, and conquer death so that we can have eternal life with Him.

THE TRUE LIGHT

You are the Christ, the Son of the living God.
MATTHEW 16:16

Christ came into this world as God's Ambassador, sent from Heaven to tell us of God's love, and to bring the war between us and God to an end.

Now we, as "ambassadors for Christ" (2 Corinthians 5:20), boldly echo the ringing conviction of the apostle Peter when he confessed, "You are the Christ, the Son of the living God." The title "Christ" means "anointed one." It is the Greek term for the ancient Hebrew word *Messiah*—the anointed one whom God would send to save His people.

Peter and his fellow Jews, the first believers of the early Christian church, recognized Jesus Christ as the Messiah promised in the Old Testament. Their world was one of discouragement and despair, but the promised Messiah shone as a beacon in the darkness, and His light has never dimmed. "In Him was life, and the life was the light of men" (John 1:4).

No matter how dark the world gets . . . no matter how dark our paths may seem . . . Jesus is still our life and light.

HOPE FOR TODAY

There will always be those who say Jesus was just a really good man—a prophet, even—but not the Son of God. In the face of deception and disbelief, our Savior asks, "Who do *you* say that I am?"

THE SUMMIT OF LOVE

How great is the love the Father has lavished on us,
that we should be called children of God!

1 JOHN 3:1 NIV

M ary and Joseph deeply loved the child God gave them, even becoming refugees to spare His life when King Herod tried to kill Him (Matthew 2:13–15).

But their love was almost nothing compared with God's infinite love for His Son. The Bible declares, "The Father loves the Son, and has given all things into His hand" (John 3:35). Can you even begin to imagine the Father's emotions that first Christmas as His dearly loved Son left Heaven for earth, knowing Jesus would one day go to the Cross, "despised and rejected by men, a Man of sorrows and acquainted with grief" (Isaiah 53:3)?

We rightly focus on God's love for us. But don't lose sight of what it cost the Father to send His beloved Son into the world. Why did He do it? Because "God so loved the world that He gave His only begotten Son, that whoever believes in Him should not perish but have everlasting life" (John 3:16).

God loves the Son—and He loves you as well.

HOPE FOR TODAY

Everything about God is more than we can fathom: His holiness, His grace, His mercy. Perhaps, the most mind-boggling of all is the relentless love for His children that sent His Son to a Cross.

THE REMEDY FOR SIN

Bless the LORD, . . . who forgives all your iniquities,
Who heals all your diseases.
PSALM 103:2–3

Jesus came into the world to save all kinds of people: rich and poor, black and white, educated and illiterate, sophisticated and ordinary—and anyone in between.

Yet only two groups of people gathered at God's invitation to pay Him homage when He was born. One was the shepherds—lowly, at the bottom of the social ladder, uneducated, unsophisticated. The other was the wise men—intellectuals, from another race and country, wealthy, respected. The two groups could hardly have been more different!

God brought both groups to Bethlehem—one by an angelic announcement, one by the appearance of a miraculous star. And by bringing both, God was telling us that Jesus is the Savior for everyone. Every person stands in need of His forgiveness and new life—and every person can know it, if he or she only repents and makes that journey to the Christ of Christmas.

No matter who you are in the eyes of others, you need Christ. And no matter what you have done, He loves you and stands ready to welcome you.

HOPE FOR TODAY

In the act of Communion, we partake of the bread and drink of the cup symbolizing the broken body and shed blood that save us all.

THE PRINCE OF PEACE

"Your faith has saved you. Go in peace."
LUKE 7:50

During the First World War, on Christmas Eve, the battlefield was strangely quiet. As the soft snow fell, the thoughts of the young men were of home and their families.

Softly one lad began to hum "Silent Night." Others took up the chorus until the trenches resounded with the Christmas song. When they finished they were astonished to hear the song echoing from the trenches across no-man's-land: in their own tongue the other soldiers also sang "Silent Night." That night they were thinking of the Prince of Peace, the Christ of Christmas.

How different this world would be if we could unite together around that "Holy Infant so tender and mild." Earth can be as Heaven with Christ. Discord can be as peace when Christ is near. Midnight gloom can be transformed into noonday brightness when He abides with us.

Full peace will come only when Christ returns. But until that day we can know His peace in our hearts and be messengers of His peace in the world as we commit our lives to Him.

HOPE FOR TODAY

Healing and forgiveness in Scripture was often followed with Jesus' instruction to "go in peace." That is what Christ brought at Christmas—peace—and He is still offering it to hearts today.

A Rainbow of Hope

The Lord is near to all who call upon Him,
To all who call upon Him in truth.
PSALM 145:18

Have you ever thought about what has happened because Christ came to the world? That Babe in the manger of Bethlehem grew up to become our crucified and risen Savior—and the world has never been the same.

His compassion has made the world more compassionate. His healing touch has made the world more humanitarian. His selflessness has made the world more self-effacing. Christ drew a rainbow of hope around the shoulders of men and women and gave them something to live for.

If Christ had not come, this world would indeed be a hopeless world. If Christ had not come, this would be a lost world. There would be no access to God, there would be no atonement for sin, there would be no forgiveness, and there would be no Savior.

Yes, Christ came into the world and made it a better place. And He will do the same for you, if you will open your life to Him.

Hope for Today

The Lord is near to those who call, and with his nearness come perfect peace, complete joy, forgiveness of sins, and a life with purpose. Call out to Him today. Seek Him while He still may be found (Isaiah 55:6).

THE KING OF KINGS

A scepter of righteousness is the scepter of Your kingdom.

PSALM 45:6

From His very birth Christ was recognized as King. Something about Him inspired allegiance, loyalty, and homage. Wise men brought Him gifts. Shepherds fell down and worshiped Him. Herod, realizing that there is never room for two thrones in one kingdom, sought His life.

As Jesus began His ministry, His claims upon people's lives were total and absolute. He allowed no divided loyalty. He demanded and received complete adoration and devotion. Mature men and women left their businesses and gave themselves in complete obedience to Him. Many of them gave their lives, pouring out the last full measure of devotion.

His words caused even His most avowed enemies to say, "No man ever spoke like this Man!" (John 7:46). And yet He was more than a poet, more than a statesman, more than a physician. We cannot understand Christ until we understand that He is the King of kings and the Lord of lords. Like Thomas, our only response must be to bow down and confess, "My Lord and my God!" (John 20:28).

HOPE FOR TODAY

Christ demands devotion. Christ described Peter's death and then told him to, "Follow Me." He tells all believers to pick up their crosses and follow Him. Faith in Christ is an all-or-nothing deal.

GOD WITH US

Behold, the virgin shall conceive and bear a Son,
and shall call His name Immanuel.

ISAIAH 7:14

I never come to Christmas without thinking of the thousands of people who are lonely and troubled at this time of year. I have had psychiatrists tell me their schedules are overloaded with people who find the Christmas season almost more than they can bear because of their loneliness and isolation.

Christmas is God's reminder that we are not alone. God revealed in the life, death, and resurrection of Jesus a reconciling love that rescues us from separation and loneliness. We are not alone; God has come down from Heaven to tell us He loves us!

During this Christmas season, you can be assured that Jesus Christ is here. He is here to give us hope, to forgive our sins, to give us a new song, to impart faith, and to heal our spiritual wounds, if only we will let Him.

The Christmas message has not changed after two thousand years. Christmas still reminds us that God is with us. If you are lonely this Christmas, welcome Christ into your life. Then ask Him to help you reach out to someone else who is lonely, and show that person His love.

HOPE FOR TODAY

The enemy twists everything good. How else could a celebration of God's coming to His people make people feel alone and unloved? Fight the lies of Satan by feasting on the truths in God's Word.

HEAVENLY HERALD

"I have come that they may have life, and that
they may have it more abundantly."
JOHN 10:10

Christmas is not just a date on the calendar. It is not just an annual holiday. It is not a day to glorify selfishness and materialism. Christmas is the celebration of the event that set Heaven to singing, an event that gave the stars of the night sky a new brilliance.

Christmas tells us that at a specific time and at a specific place a specific Person was born. That Person was (in the words of an ancient Christian creed) "God of God, Light of Light, very God of very God"—the Lord, Jesus Christ.

From the lips of Him who came fell these words: "The Son of Man has come to seek and to save that which was lost" (Luke 19:10). Like piercing trumpets, these words heralded the breaking in of the Divine to human history. They declared that Heaven had come to our rescue and that God had not left us to stumble alone on Earth's pathway. What a wonderful and glorious hope we have because of that first Christmas!

HOPE FOR TODAY

That first Christmas proved for all time that we are not forgotten, unloved, or unwanted. Our God saw us in our wretched state and, like the father of the prodigal son, came running to our rescue.

A HEALING WORD

"I have called you friends."
JOHN 15:15

Christ came into a world that had problems much like the ones we grapple with today. Life was short, disease was rampant, nations chafed under the heel of Roman rule, and slavery was universal. Widows, orphans, the disabled, and the chronically ill had no social safety net to see them through the rough times.

To those without the joy of living, Jesus said, "I have come that they may have life, and that they may have it more abundantly" (John 10:10).

To those who bore the chafing burden of the guilt of sin, He said, "Be of good cheer; your sins are forgiven you" (Matthew 9:2).

To the friendless He said, "No longer do I call you servants . . . but I have called you friends" (John 15:15). He had a healing word for everyone.

On the surface the world has changed radically since that first Christmas. But deep inside, our problems are the same—for they are problems of the heart. And Christ still comes to us to cleanse our guilt, give us hope for the future, and heal our hurts with His love.

HOPE FOR TODAY

What is it that your heart longs for? Freedom, friendship, forgiveness? Christ came to fill every need, break every chain, and bring salvation to a lost and dying world.

LOOKING FOR PEACE

"Glory to God in the highest,
and on earth peace."
LUKE 2:14

The centuries have rolled by, and still the world longs for and looks for the peace the angels sang about on that first Christmas morning. Even the land of Jesus' birth often seems torn by violence and conflict. "Where is His peace?" you ask.

I'll tell you where it is. It abides in the hearts of all who have trusted His grace. And in the same proportion that the world has trusted in Christ, it also has peace. Yet our world continues to be torn by wars and unrest. I know of no country that is completely safe or completely at peace.

The greatest war of all, however, is the war between God and us, as we stubbornly rebel against His authority and defiantly seize control of our lives apart from Him. But now the war can be over, as we yield ourselves to Christ as our Lord. Then we have peace—peace with God, peace in our hearts, and peace with one another. Is the war over in your life?

HOPE FOR TODAY

Lord, I could never do for myself what You have done. I give complete control of my life to You. Fill me with Your peace, and let me be an instrument of that peace to a broken and hurting world.

ROOM FOR JESUS

She brought forth her firstborn Son, . . . and laid Him in a manger, because there was no room for them in the inn.

LUKE 2:7

No room for Jesus? No room for the King of kings? No, but room for others and for other things. There was no room for Jesus in the world that He had made—imagine!

Things have not really changed since that Bethlehem night over two thousand years ago. God is still on the fringes of most of our lives. We fit Him in when it is convenient for us, but we become irritated when He makes demands on us. If God would only stay in His little box and come out when we pull the string!

Our lives are so full. There is so much to be done. But in all our busy activities are we in danger of excluding from our hearts and lives the One who made us?

"Oh, come to my heart, Lord Jesus; there is room in my heart for You."

HOPE FOR TODAY

We may not say it with our words, but do our attitudes and actions declare, "There's no room for You here, Lord"? Does the way we spend our time, energy, and resources leave any room for Christ in our lives?

THE SUFFERING SERVANT

He was wounded for our transgressions.

ISAIAH 53:5

Jesus' life began in the midst of persecution and peril. He came on a mission of love and mercy, sent by the Father. An angel announced His conception and gave Him His name. The heavenly host sang a glorious anthem at His birth. By the extraordinary star, the very heavens indicated His coming. He was the most illustrious child ever born—the holy child of Mary, the divine Son of God.

Yet no sooner did He enter our world than Herod decreed His death and labored to accomplish it. Warned by God in a dream, Joseph fled Bethlehem at night, taking Mary and the baby Jesus to Egypt until Herod's death finally made it safe to return.

The Son of the eternal Father, Jesus entered time and was made in the likeness of man. He assumed our human nature with all its infirmities, and weakness, and capacity for suffering. He came as a child of the poorest parents. His entire life was one long pathway of humiliation.

Now He is in Heaven, no longer limited by time and space. And someday He will come again—this time in glory—to take us to Himself.

HOPE FOR TODAY

We won't fully grasp all that Christ gave up to come to earth until we see Heaven for ourselves. Once there, I wonder, would we give any of it up to return to earth?

GOD'S WISDOM

How unsearchable are His judgments and His ways past finding out!
ROMANS 11:33

The end of another year is approaching, and people are already predicting what the new year holds. A year from now most of them probably will have missed the target!

The fact is, no one knows the future—except God. We even know so little about the world in which we live. No doubt scientists will continue to uncover astonishing facts about the universe. But even then, they will know only a miniscule amount compared with the total sum of potential knowledge.

But God is infinite! He knows it all—because He created it in the first place. We will always be bewildered and confused by what we don't know, if we are honest. We don't even know our immediate futures; as James said, "You do not know what will happen tomorrow" (James 4:14).

What should this mean? It should give us humility before God, and it should give us trust—trust in the God who does know our futures, and who works all things for His glory. You can trust all your tomorrows to Him!

HOPE FOR TODAY

We don't need to fear the unknown or worry about what tomorrow holds. God has already seen tomorrow, and nothing is unknown to Him. We just need to follow Him one day at a time.

PASS ALONG COMFORT

Blessed be the God . . . of all comfort.
2 CORINTHIANS 1:3

A dear friend and trusted counselor once told me that sometimes the greatest test comes to us when we ask God the question, "Why?"

As Charles Hembree once pointed out, "In the full face of afflictions it is hard to see any sense to things that befall us, and we want to question the fairness of a faithful God. However, these moments can be the most meaningful of our lives."

Alexander Nowell once said, "God does not comfort us that we may be comforted but that we may be comforters." We are to pass along the comfort with which God has comforted us.

Look around you. There are countless opportunities to comfort others, not only in the loss of a loved one, but also in the daily distress that so often creeps into our lives. One of Paul's companions on some of his missionary journeys was named Joseph, but "the apostles called [him] Barnabas (which means Son of Encouragement)" (Acts 4:36 NIV). Will you be a Barnabas to someone today?

HOPE FOR TODAY

Children often enter a situation asking, "Who will be my friend?" The better question would be, "To whom can I be a friend?" Adults, too, often ask the wrong question. Don't ask, "Why did I suffer?" Ask, "Who can I comfort?"

BRING GLORY TO GOD

Present . . . your members as instruments of righteousness to God.
ROMANS 6:13

When you serve sin, your body is dedicated to the service of sin. Your appetites, whetted by Satan, rage unthrottled. Your God-given creative impulses are sacrificed to Satan on the altar of lust. A sinner, in a sense, is a dedicated person, yielded to his appetites and selfish desires.

But when Christ comes into the human heart we are to yield our bodies to Him. Our human frame is often a rebellious and unruly servant. Only through rigid discipline and the help of the Holy Spirit are we able to master it and bring it into complete subjection to Christ. We must guard against appetites that blight the conscience, wither the soul, and weaken our witness for Christ.

Perhaps many things are lawful, but are they moral? Are they a harmful example to others?

As long as we are in this world, our old nature will try to defeat us and turn us away from Christ. But learn to recognize the warning signs, and commit your mind and body to Christ "as instruments of righteousness."

HOPE FOR TODAY

Keep me in Your Word, God, so that I will know Your will. Teach me to find my identity and worth in You so that I don't seek it in the world. Make me an instrument of righteousness in Your right hand.

GOD'S GIFTS TO US

We have different gifts, according to the grace given us.

ROMANS 12:6 NIV

If you are a parent, you've undoubtedly had the experience of having your children complain after Christmas is over, disappointed they didn't get the gift they wanted or bored with the ones they received. It's not an easy problem to solve!

God our Father has given gifts to each of us, and I pray we may never become discontent or bored with them. The greatest gift of all, of course, is the gift of His Son. But the Bible also teaches God has given us other gifts—gifts that come from the Holy Spirit's ministry in our lives. These are the gifts of the Spirit, and they include everything from the gift of preaching to the gift of hospitality. None of us has every gift, but every Christian has at least one, to be used for one purpose: to build up Christ's body, the church (Ephesians 4:11–12).

What spiritual gift has God given you? Don't worry about those gifts you don't have. Be content with those God has given you, and use them for His glory.

HOPE FOR TODAY

We have a purpose that is ours alone, and our gifts and talents help us fulfill that purpose. We will never be more satisfied than when we are using our God-given gifts to fulfill His will in our lives.

THE CITY OF GOD

There shall be no night there. . . . And they shall reign forever and ever.
REVELATION 22:5

M any years ago I was visiting the dining room of the United States Senate. As I was speaking to various people, one of the senators said, "Billy, we're having a discussion about pessimism and optimism. Are you a pessimist or an optimist?" I smiled and said, "I'm an optimist." He asked, "Why?" I replied, "I've read the last page of the Bible."

The Bible speaks about a heavenly city whose builder and maker is God, where those who have been redeemed will be superior to angels. It speaks of "a pure river of water of life, clear as crystal, proceeding from the throne of God and of the Lamb" (Revelation 22:1). It says, "There shall be no night there: They need no lamp nor light of the sun, for the Lord God gives them light. And they shall reign forever and ever."

As another year ends, no doubt you have had your share of joys and disappointments. Don't live in the past, but "be patient and stand firm, because the Lord's coming is near" (James 5:8 NIV).

HOPE FOR TODAY

We can't cling to the successes or failures of the past. Each new day brings a new opportunity to live for Christ, to share His gospel, and to build His kingdom. Let's be about our Father's business.

About the Author

Billy Graham, world-renowned preacher, evangelist, and author, has delivered the gospel message to more people face-to-face than anyone in history and has ministered on every continent of the world in more than 185 countries. Millions have read his inspirational classics, including *Angels, Peace with God, The Holy Spirit, Hope for the Troubled Heart, How to Be Born Again, The Journey, Nearing Home, Where I Am,* and *The Reason for My Hope.*

My Devotional Thoughts